The North Dakota State Constitution

The Oxford Commentaries on the State Constitutions of the United States
G. Alan Tarr, Series Editor

Professor G. Alan Tarr, Director of the Center on State Constitutional Studies at Rutgers University, serves as General Editor for this important new series which in its entirety will cover each of the 50 states. Each volume of The Oxford Commentaries on the State Constitutions of the United States contains a historical overview of the state's constitutional development, plus a section-by-section analysis of the state's current constitution. Other features included in the volumes are the text of the state's constitution, a bibliographic essay, table of cases, and index. This series provides essential reference tools for those investigating state constitutional development and constitutional law.

The North Dakota State Constitution

James E. Leahy

Foreword by Chief Justice Gerald W. VandeWalle

THE OXFORD COMMENTARIES ON THE STATE CONSTITUTIONS OF THE UNITED STATES
G. Alan Tarr, Series Editor

OXFORD
UNIVERSITY PRESS

OXFORD
UNIVERSITY PRESS

Oxford University Press, Inc., publishes works that further Oxford University's objective of excellence in research, scholarship, and education.

Oxford New York
Auckland Cape Town Dar es Salaam Hong Kong Karachi Kuala Lumpur Madrid Melbourne
Mexico City Nairobi New Delhi Shanghai Taipei Toronto

With offices in
Argentina Austria Brazil Chile Czech Republic France Greece Guatemala Hungary Italy
Japan Poland Portugal Singapore South Korea Switzerland Thailand Turkey Ukraine
Vietnam

Previously published in 2003 by Greenwood Press

Published by Oxford University Press, Inc.
198 Madison Avenue, New York, New York 10016

Library of Congress Cataloging-in-Publication Data

Leahy, James E., 1919–
The North Dakota state constitution : a reference guide/James E. Leahy; foreword by Gerald W. VandeWalle.
p. cm.—(The Oxford commentaries on the state constitutions of the United States)
Includes bibliographical references and index.
ISBN 978-0-19-977873-7 (hardback)
1. Constitutions—North Dakota. 2. Constitutional law—North Dakota.
I. North Dakota. Constitution. II. Title.
KFN9001 1889.A6 L435 2011
342.78402—dc22 2010054190

Note to Readers
This publication is designed to provide accurate and authoritative information in regard to the subject matter covered. It is based upon sources believed to be accurate and reliable and is intended to be current as of the time it was written. It is sold with the understanding that the publisher is not engaged in rendering legal, accounting, or other professional services. If legal advice or other expert assistance is required, the services of a competent professional person should be sought. Also, to confirm that the information has not been affected or changed by recent developments, traditional legal research techniques should be used, including checking primary sources where appropriate.

(Based on the Declaration of Principles jointly adopted by a Committee of the American Bar Association and a Committee of Publishers and Associations.)

■ COPYRIGHT ACKNOWLEDGMENTS

The author and publisher are grateful for permission to reproduce material from the following:

Crockett, Richard B. *Constitutional Autonomy and the North Dakota State Board of Education.* 54 North Dakota Law Review 530 (1977–1978). Reproduced by permission.

Lamar, Howard Roberts. *Dakota Territory, 1861–1889.* Fargo: Institute for Regional Studies, 1997. Reproduced by permission of the copyright holder, Yale University Press, New Haven, CT.

Leahy, James E. *"The Constitution Is What the Judges Say It Is."* 65 North Dakota Law Review 491, 499 Note 50 (1989). Reproduced by permission.

Meschke, Herbert L., and Lawrence D. Spears. *Digging for the Roots: The North Dakota Constitution and the Thayer Correspondence.* 65 North Dakota Law Review 343 (1989). Reproduced by permission.

Reprinted from *History of North Dakota* by Elwyn B. Robinson by permission of the University of Nebraska Press. Copyright © 1966 by the University of Nebraska Press. Copyright © renewed 1994 by the University of Nebraska Press.

Smith, Thomas O. *State Lands! What Are We Doing.* 51 North Dakota Law Review 477 (1975). Reproduced by permission.

Sovereign Immunity: An Outdated Doctrine Faces Demise in a Changing Judicial Arena. 69 North Dakota Law Review 401 (1993). Reproduced by permission.

Sovereign Immunity—Judicial Abrogation of North Dakota's Sovereign Immunity Results in Its Possible Legislative Reassertion and Legislation to Provide Injured Parties a Remedy for the Torts Committed by the State or Its Agents. 71 North Dakota Law Review 761 (1995). Reproduced by permission.

Tabor, Sandra. *Apportionment in North Dakota: The Saga of Continuing Controversy.* 57 North Dakota Law Review 447 (1981). Reproduced by permission.

Vogel, Robert. *Justice Robinson and the Supreme Court of North Dakota.* 58 North Dakota Law Review 83 (1982). Reproduced by permission.

Vogel, Robert. *Sources of the North Dakota Constitution.* 65 North Dakota Law Review 331 (1989). Reproduced by permission.

Every reasonable effort has been made to trace the owners of copyright materials in this book, but in some instances this has proven impossible. The author and publisher will be glad to receive information leading to more complete acknowledgments in subsequent printings of the book and in the meantime extend their apologies for any omissions.

To my wife, La Vern, for her patience, understanding, and love

CONTENTS

■ SERIES FOREWORD

In 1776, following the declaration of independence from England, the former colonies began to draft their own constitutions. Their handiwork attracted widespread interest, and draft constitutions circulated up and down the Atlantic seaboard, as constitution-makers sought to benefit from the insights of their counterparts in sister states. In Europe, the new constitutions found a ready audience seeking enlightenment from the American experiments in self-government. Even the delegates to the Constitutional Convention of 1787, despite their reservations about the course of political developments in the states during the decade after independence, found much that was useful in the newly adopted constitutions. And when James Madison, fulfilling a pledge given during the ratification debates, drafted the federal Bill of Rights, he found his model in the famous Declaration of Rights of the Virginia Constitution.

By the 1900s, however, few people would have looked to state constitutions for enlightenment. Instead, a familiar litany of complaints was heard whenever state constitutions were mentioned. State constitutions were too long and too detailed, combining basic principles with policy prescriptions and prohibitions that had no place in the fundamental law of a state. By including such provisions, it was argued, state constitutions deprived state governments of the flexibility they needed to respond effectively in changing circumstances. This—among other factors—encouraged political reformers to look to the federal government, which was not plagued by such constitutional constraints, thereby shifting the locus of political initiative away from the states. Meanwhile, civil libertarians concluded that state bills of rights, at least as interpreted by state courts, did not adequately protect rights and therefore looked to the federal courts and the federal Bill of Rights for redress. As power and responsibility shifted from the states to Washington, so too did the attention of scholars, the legal community, and the general public.

During the early 1970s, however, state constitutions were "rediscovered." The immediate impetus for this rediscovery was former President Richard Nixon's appointment of Warren Burger to succeed Earl Warren as Chief Justice of the United States Supreme Court. To civil libertarians, this appointment seemed to signal a decisive shift in the Supreme Court's jurisprudence, because Burger was expected to lead the Court away from the liberal activism that had characterized the Warren Court. They therefore sought ways to safeguard the gains they had achieved for defendants, racial minorities, and the poor during Warren's tenure from erosion by the Burger Court. In particular, they began to look to state bills of rights to secure the rights of defendants and to support other civil-liberties claims that they advanced in state courts.

The "new judicial federalism," as it came to be called, quite quickly advanced beyond its initial concern to evade the mandates of the Burger Court. Indeed, less than two decades after it originated, it became a nationwide phenomenon. For when judges and scholars turned their attention to state constitutions, they discovered an unsuspected richness. They found not only provisions that paralleled the federal Bill of Rights, but also constitutional guarantees of the right to privacy and of gender equality, for example, that had no analogue in the U.S. Constitution. Careful examination of the text and history of state guarantees revealed important differences between even those provisions that most resembled federal guarantees and their federal counterparts. Looking beyond state declarations of rights, jurists and scholars discovered affirmative constitutional mandates to state governments to address such important policy concerns as education and housing. Taken altogether, these discoveries underlined the importance for the legal community of developing a better understanding of state constitutions.

Yet the renewed interest in state constitutions has not been limited to judges and lawyers. State constitutional reformers have renewed their efforts with notable success: since 1960, ten states have adopted new constitutions and several others have undertaken major constitutional revisions. These changes have usually resulted in more streamlined constitutions and more effective state governments. Also, in recent years political activists on both the left and the right have pursued their goals through state constitutional amendments, often enacted through the initiative process, under which policy proposals can be placed directly on the ballot for voters to endorse or reject. Scholars too have begun to rediscover how state constitutional history can illuminate changes in political thought and practice, providing a basis for theories about the dynamics of political change in America.

James E. Leahy's excellent study of the North Dakota Constitution is the latest volume in the series, The Oxford Commentaries on the State Constitutions of the United States, which reflects this renewed interest in state constitutions and will contribute to our knowledge about them. Because the constitutional tradition of each state is distinctive, the volume begins with the history and development of the North Dakota Constitution. It then provides the complete text of North Dakota's current constitution, with each section accompanied by commentary that explains the provision and traces its origins and its interpretation by the courts and by other governmental bodies. Finally, the book concludes with a table of cases cited in the history and the constitutional commentary, as well as a subject index.

G. Alan Tarr

■ FOREWORD

The North Dakota Constitution is lengthy when compared with the U.S. Constitution. The Legislature has proposed and the citizens have approved amendments to shorten the document, but it arguably remains too detailed. Finding one's way through its provisions and understanding its diverse phrasing is often a daunting task for the legal and judicial practitioner as well as the constitutional scholar.

Professor James E. Leahy has written one of the very few (if not the very first) comprehensive discussions and reviews of the North Dakota Constitution and the legal decisions construing it. From the opening paragraphs discussing the territory that was to become North Dakota; to the description of its native people, the establishment of the territorial and state government, and its politics; to a description of the state's topography; to the substantive provisions of our North Dakota Constitution; Professor Leahy has researched and written a book that teaches its readers without being unduly pedagogic. The book will be of interest, even to casual readers. Most importantly, it is a splendid reference for lawyers and litigants who are researching the meaning of the individual provisions of the North Dakota Constitution. Well laid out, the work provides easy and logical access to the constitution, the legislative enactments implementing the constitution's provisions, and the North Dakota and U.S. Supreme Court cases construing the constitution. The references to those cases often include the apposite quotations from the opinions.

The North Dakota Supreme Court has often entreated lawyers and litigants, urging a specific interpretation of an allegedly ambiguous constitutional provision, to give the Court the rationale for the construction desired, other than the wish it were so. More often than not, that entreaty has not been heeded because lawyers and litigants have found few resources to justify their rationale. Professor Leahy's book is not the only source to fill the void, but it is a significant work that vastly increases the resources available to study and construe the North Dakota Constitution. Scholars, lawyers, judges, and court watchers would do well to examine this important work when beginning their odyssey through the North Dakota Constitution.

Gerald W. VandeWalle
Chief Justice
The North Dakota Supreme Court

The Constitution shall be republican in form, and make no distinction in civil or political rights on account of race or color, except as to Indians not taxed, and not to be repugnant to the Constitution of the United States and the principles of the Declaration of Independence.

The Enabling Act, Section 4.

PART ONE

The History of the North Dakota Constitution

THE EXPLORERS

The land that became the State of North Dakota was part of the territory included in the Louisiana Purchase in 1803. It was explored by Meriwether Lewis and William Clark at the request of President Thomas Jefferson. This expedition spent the winter of 1804–1805 in Mandan Indian country where they built Fort Mandan on the Missouri River at a point near Bismarck, the state's present capital city. The explorers experienced a climate of extremes; warm days and cool nights, hot summers and cold winters, not much rain but lots of sunshine.

Long before the United States acquired the territory, French fur traders had visited the area and set up trading posts. One of the first traders was Pierre Gaultier de Varennes, sieur de la Verendrye of France, who entered the territory from Canada in 1738.

La Verendrye left Canada with a party of 13 men in October 1738 with the intent of meeting the Indians settled near what is now Bismarck/Mandan, North Dakota. The party arrived at the Mandan Indian village in December 1738. Elwyn B. Robinson describes La Verendrye's meeting with the Indians living there.

> As La Verendrye's party approached the village, which was still several days' journey away, some of the Mandans came out to greet them. . . . A Mandan chief, speaking Assiniboin, welcomed La Verendrye with expressions of great joy and begged him to

> stay at his village—the smallest of the six and the only one at some distance from the Missouri River. When they arrived, the Mandans carried La Verendrye into the village and begged to be made his children. He fulfilled their request by putting his hands on the head of each chief.[1]

Other settlers came down from Canada in 1812 and settled at Pembina in the northeast corner of the territory.

> Slowly the fur hunters and traders were replaced by ranchers and farmers. Steamboats began to ply the Red and Missouri rivers. The federal government then set up military posts to protect the settlers from the Sioux Indians, who were making a last fight for their hunting grounds. The first such post was Fort Abercrombie, on the Red River, [near present-day Wahpeton] authorized in 1858.
>
> The coming of the railroads brought throngs of new settlers to work the rich wheatland. During the 1870s and 1880s railroads pushed across the state. They advertised for farmers who would ship rich grain crops to the East. The vast acres that the railroads received from the government along their rights-of-way were sold at low rates. Sod houses dotted the prairies as land-hungry settlers staked out homesteads. From the mid-1870s to mid-1890s, bonanza farms of 3,000 acres . . . often made large profits growing wheat or raising cattle.[2]

THE NATIVES WERE THERE

When the fur traders came into the territory, a number of Indian tribes were already living there. These included the Arikara, Assiniboin, Cheyenne, Cree, Crow, Dakota, Hidatsa, Mandan, and Yanktonai tribes. In a journal kept about his travels, the French explorer La Verendrye wrote about the Mandans:

> This tribe is mixed white and black. The women are fairly good looking, especially the light colored ones; many of them have blond or fair hair. Both the men and the women of this tribe are very industrious. Their lodges are large and spacious, and are separated into several apartments by broad planks. Nothing is left lying about, for all their belongings are kept in large bags which are hung on posts. Their beds are made like tombs, surrounded by skins. All go to bed naked, men and women. The men are always naked and for covering they use buffalo robes. Most of the women go naked like the men, with this difference, that they wear a loin cloth about a hand breadth wide and a span long, sewed to a girdle in front. . . . Their fort has a great number of caches in which are stored such things as corn, meat, fat, dressed buffalo robes and bearskins. . . . They make wicker work very skillfully, both flat and in the form of baskets. They use earthen pots for cooking their food which they manufacture like

[1] *Compton's Interactive Encyclopedia*, "North Dakota" (Softkey Multimedia, 1999).

[2] Id.

> many other tribes. They are for the most part great eaters and they are extremely fond of feasting.... The men are of good size and tall, very alert and for the most part good looking. They have fine features and are very affable. Most of the women do not have the Indian features. The men take part in a sort of ball play in the open places.[3]

Author Conrad W. Leifur describes the Indian people: "White men often called the Indians savages. Yet, they were better than the whites in many of the common virtues, such as honesty, truthfulness, reverence for their gods or spirits (of which they had several), self-denial, love for their families, and the ability to suffer without complaint. Although they were not educated as white men understand education, they were very intelligent."[4]

As more and more traders and settlers came into the region, conflicts arose between them and the Indians. As time went on, the Indians were forced to give up their land and go on reservations.

> With the introduction of guns and the westward movement of trappers and pioneers, the fate of the bison and Plains culture was, however, soon sealed. By 1880 bison no longer existed in sufficient numbers to permit the summer hunts, tribes were being shunted to reservations, and the Great Plains culture was essentially destroyed. The often-fierce and bloody conflicts between the Plains Indians and whites culminated in 1890, when a group of Sioux followers of the revivalistic ghost dance movement encountered cavalry units at Wounded Knee, South Dakota, where nearly 300 native Americans, mainly women and children, were massacred by the 7th Cavalry, Gen. George Armstrong Custer's former unit.
>
> Although the resistance of the Plains peoples was eventually broken, many of the most powerful tribes escaped being driven outside their own territories. Although on the reservations they had little or no opportunity to maintain their traditional way of life, certain aspects of Plains culture have nevertheless been preserved, although in adjusted form.[5]

THE SETTLERS CAME

As the Indians were moved to reservations, and the fur trade diminished, farms and ranches came into being. Helped by steamboats on the Red and Missouri Rivers, and railroads from the east, settlers began to migrate into the territory.

Elwyn B. Robinson describes the beginnings of a settler's life in the state.

> When the settler arrived with his wagon, stock, and household goods, he had many things to do. He and his family might sleep in or under the wagon the first few nights,

---

[3] Elwyn B. Robinson, *History of North Dakota* (Lincoln: University of Nebraska Press, 1986), p. 31.

[4] Conrad W. Leifur, *Our State North Dakota* (New York: American Book Company, 1953), p. 105.

[5] *Grolier Multimedia Encyclopedia, 1999* "Indians, American, (II)" (Grolier Interactive, 1999).

> or they might have a tent. Water was an immediate necessity; the settler had to find a spring, dig a shallow well, or haul water from a stream. . . .
>
> The pioneer hurried to provide a house. If he were near the wooded banks of a river, he generally built a low log cabin of two rooms. . . .
>
> On the open prairie, the newcomer might build a 14 by 16-foot sod house, laying up tiers of sod. Windows were small. The walls, sometimes two and one-half feet thick, were often boarded on the inside and whitewashed.[6]

Most of the settlers broke sod and started farming. Small towns sprang up throughout the territory. Soon there were banks, harness shops, lumber yards, grain elevators, livery stables, poolrooms, and saloons. Doctors, lawyers, and druggists followed. Newspapers were started, churches organized, and the postal service began.

Robinson writes: "Mail and visits to town boosted the settlers' morale. They also drew together to combat loneliness of the empty prairie. . . . Sundays they would gather in each other's homes to visit. The young people often organized dances and card parties, either in homes or in hotels. A home which had a reed organ would become a social center where neighbors gathered to sing and make taffy."[7]

Education started in the homes. Mothers would read aloud to their children. An older child would help the younger ones. Soon neighbors got together, built a school, and hired a teacher. "In 1874, Ida C. Hall, seventeen, began teaching the first school in Jamestown in a small shed without even a chair for the teacher. She boarded at the railroad section house."[8] Religious services also began in the home. There was Bible reading, family prayers, and catechism.

Pioneer life was very demanding. People were isolated in the wintertime; floods came in the springtime; and the summers required hard labor to work the sod and to get the crop in.

Life was very difficult for women. Their homes were drab, with dirt floors and leaky roofs. There were few doctors so the women had to have babies without them, and take care of any sickness that the family had. Sometimes their husbands were required to seek work away from home, leaving the wife and children by themselves. For many women, the burdens of life were increased because "they were often persons of refinement and education from well-to-do homes. . . . Coming from forested, hilly country, many must have been shocked when they first saw the vast, flat treeless plain."[9]

---

[6] Robinson, supra note 3, p. 159.

[7] Id., p. 166.

[8] Id.

[9] Id., pp. 169–170.

THE ARMY RULED

As the settlers came and conflicts arose between them and the Indians, the Army was sent to maintain order. Forts were built, particularly along the Red River in the east and the Missouri River in the west. It is reported that in 1873 there were 2,652 troops in that part of the territory that became North Dakota.[10]

Author Robinson describes the plight of the Indians as the Army increased in numbers.

> The army forts, the agencies and reservations, and the disappearance of wild game confronted the Indians with a problem of readjustment. A free people ruling a vast, semiarid grassland, they had developed a way of life centering on the buffalo. But as the herds disappeared, their adaptation to the environment broke down. At the same time, the army was taking away from them both their freedom and their control of the country. The army put them on reservations and they were compelled to submit, for they were now dependent upon the government for subsistence.[11]

THE CONSTRUCTION OF THE RAILROADS

Howard Roberts Lamar has written: "It would be difficult to exaggerate the vital role the railroad played in shaping the Territory's political and economic history. The struggle to secure a railroad is, in fact, a key and binding factor which gives meaning to Dakota politics for the years 1869-74. Since the builders of the first line were also the leading political figures in Dakota, regardless of party or position, the railroad issue was often the most important political issue."[12]

In order to promote expansion of the West, Congress gave huge amounts of land to the railroads. The Northern Pacific, for example, received 20 sections of land per mile in Minnesota and Oregon, and 40 sections per mile in Dakota, Montana, Idaho, and Washington.[13] While this grant of land played a vital part in the growth of the state, it had its downside as well. "The land grant," Robinson writes, "24 percent of the state's area, gave the Northern Pacific a huge economic stake in the government. So for years the railroads and the people struggled for control. Who would dominate the government and economy of North Dakota?"[14]

---

[10] Id., p. 176.

[11] Id., p. 177.

[12] Howard Roberts Lamar, *Dakota Territory, 1861–1889* (Fargo: Institute for Regional Studies, 1997), p. 130.

[13] Robinson, supra note 3, p. 125.

[14] Id., p. 198.

THE BONANZA FARMS

The eastern part of the territory, particularly the Red River Valley, proved to be adaptable to the growing of wheat and therefore huge farms were created, commonly referred to as "bonanza" farms. The first of such farms was established by purchase of land from the Northern Pacific Railroad by George W. Cass, its president, and Benjamin Cheney, a director. They bought 13,440 acres of land near Casselton and hired Oliver Dalrymple to manage them. But they were not the only ones. It is reported that from 1873 to 1878, the railroad sold 1,700,000 acres of land in what became Minnesota and North Dakota.

The scale of operations on bonanza farms was spectacular. They were adapted to a wheat country where extensive agriculture was required by scant rainfall and hence relatively low yields per acre. In 1879, Dalrymple was using 400 horses and mules, 100 broadcast seeders, 50 harrows, and 115 self-binding harvesters. He employed 400 men in the harvest rush. By 1880 he had charge of 55,000 acres, though less than half the land was under cultivation.[15]

THE CREATION OF DAKOTA TERRITORY

President James Buchanan signed the bill creating Dakota Territory on March 2, 1861, two days before his term as president ended. Dakota Territory included the present states of North and South Dakota and parts of present Wyoming and Montana. The western boundary of the Territory was set at Wyoming's eastern boundary when it became a state in 1868.

Shortly after becoming president in 1861, Abraham Lincoln appointed his longtime friend and family physician William Jayne of Springfield, Illinois, as the Territory's first governor. At the time, Captain J.B.S. Todd was thought to be the prime candidate for governor. Todd had lived in the area for many years, had been involved in the development of the city of Yankton, and was a very successful promoter. He was also a cousin of President Lincoln's wife, Mary Todd Lincoln.

When the time came to select a capital for the Territory, Governor Jayne selected Yankton. It is believed that Mary Todd Lincoln played a part in this selection because Yankton was considered to be "Captain Todd's town."[16]

Author Leifur has written: "In many ways the government during territorial days was similar to that in statehood. As has been said, there was a governor and a legislature. Likewise, the territory was divided into counties, although these counties were much larger than those of the present day. They had about the same group of officials as we have today, but the most important officer in the

---

[15] Id., p. 138.

[16] Lamar, supra note 12, p. 71.

county in those days was the sheriff, with the treasurer next."[17] The governor and most of the Territory's other officials were appointed by the president, but legislators and local officers were elected. The population of the Territory had grown to about 300,000 by the early 1880s.

A FEW OF THE PROMINENT CITIZENS

Dr. William Jayne

Author Lamar describes Dr. William Jayne as: "A tall, lanky man of thirty-six years, with a hawklike nose and piercing eyes. Jayne possessed a strong temper and so little political subtlety that he was to split rather than unite the infant Republican party of Dakota in its first years. In his fight to seize political control of Dakota, he ran up against Captain Todd, whose more adroit maneuvers finally forced Jayne to return to Springfield in defeat."[18]

Captain John B. S. Todd

Captain John B. S. Todd came to the territory in 1855 with General W. S. Harney's march against the Sioux Indians. "Seeing the opportunities offered by the new country soon to be opened to settlement, . . . [Todd] resigned his commission, became a sutler at Fort Randall, and formed a trading and land company."[19]

Alexander McKenzie

One of the more powerful men in the territory was Alexander McKenzie, who had been elected Sheriff of Burleigh County at the age of 24. Author Leifur describes McKenzie as having

> plenty of money behind him, and by granting important favors to those in power, he was able to prevent the passage of laws that might hurt the railroads. He was very clever at handling people. He could be ruthless with them as well as generous. And when generous, they did not know whether it was because he liked them or whether he was planning to ask for a return favor sometime. In a short time he was representing the interests of the banks, insurance companies, and elevator and lumber companies, as well as those of the railroads. And the more interests he took on, the more prosperous and powerful he became.[20]

---

[17] Leifur, supra note 4, p. 258.
[18] Lamar, supra note 12, p. 66.
[19] Robinson, supra note 3, p. 127.
[20] Leifur, supra note 4, p. 296.

The so-called "McKenzie Machine" continued to be a force in North Dakota politics well into the early 1900s.[21]

Nehemiah G. Ordway

Nehemiah G. Ordway became the seventh Governor of the Territory in 1880. Author Robinson wrote about him: "Ordway was a tall and distinguished-looking leader; his sanctimonious manner hid an able, scheming mind. He brought a number of people with him [from New Hampshire]—his son was to become territorial auditor—and soon built up a powerful political machine, using the patronage of public-land-sales advertising to enlist newspaper editors."[22]

Ordway made an alliance with McKenzie, and together they pulled off a coup that moved the territorial capital from Yankton to Bismarck, which was on the east-west line of the Northern Pacific Railroad. President Chester Arthur removed Ordway as governor in June 1884 because of corrupt dealings.

Chief Four Bears

Brent Lloyd Wills describes Chief Four Bears:

> All the pride and the splendor which had been developed in the red man before the arrival of the white seems to have been brought together and to have survived in Four Bears. He was wise and strong in tribal council. He was mighty in war. He was the greatest warrior of them all. He led his people against their enemies. . . .
>
> Throughout his life Chief Four Bears was a good and true friend of the white man. He believed that both races could benefit by sharing, by working together, exchanging ideas and goods in peaceful and friendly brotherhood. He welcomed white men to the Mandan villages and showed them every kindness.[23]

Theodore Roosevelt

Although not a North Dakotan, Theodore Roosevelt played a part in the development of the territory.

> Theodore Roosevelt first came to North Dakota in September, 1883, on a hunting trip. His headquarters on this trip was at the Chimney Butte Ranch, also known as the Maltese Cross, from the shape of its cattle brand. . . . The house was a log structure

---

[21] Robinson, supra note 3, pp. 230–231.

[22] Id., p. 200.

[23] Brent Lloyd Wills, *North Dakota Geography and Early History* (Grand Forks: University of North Dakota Press, 1967), pp. 76–77.

> of one room. Here Roosevelt stayed for about three weeks with the three cowboys whose home it was. . . . Roosevelt made several hunting trips far into the Badlands country. On one of these trips he shot his first buffalo. Before returning to the East he bought the ranch, . . . He hoped to come out here often, for he liked the country and he liked to hunt. Although of a rugged personality, he was not very strong physically and he hoped to build himself up by living a vigorous outdoor life in the stimulating North Dakota air. It may perhaps be said that North Dakota gave Theodore Roosevelt the health and strength to make him the great man that he later became.[24]

Roosevelt became involved in the ranching in the area, including becoming chairman of the Stockmen's Association. Because of his thick glasses, he was referred to as "Four Eyes."

Linda Warfel Slaughter

Linda Warfel Slaughter came to the Territory in the early 1870s with her husband, an army surgeon who was stationed at Fort Rice, just south of Mandan. "Linda Slaughter," author Leifur declares,

> was one of the most talented of North Dakota pioneer women. She was a writer, painter, lecturer, nurse, and an excellent cook. . . . She taught the first Sunday school in a tent. On July 7, 1873, she became the first teacher of a public school. When the schools of the county were organized, she became the first county superintendent of schools. When Bismarck was granted a post office, she became the first postmistress. In honor of all her achievements, when the telegraph services reached Bismarck, she was selected to write the first telegram to be sent from there.[25]

THE CAPITAL IS HIJACKED TO BISMARCK

In response to a movement in the Territorial Legislature, a bill was passed setting up a nine-member commission to choose a new site for the capital. The commissioners were required to meet in Yankton for the purpose of organization. In order to do so, the commissioners met in Sioux City and agreed upon an organization. They then took a train to Yankton, arriving there at 3:00 in the morning. The organization was then agreed upon and the train left town, making stops at the various towns interested in being the capital.

"Bismarck," Leifur writes, "put on the best show of entertainment for the commission and also made the best bid. Its offer was one hundred thousand

---

[24] Leifur, supra note 4, pp. 279–280.

[25] Id., p. 248.

dollars and 320 acres of land. This offer was accepted and Bismarck became the territorial capital. The cornerstone of the new capital was laid on September 5, 1883."[26]

THE TERRITORIAL GOVERNMENT

The territorial government first met in 1862. There were 13 members in the House and 9 in the Senate. "Each of these members," Leifur notes, "seemed to have very definite ideas as to how the territory should be run, and seldom did they agree on anything. The second legislature was no better than the first. It was not even agreed as to who were legally elected members of the house. There were two groups which claimed the honor, so there were two houses, meeting in two different places. Finally, after much argument, one house was agreed upon, and business proceeded."[27]

THE FARMERS ORGANIZE

In the early 1880s, farmers in the Territory found themselves at the mercy of the Minneapolis millers who had organized to eliminate competition in the purchase of grain. The millers and other large purchasers of grain controlled the elevators which bought the grain and the grain terminals in Minnesota. When these large purchasers of grain combined with the railroads, the independent buyers were forced out of business.

Robinson describes the situation as it then existed: "With such rigid control, the . . . [monopoly] could and did abuse the farmers with low grading and low prices, with false weights and excessive dockage. The farmers, helpless before the combination of the railroads and the large purchasers of wheat, were the victims of irregularity and intentional fraud."[28]

As a result, the farmers organized the Dakota Farmers' Alliance and began to seek help in the political arena. Although the Alliance was successful in electing its members to the Territorial Legislature, they were not successful in obtaining the kind of legislation that would give them relief. Robinson sums up the Alliance's efforts: "For all their struggles, the farmers could not break the grip of the railroads, the elevator monopoly, and their allies upon the government or the economy of Dakota."[29]

---

[26] Id., pp. 261–262.

[27] Id., p. 259.

[28] Robinson, supra note 3, p. 203.

[29] Id., p. 207.

THE CREATION OF THE TWO DAKOTAS

The people in the southern part of the Territory, being unhappy that the capital had been moved to Bismarck, called constitutional conventions in 1883 and again in 1885 hoping to become a state separate from the Territory. These efforts failed, but did spark interest in the creation of two states. The Republican platform of 1888 called for the admission of two states, and the Omnibus Bill of February 22, 1889 authorized the creation of constitutions for North Dakota, South Dakota, Montana, and Washington.[30]

> Statehood was a quiet revolution, accomplished by less than two hundred men. The first leaders were Yankton politicians, but all came from southern Dakota and all were Republicans. With a few exceptions, they were conservative, middle-class business and professional men—bankers, lawyers, ministers, railroad employees, and newspaper editors. They were of the older American stock and came from New England, New York, or the states of the Old Northwest. They were Republicans because Dakota was a one-party region—a result of the long years of territorial status when the Republican party had control of the United States government.
>
> These men wished to throw off outside control. They were tired of the President's appointing the governor and other officials from outside the territory. They aspired to win elective office themselves.[31]

Among those opposing statehood were Ordway, McKenzie, and their followers and the railroads. The railroads were opposed because of lenient territorial laws and their ability to influence decisions made in Washington concerning the Territory.

The Enabling Act required the convening of a constitutional convention of 75 members, 3 to be elected from each of the 25 districts in the Territory. These delegates were elected in May 1889 and the Convention opened in Bismarck on July 4. Author Robinson writes: "A big parade celebrated the event; five hundred Sioux from Standing Rock, led by Sitting Bull, who carried a huge American flag, took part."[32]

THE CONSTITUTIONAL CONVENTION

Many of the prominent men of the Territory were delegates to the Constitutional Convention. Most were from the eastern counties and were under 50 years of age. There were 51 Republicans, 19 Democrats, 2 Prohibitionists, 2 Populists,

---

[30] Id., p. 203.

[31] Id., p. 199.

[32] Id., p. 208.

and 1 Independent. One-third of the delegates were lawyers, 29 were farmers, and 23 of them were foreign born. Only 10 were Scandinavian.[33]

The Convention's organization was similar to the present-day State House of Representatives, with a presiding officer, clerks, sergeant at arms, watchman, messenger, chaplain, and official stenographer. Committees were formed for the various types of legislation to be considered.

On July 20, Delegate Erastus A. Williams presented the Convention with a proposed constitution prepared by Professor James Bradley Thayer of Harvard Law School, at the request of Henry Villard, Chairman of the Board of Directors of the Northern Pacific Railroad. "Thayer's draft," Robinson notes, "was a carefully constructed model constitution, not a dishonest effort to create a government favorable to the railroads."[34]

Among the more difficult problems facing the delegates was whether the constitution should be similar to the U.S. Constitution (i.e., rather short) or whether it should be long and more specific in its provisions.

Judge Thomas M. Cooley, a visiting statesman, when addressing the Convention, "told the delegates that they must trust the government: 'Don't in your constitution-making legislate too much. . . . You have got to trust somebody in the future and it is right and proper that each department of government should be trusted to perform its legitimate function.'"[35] The fact that the final document is very long, with several of the articles containing more than 20 sections, indicates that the delegates did not follow Judge Cooley's admonition.

The issue of prohibition was also a difficult one, as was the location of the state's numerous public institutions. The question of prohibition was submitted to the voters as a separate issue at the election to approve the constitution. At that election, held October 1, 1889, the constitution was approved by a vote of 27,441 to 8,107, but prohibition passed by less than 1,200 votes. In dealing with the location of the state's institutions, the delegates made that part of the constitution by including Article XIX, which designates the number and location of each.

Author Robinson discusses what the delegates accomplished in writing the Convention:

> In addition to establishing the framework of the state government, the constitution guarantees basic human rights and a democratic society in the American tradition. First come the liberties of the individual: freedom of worship, habeas corpus, jury trial, freedom of speech and publication, the right of assembly, and no imprisonment

---

[33] Id.

[34] Id., p. 209.

[35] Id., p. 210.

for debt. The convention granted suffrage to all males twenty-one years of age who were citizens or who, though of alien birth, had declared their intention of becoming citizens not less than one nor more than six years before the election, and also to civilized persons of Indian descent who had severed tribal relations two years before the election. Women might vote in school elections.

Married women could control their own property. Hiring children under twelve to work in mines and factories was prohibited. Corporations were forbidden to exchange black lists. The first legislative assembly was required to establish a system of free public education extending from the primary grades through the collegiate level.[36]

At the October 1 election, the people elected legislators and state officials, including three supreme court justices and congressmen. And on November 2, 1889, President Benjamin Harrison declared North Dakota a state and John Miller became the first governor. Women did not receive the full right to vote until the adoption of the Nineteenth Amendment to the U.S. Constitution, which the State Legislature ratified in 1919.

NORTH DAKOTA POLITICS

When the movement for statehood began, the first leaders were Republicans. "Statehood leaders," Robinson writes, "had nothing but contempt for the graft and corruption of the territorial system. They brought into the movement reformers, lawyers, and members of women's clubs. But the Democrats—the workmen of the towns and the Black Hills, the saloon element, and some of the merchants—took little interest in the movement."[37]

Some members of the Farmers' Alliance, not having much political success, joined with the Prohibitionists to form the Independent Party of North Dakota in 1890.

Many of the members of the Alliance, however, did not join the Independent Party and therefore all of the Republican candidates were elected in November. But the Independent Party did not give up, and succeeded in taking over most of the state offices in the election of 1892. The administration of the party's choice for governor, Eli C. D. Shortridge, however, was a failure and the Republican Party came back into power in the election of 1894.

---

[36] Id., p. 214. See: Robert Vogel, *Sources of the North Dakota Constitution*, 65 North Dakota Law Review (1989), p. 331; Herbert L. Meschke and Lawrence D. Spears, *Digging for Roots: The North Dakota Constitution and the Thayer Correspondence*, 65 North Dakota Law Review (1989), p. 343.

[37] Robinson, supra note 3, p. 199.

The movement for reform saw new life with the organization of the Nonpartisan League by Arthur C. Townley in 1915. In describing Townley, Robinson wrote:

> He was born and raised on a farm in Brown's Valley, Minnesota, graduated from high school at Alexandria, read voraciously on politics and economics under the tutelage of a radical tailor, and taught country school. In 1907, at the age of twenty-seven, he began to farm in the Golden Valley country near Beach, North Dakota. He soon plunged in flax, borrowing heavily for power machinery. When in 1912 an early frost and a break in flax prices wiped out his returns, he went bankrupt with debts of eighty thousand dollars. An embittered Townley turned to socialism.[38]

The League grew rapidly and was able to win the governorship and a majority in the House of Representatives in the November 1916 election and a majority of both houses of the Legislature in 1918.

The League-controlled Legislature established an Industrial Commission to manage all businesses in the state; created the Bank of North Dakota for the deposit of all state and local government funds; and ordered the construction of the North Dakota Mill and Elevator to encourage the manufacture and distribution of farm products.

The Legislature also "enacted a workmen's compensation law and also an eight-hour day and minimum-wage law for women. It limited the use of injunctions in labor disputes."[39]

The League suffered a setback in a recall election held October 28, 1921, when candidates of the Independent Voters Association defeated three League officeholders.

The candidacy of Franklin D. Roosevelt for the office of President of the United States in 1932 gave the League an opportunity to return to power in North Dakota. During the early years of the League, one of its prominent members was William Langer who, after being elected as state's attorney for Morton County in 1914, immediately began a campaign against bootleggers.

Prior to the election in 1932, Langer had spent personal funds to finance the resurrection of the League and was the League's candidate for governor in that election, which he won. Langer was elected to the U.S. Senate in November 1940.

In 1932, the League also captured control of the Legislature and all state offices. At this time, League members were candidates in the Republican primary election.

During this period, when the League's candidates were running and winning in the Republican primary election, an anti-Langer and League movement

[38] Id., p. 328.

[39] Id., p. 343.

brought about the creation of the Republican Organizing Committee. This was an attempt to bring about a realignment of the political parties in the state, and that did take place in 1956 when the Nonpartisan League moved to the Democratic Party and Republicans came together in one Republican Party.

Although North Dakota does not require voters to register as members of a particular political party, the Republican Party has been the predominant party on the state level for many years. There are exceptions, as indicated by the election of three Democratic governors (i.e., William L. Guy [1961–1973], Arthur A. Link [1973–1981], and George Sinner [1985–1993]).

State Democrats have been successful on the national level in recent years, electing both U.S. Senators Byron Dorgan and Kent Conrad and the state's lone member of the U.S. House of Representatives, Earl Pomeroy.

THE NORTH DAKOTA SUPREME COURT

Article VI, Section 2 of the state constitution creates the Supreme Court and gives it both original and appellate jurisdiction. Three justices were elected at the time of the adoption of the constitution. They were Joseph M. Bartholomew, Alfred Wallin, and Guy C. H. Corliss. Bartholomew became the first chief justice.

Chief Justice Bartholomew grew up in Wisconsin, served in the Army during the Civil War, and, after studying law in a law office, was admitted to the bar in Wisconsin. He came to Dakota Territory in 1883 and set up a practice in LaMoure County.

Justice Wallin was born in New York, but spent his boyhood in Michigan where his father practiced medicine. The justice graduated from the law department of the University of Michigan and started to practice law in St. Peter, Minnesota, in 1865. He came to Dakota Territory in January 1883 where he joined the firm of Wilson & Ball in Fargo.

After completing high school, Justice Guy C. H. Corliss did not attend school again. Born in New York State, Justice Corliss studied law in a law office and was admitted to the New York Bar in June 1876. In the fall of 1898, the justice moved to Grand Forks where he practiced law until he was elected to the Supreme Court.

Justice Corliss is described as "one of the most learned members of the legal profession in North Dakota, . . . [who] gained his knowledge and high station by dint of his own efforts. He has studied always with the idea of strengthening his mind and character, and he now stands at the head of the North Dakota bar."[40]

---

[40] *Compendium of History and Biography of North Dakota* (Chicago: Geo. A. Ogle & Co., 1900), p. 204.

One of the more colorful justices was James E. Robinson, who was on the Court from 1915 to 1923. Former North Dakota Supreme Court Justice Robert Vogel describes Justice Robinson:

> He was a veteran of the Civil War and was seventy-five years of age when he took office. He had a full beard and looked like an Old Testament prophet. . . . He is reputed to have worn his hat regularly in the courtroom and to have walked out of the courtroom in the middle of arguments if he thought he had heard enough from the lawyer arguing the case. He read the briefs in advance and, if he decided the case was a simple one, he would write a tentative opinion and send it to the lawyers before oral argument so they could save the trip to Bismarck if they agreed with the opinion. . . .
>
> There are several things about Robinson's opinions that are striking to a lawyer-reader. The most astonishing is Robinson's attitude toward prior decisions (precedents). He not only did not feel obligated to follow them—he usually disregarded them completely.[41]

Justice Robinson discussed his disdain for precedents in a dissenting opinion: "In this case there is no use of talking of res judicata or the force of any prior decision binding on this court. Though it is the custom of courts to adhere to their own blunders and pile error on error, the nefarious custom is not a law, and the custom is of less force when a party invokes a prior decision made by a bare majority of one judge, or by three judges, voting against three judges including the trial judge."[42]

THE U.S. CONSTITUTION VERSUS THE NORTH DAKOTA STATE CONSTITUTION

In discussing the differences between the two constitutions, the North Dakota Supreme Court has pointed out: "Congress can pass no laws but such as the Constitution authorizes, either expressly or by clear implication; while the state Legislature has jurisdiction of all subjects on which its legislation is not prohibited. The law making power of the state, it is said in one case, recognizes no restraints and is bound by none except such as are imposed by the Constitution."[43]

However, a subject that has spawned much debate among the justices is how the North Dakota Supreme Court should interpret those sections of the state constitution which deal with civil rights. Justice Beryl Levine expressed one side

---

[41] Robert Vogel, *Justice Robinson and the Supreme Court of North Dakota*, 58 North Dakota Law Review 83 (1982), pp. 84–85.

[42] McHenry County v. Brady, 163 N.W. 540, 549 (1917).

[43] State v. First State Bank, 202 N.W. 391, 396 (1924).

of that argument when she wrote: "I adhere to the position that our state constitution ought to have a life of its own in the area of fundamental rights and individual liberties. Otherwise it becomes a mere appendage to the United States constitution and I cannot accept the notion that a state's sovereign law should be reduced to a mere 'me too' or 'ditto.' That flies in the face of federalism and disregards the structure and substance of the American polity."[44]

This brought a response from Justice Gerald W. VandeWalle: "Although I agree we need not merely echo the United States Supreme Court in applying our own constitutional provisions which are identical to the Federal Constitution, I cannot agree that the interpretation and application of those provisions should merely reflect the philosophy or views of the particular justices who happen to be sitting at the time the issue of the application and interpretation of our State Constitution is raised."[45]

THE TOPOGRAPHY OF THE STATE

The north-flowing Red River forms the eastern boundary of North Dakota. The soil, for approximately 30–40 miles west of the river, is excellent for growing hard spring wheat and durum. This area, therefore, has been referred to as the breadbasket of the world.

The land for approximately 200 miles west of the Red River Valley is a rolling plain with few hills. Much farming is also carried on here. The International Peace Garden State Park is located here along the U.S.–Canadian border, 888 acres of which are in the United States and 1,300 acres of which are in Canada. This park is located in the Turtle Mountains and contains a large, beautiful formal garden.

The far western part of the state is more rugged with buttes that rise up to 400 feet above the plains. Many cattle ranches are located throughout this area as well as lignite coal mines and oil wells. The Theodore Roosevelt National Park, which is also located in this region, contains badlands, petrified forests, a Painted Canyon, and buffalo.

Author Leifur describes this area: "The Badlands are not only beautiful and of exceptional geologic interest but they furnish recreation for people who enjoy the atmosphere provided by a ranch country so typical of the West. The vegetation is unique and interesting as is the bird and mammal life. Hiking or saddle-horse trips through the rugged canyons of the Little Missouri River provide many thrills for park visitors."[46]

---

[44] State v. Ringquist, 433 N.W.2d 207, 217 (1988).

[45] Id. at 46.

[46] Leifur, supra note 4, p. 570.

There are many lakes and rivers in the state containing a variety of fish. The largest lake is Lake Sakakawea, which was formed by building a dam on the Missouri River northwest of Bismarck.

Deer flourish throughout most of the state, and pronghorn antelope are found in the far western region. Upland game, such as pheasants, grouse, and ducks allow for annual hunting seasons.

The climate of North Dakota can best be described as harsh in the winter, with hot summers and beautiful springs and falls. Annual rainfall varies from around 21 inches in the Red River Valley to 15 inches in the far western part of the state.

PART TWO

The North Dakota Constitution and Commentary

Preamble

We, the people of North Dakota, grateful to Almighty God for the blessings of civil and religious liberty, do ordain and establish this constitution.[1]

The delegates to the Convention considered several different versions of a Preamble. One of those under consideration reads as follows:

Almighty God, in his infinite mercy, having prospered us as a territory, and looking to him for a blessing upon our present endeavor to secure and transmit unimpaired to succeeding generations the liberty we now enjoy, and that we may form a more perfect government, establish justice, insure peace and domestic tranquility, provide for the common defense and promote general prosperity to ourselves and our posterity, do ordain and establish this Constitution for the State of North Dakota.[2]

[1] An attempt was made at the Constitutional Convention in 1889 to strike the words "Almighty God" from the Preamble. (Journal of the Constitutional Convention for North Dakota Held at Bismarck, Thursday, July 4 to August 17, 1889, pp. 357–360.)

[2] Journal of the Constitutional Convention for North Dakota, p. 157.

Article I

Declaration of Rights

ALL INDIVIDUALS . . . HAVE CERTAIN INALIENABLE RIGHTS

Section 1. All individuals are by nature equally free and independent and have certain inalienable rights, among which are those of enjoying and defending life and liberty; acquiring, possessing and protecting property and reputation; pursuing and obtaining safety and happiness; and to keep and bear arms for the defense of their person, property, and the state, and for lawful hunting, recreational, and other lawful purposes, which shall not be infringed.

In commenting on this section, the North Dakota Supreme Court has written: "This section embodies the essence of the statement of the "self-evident truths" set forth in the Declaration of Independence, and the words and terms used, whether in the Declaration of Independence, the Constitution of the United States, or the Constitutions of the several states, convey a commonly accepted meaning."[3]

The Court then pointed out that Section 12 of Article I also defines and declares the existence of certain rights. "We will consider these two sections together," Justice William L. Nuessle wrote, "because the second supplements and supports the first which defines and declares the inherent rights of men,

---

[3] State v. Cromwell, 9 N.W.2d 914, 918 (1943).

while the second protects and guarantees the exercise and enjoyment of those rights."[4]

Enjoying and Defending Life and Liberty

The word "liberty" in this section has been the subject of court interpretation. For example, in *State v. Woodmanse*,[5] the Supreme Court held that the word liberty does not give an individual the unqualified right to be a banker. The Court acknowledged that "the provision relative to personal liberty found in our constitution might be violated by enactment of a statute which operated to deprive a citizen of the right to pursue a lawful trade or avocation."[6] The Court pointed out, however, that the business of banking had always been the subject of state regulation.

Although the question of the meaning of the word liberty was before the Court a number of times after *Woodmanse*, the result in most of the cases was the same. For example, the Court held that Section 1 was not violated when the state prohibited liquor sales,[7] required the licensing of cream stations,[8] plumbers,[9] water softener installers,[10] dealers in securities,[11] garbage collectors,[12] and house movers.[13] Furthermore, the right to liberty does not include the right to be a bootlegger,[14] nor to inherit or to take by will or to devise and bequeath one's property.[15]

The Court did, however, strike down a law requiring professional photographers to secure a state license. The Court referred to those parts of sections 1 and 13 (now Section 12) which protect people from being "deprived of life, liberty or property without due process of law."[16]

In striking down the photographer's licensing law, the Court asked and answered the question: "Are the means of the regulation contained . . . [in the statute] reasonably required and appropriate for . . . [protection of the public]? We do not think so."[17]

---

[4] Id.

[5] 46 N.W. 970 (1890).

[6] Id., p. 971.

[7] State v. Fargo Bottling Works Co., 124 N.W. 387 (1910).

[8] Cofman v. Ousterhous, 168 N.W. 826 (1918).

[9] State ex rel. City of Bismarck v. District Court, 253 N.W. 744 (1934).

[10] Bob Rosen Water Conditioning Co. v. City of Bismarck, 181 N.W.2d 722 (1970).

[11] State v. Goetz, 312 N.W.2d 1 (1981).

[12] Tayloe v. City of Wahpeton, 62 N.W.2d 31 (1953).

[13] Johnson v. Elkin, 263 N.W.2d 123 (1978).

[14] State ex rel. Germain v. Ross, 170 N.W. 121 (1918).

[15] Moody v. Hagen, 162 N.W. 704 (1917).

[16] State v. Cromwell, supra note 1, p. 922.

[17] Id. at 921.

This reasonableness test is consistent with the approach taken by the U.S. Supreme Court when dealing with the concept of due process guaranteed by the Fifth and Fourteenth Amendments to the U.S. Constitution.[18]

When Harold J. Odegaard was charged with failure to wear a crash helmet while riding a motorcycle as required by North Dakota law, he argued that the statute violated the liberty provisions of Sections 1 and 12. A majority of the Court disagreed and affirmed his conviction. The justices did not specifically say that the helmet law infringed upon any right guaranteed by Sections 1 and 12. They simply said that there was "a real and substantial relationship between the exercise of the police powers contained in our crash helmet statute and the public health, safety and welfare. It follows that the statute in no way violates any of the provisions of our state or federal constitutions."[19]

To Keep and Bear Arms

In *State v. Ricehill,*[20] the Court had its first opportunity to interpret the phrase in Section 1 "to keep and bear arms for the defense of their person, family, property and the state . . . which shall not be infringed." Ricehill, a previously convicted felon, was charged with and found guilty of violating a state law making it a criminal offense for a person convicted of a felony to possess a firearm. On appeal to the Supreme Court, Ricehill argued that Section 1 gave people the absolute right to bear arms. The Court disagreed.

Writing for the Court, Justice Gerald W. VandeWalle declared: "We disagree with such a broad reading of the provision. Instead, we believe our Constitution's protection of the right to keep and bear arms is not absolute; although it prevents the negation of the right to keep and bear arms, that right nevertheless remains subject to reasonable regulation under the State's police power."[21]

ALL POLITICAL POWER IS INHERENT IN THE PEOPLE

Section 2. All political power is inherent in the people. Government is instituted for the protection, security and benefit of the people, and they have a right to alter or reform the same whenever the public good may require.

Section 2 states a truism: the political power belongs to the people. Referring to this power, the Court has interpreted it this way: "The words of section 2 have the deepest significance; the words have such a profound meaning, and are such

[18] See: United States v. Caroline Products Co., 304 U.S. 144 (1938); N. D. State Board of Pharmacy v. Snyder's Drug Stores, Inc., 414 U.S. 156 (1973).

[19] State v. Odegaard, 165 N.W.2d 677, 680 (1969). Section 12 was formerly Section 13 of Article I.

[20] 415 N.W.2d 481 (1987). See also: Kasprowicz v. Finck, 574 N.W.2d 564 (1998).

[21] Id. at 483. The phrase "to keep and bear arms, etc." was added by an initiated amendment to the constitution adopted Novermber 6, 1984.

a lucid revealment of the place where political power is lodged for the benefit of the people, as should make a vivid impression on the minds of all. Each generation of people inherit this great and far-reaching political power from the preceding generation."[22]

Because all political power resides with the people, the Court has interpreted the North Dakota Constitution as being one of *limitations* upon government, unlike the U.S. Constitution, which is a grant of power to government.[23]

Relying on Section 2, the Court has held that a County Board of Commissioners has little discretion in the incorporation of a village if the citizens desiring to incorporate have complied with the statutes related to incorporation.[24]

THE FREE EXERCISE AND ENJOYMENT OF RELIGIOUS PROFESSION AND WORSHIP . . . SHALL BE FOREVER GUARANTEED

> **Section 3.** The free exercise and enjoyment of religious profession and worship, without discrimination or preference shall be forever guaranteed in this state, and no person shall be rendered incompetent to be a witness or juror on account of his opinion on matters of religious belief; but the liberty of conscience hereby secured shall not be so construed as to excuse acts of licentiousness, or justify practices inconsistent with the peace or safety of this state.

The foundation for Section 3 and the other sections of Article I that guarantee certain rights, can be traced back to the organization of the Dakota Territory in 1861. The Organic Law, adopted by the Congress March 2, 1861, to organize the Dakota Territory, contains the requirement "that the Constitution and all laws of the United States . . . shall have the same force and effect within the said territory of Dakota as elsewhere within the United States." That, of course, includes all of the rights guaranteed by the first ten amendments to the U.S. Constitution commonly referred to as the Bill of Rights.

Also, when the time came to create the states of North Dakota, South Dakota, Montana, and Washington, The Enabling Act of February 22, 1889, included the following provision with regard to religious beliefs: "First. That perfect toleration of religious sentiment shall be secured, and that no inhabitant of said states shall ever be molested in person or property on account of his or her mode of religious belief."

The North Dakota Supreme Court has considered six cases involving the state's compulsory school attendance laws and upheld those laws in all six cases. In five of these cases, the Court held that the laws did not violate the First

[22] State v. Hall, 171 N.W. 213, 214–215 (1919).

[23] State ex rel. Agnew v. Schneider, 253 N.W.2d 184, 187 (1977).

[24] State ex rel. Brunelle v. Sutton, 3 N.W.2d 106 (1942).

Amendment to the U.S. Constitution.[25] In the sixth case, the Court relied upon Article I, Section 3 of the North Dakota Constitution and reached the same result.[26] The Court reached these decisions even though the parents involved argued that these laws violated their right to freedom of religion protected by both the First Amendment and Section 3.

Writing for the Court in a case decided under Section 3, Justice Paul Sand explained:

> This illustrates that the interest of the state and the interests of individuals regarding their religious beliefs or convictions must be harmonized and balanced with the interests of the state so as to preserve the separate interests as much as possible without infringing upon the respective rights more than is necessary. The interests of neither one is absolute. We believe the stated constitutional mandate and objective establishes the compelling state interest and outbalances the resulting strain or imposition on the defendants' religious beliefs. Under the posture of this case we have available to us no other viable alternatives.[27]

When presented with the question whether a teacher certification requirement placed an unconstitutional burden on the religious beliefs of parents who home school their children, the Court held that it did not. The Court found no violation of the First Amendment, and bypassed the question of whether the certification requirement violated Section 3.[28]

The Court addressed the question of whether Sunday closing laws infringe upon religious beliefs in a case involving C. W. Temple and Clara Wright, who were arrested, charged with, and convicted of operating a theater on Sunday in violation of state law. The Court first said that it was not necessary to discuss the impact of the law on religion, but then discussed that issue at great length. "The law here in question," Justice B. F. Spalding declared, "in no manner interferes with the religious convictions or scruples of any inhabitant of the state. It neither prescribes for nor compels the petitioners or others to observe any form of religious worship. It creates no establishment of religion. The wills and consciences of all of the people are left free in this respect."[29]

The Establishment of Religion

Although Section 3 does not contain a clause specifically prohibiting the establishment of religion, the Court has interpreted that section as being similar to

---

[25] James E. Leahy, *"The Constitution Is What the Judges Say It Is,"* 65 North Dakota Law Review 491, 499 Note 50 (1989).

[26] State v. Rivinius, 328 N.W.2d 220 (1982).

[27] Id. at 229.

[28] State v. Patzer, 382 N.W.2d 631, 639 (1986). See also: State v. Melin, 428 N.W.2d 227 (1988).

[29] State v. Barnes, 132 N.W. 215, 218 (1911).

the establishment clause of the First Amendment to the U.S. Constitution. Such a case was *Bendewald v. Ley*.[30] This case involved a dispute between two church groups, each claiming the ownership of the church property. In concluding that the courts should not become involved in the dispute, the Court wrote: "The civil authority, both legislative and judicial, are traversing, under our Constitutions, both national and state, in forbidden and prohibited territory when they assume to legislate, or to interpret laws which undertake to define and interpret doctrinal and ecclesiastical questions, so as to be binding upon individuals or interfere with the determination of the individual conscience with reference thereto."[31]

Those parts of Section 3 prohibiting a religious qualification for being a juror, and preventing the use of religion to excuse licentiousness have not been construed by the North Dakota Supreme Court.

EVERY MAN MAY FREELY WRITE, SPEAK AND PUBLISH

> **Section 4.** Every man may freely write, speak and publish his opinions on all subjects, being responsible for the abuse of that privilege. In all civil and criminal trials for libel the truth may be given in evidence, and shall be a sufficient defense when the matter is published with good motives and for justifiable ends; and the jury shall have the same power of giving a general verdict as in other cases; and in all indictments or informations for libels the jury shall have the right to determine the law and the facts under the direction of the court as in other cases.

In construing this section, the Supreme Court has said:

> Few rights guaranteed by the Constitution are more valuable than those of freedom of speech and liberty of the press, which are guaranteed by the section quoted. But freedom does not mean unrestrained license. The fact that a right is guaranteed does not mean that there is also granted a license to abuse that right. Our Constitution expressly recognizes this; for while it guarantees to every man the right to "freely write, speak and publish his opinions on all subjects," and makes it permissive to publish the truth with good motives and for justifiable ends, it also provides that one who abuses that privilege shall be responsible therefor.[32]

One of the recognized methods of speaking is peaceful picketing. While the Court has agreed to that generalization, it has also held that peaceful picketing for an unlawful purpose is not protected by the North Dakota State Constitution. The Court reached that decision when it upheld an injunction granted against persons picketing for the purpose of securing union shops at several construction companies.

---

[30] 168 N.W. 693, 696 (1917).

[31] Id. p. 696. See also: State v. Burckhard, 579 N.W.2d 194, 196 (1998).

[32] Englund v. Townley, 174 N.W. 755, 757 (1919).

Because both closed and union shops were prohibited under North Dakota law, the Court, quoting from a U.S. Supreme Court case, declared: "'Peaceful picketing is now recognized as an exercise of the right of free speech and therefore lawful. . . . However it cannot be made the cover for concerted action against an employer in order to achieve an unlawful or prohibited object, such as to compel an employer to coerce his employees to join a union.'"[33]

Although the Supreme Court did not mention Section 4 when it upheld the convictions of Mary Heath, Carol Dorsey, and Dwight Redfern, the central issue in their cases was the right to engage in peaceful picketing. The defendants were teachers who were arrested for ignoring a court order against picketing the school district. In discussing peaceful picketing, the Court pointed out: "Picketing, even though it is peaceful and without violence and disorder, and even though it does not actually obstruct a governmental function, if used for the purpose of fostering and supporting an illegal strike against a governmental employer, is unlawful and may be enjoined."[34]

Section 4 also protects the right to publish one's opinions. One freedom which the press wants is the right to attend criminal trials. The Court has considered that question in two cases. In one, the Court upheld a lower court's decision to close a preliminary hearing, being of the opinion that such a hearing was not a pretrial hearing nor a trial. In so holding, Justice Paul Sand wrote for the Court: "The news media under the North Dakota Constitution does not have any greater right than it has under the United States Constitution. Consequently, the opinions of the United States Supreme Court on this topic have full application in this state."[35]

In the second case, the Court sent the case back to the trial court because that court had not made factual and legal findings to support closing the preliminary hearing.[36]

Six months after this decision, the U.S. Supreme Court held that there was "a qualified First Amendment right of access to criminal proceedings [which] applies to preliminary hearings."[37] Because the North Dakota Supreme Court had said that "the opinions of the United States Supreme Court on this topic have full application in this state,"[38] preliminary hearings in North Dakota must now be open to the press unless it is necessary to close them to protect the defendant's right to a fair trial.

---

[33] Minor v. Building and Construction Trades Council, 75 N.W.2d 139, 154 (1956).

[34] State v. Heath, 177 N.W.2d 751, 756 (1970).

[35] Dickinson Newspapers, Inc. v. Jorgensen, 338 N.W.2d 72, 79 (1983).

[36] Minot Daily News v. Holum, 380 N.W.2d 347 (1986).

[37] Press-Enterpise Co. v. Superior Court, 478 U.S. 1, 13 (1986).

[38] Supra note 33, p. 79.

CITIZENS HAVE A RIGHT, . . . TO ASSEMBLE TOGETHER

> **Section 5.** The citizens have a right, in a peaceable manner, to assemble together for the common good, and to apply to those invested with the powers of government for the redress of grievances, or for other proper purposes, by petition, address or remonstrance.

The case of Charles A. Niska presented the Court with a somewhat unusual right-to-assemble question. Niska was being prosecuted for practicing law without a license. He had drafted some pleadings for Richard Schmidt and had represented Schmidt in three civil cases and one criminal case. When brought to trial, Niska argued that he was "exercising his right of assembly by associating with Schmidt to give him legal advice."[39]

While the Supreme Court recognized that Niska and Schmidt had a right to associate, the Court pointed out "the right to associate for expressive purposes is not absolute. Infringements on that right may be justified by regulations adopted to serve compelling state interests, unrelated to the suppression of ideas, that cannot be achieved by means significantly less restrictive of associational freedoms."[40]

To Apply to . . . Government . . . by Petition

The right to petition came before the Court when Melford Haugen, Jarl Hegvick, and Bernice Hegvick, appealed their conviction for threatening public servants. The defendants had lost their land, and in an attempt to reclaim it "commenced lawsuits against everyone they thought might be connected with the subject matter of their grievances."[41]

The defendants also prepared and sent to the county commissioners, letters, titled "'Re: CONSTRUCTIVE NOTICE AND DEMAND.'"[42] In the letters, the defendants threatened to commence civil and criminal actions against the commissioners for damages.

Having been found guilty of threatening the commissioners, the defendants appealed to the Supreme Court, which reversed. The Court said: "Construing . . . [the statute] in accordance with its legislative history, the First Amendment, and our state constitutional provision guaranteeing the right of the people to apply to public officials for redress of grievances by remonstrance, we conclude that the defendants' 'Constructive Notice and Demand' letters do not fall within the proscription of the statute."[43]

---

[39] State v. Niska, 380 N.W.2d 646, 650 (1986).

[40] Id.

[41] State v. Haugen, 392 N.W.2d 799, 800 (1986).

[42] Id.

[43] Id., pp. 804–805.

NEITHER SLAVERY NOR INVOLUNTARY SERVITUDE . . . SHALL EVER BE TOLERATED IN THIS STATE

Section 6. Neither slavery nor involuntary servitude, unless for the punishment of crime, shall ever be tolerated in this state.

The Supreme Court has not decided any cases involving this section.

EVERY CITIZEN . . . SHALL BE FREE TO OBTAIN EMPLOYMENT

Section 7. Every citizen of this state shall be free to obtain employment wherever possible, and any person, corporation, or agent thereof, maliciously interfering or hindering in any way, any citizen from obtaining or enjoying employment already obtained, from any other corporation or person, shall be deemed guilty of a misdemeanor.

Relying on this section, the Legislature gave workers the right "to decline to associate with his fellows, but that he also has full freedom of association, self-organization, and designation of representatives of his own choosing."[44] Later the Labor Code was amended as follows:

> **Right to work not to be abridged by membership or nonmembership in labor union.** The right of persons to work may not be denied or abridged on account of membership or nonmembership in any labor union or labor organization, and all contracts in negation or abrogation of such rights are hereby declared to be invalid, void, and unenforceable.[45]

In *Minor v. Building and Construction Trades Council*,[46] the Supreme Court, relying on Section 7, upheld the above statutes when it approved an injunction against union officials prohibiting them from picketing several contractors in an attempt to force the adoption of a union shop.

"Both closed and union shops," Justice G. Grimson declared, "are prohibited under these North Dakota laws. Any attempt to impose an all union shop or to procure a contract of employment requiring or resulting therein is in defiance of the clear, public policy of this state."[47]

THE RIGHT OF THE PEOPLE TO BE SECURE

Section 8. The right of the people to be secure in their persons, houses, papers and effects, against unreasonable searches and seizures shall not be violated; and no

---

[44] NDCC Section 34-08-02.
[45] NDCC Section 34-01-14.
[46] 75 N.W.2d 139 (1956).
[47] Id., p. 149.

warrant shall issue but upon probable cause, supported by oath or affirmation, particularly describing the place to be searched

Searches Made with a Warrant

This section affirms the principle that the best way for people "*to be secure in their persons, houses, papers and effects,*" is to require law enforcement to secure a warrant before making a search. Cases in which officers have made a search without a warrant will be discussed hereafter.

In requesting a warrant, the officer is required to present sufficient facts to enable the magistrate to determine whether there is probable cause to believe that a crime is being or has been committed. When the facts indicate that the officer's information came from an informant, the Supreme Court has said the "requirements are to be more strictly applied when the informant is an unnamed informant from the 'criminal milieu,' than when the informant is a named good citizen informant, an innocent victim of the crime, or otherwise is a disinterested observer."[48]

The Supreme Court, however, has pointed out: "Probable cause to search does not require the same standard of proof necessary to establish guilt at trial; rather, probable cause to search exists if it is established that certain identifiable objects are probably connected with criminal activity and are probably to be found at the present time at an identifiable place."[49]

When a court is called upon to determine whether the magistrate had probable cause to issue the warrant, the court must examine the facts, "and substantial deference will be given to the . . . [magistrate's] determination of probable cause."[50] The magistrate, however, must be "performing his 'neutral and detached' function and not serving as merely a rubber stamp for the police."[51]

When seeking a search warrant, the officer's affidavit must be given under oath,[52] and must contain a statement of facts, not just suspicions that a crime is being committed. For example, in reversing the conviction of Mark Handtmann for certain drug-related offenses, the Supreme Court said: "Handtmann's 'reputation' may have made the police suspicious about the presence of evidence of criminal activity at the defendants' house, but that suspicion, without anything more specific about these defendants, does not amount to probable cause to search their house."[53]

---

[48] State v. Schmeets, 278 N.W.2d 401, 408 (1979).

[49] State v. Ringquist, 433 N.W.2d 207, 212 (1988).

[50] State v. Berger, 285 N.W.2d 533, 537 (1979).

[51] Id.

[52] Supra note 46, p. 405.

[53] State v. Handtmann, 437 N.W.2d 830, 835 (1989).

In securing sufficient facts to meet the probable cause requirement for the issuance of a warrant, officers sometimes must rely upon information supplied by informants. In such cases, the "magistrate must be informed of enough underlying circumstances to enable him to determine that the informant's observations regarding the commission of a crime were accurate . . . and that the informant was credible or his information was reliable. . . . Both prongs must be met."[54]

Sometimes informants are ordinary citizens, and they "are presumed to be reliable."[55] The Court cautions, however, that the "reliability should be evaluated and verified by independent police investigation, if possible."[56]

Search warrants must identify the property to be seized. Detective Stancel obtained a search warrant to locate and seize "'various items which I have reason to believe have been recently stolen in Williams County which are evidence of crimes recently committed.'"[57] With this warrant in hand, detective Stancel went to the farm of James Schmitz where he seized several of the items he thought to have been stolen.

Schmitz was charged with and convicted of theft. On appeal, Schmitz argued that the warrant was defective as not specifically identifying the items to be seized. The Supreme Court agreed, taking note of the fact that: "On its face, the warrant authorized a search *anywhere* on Schimtz's farm for *anything* that might be stolen. . . . The officers might have been looking for anything from stolen vehicles, livestock, or farm implements to stolen cash, credit cards, or jewelry. The warrant set no limits."[58]

The place to be searched must also be specifically identified in the warrant; a search for property in the wrong place is an unlawful search and any evidence found therein cannot be used against the defendant. Such was the situation in the case of Orlynn M. Erickson when officers searched the east side of a duplex although the warrant applied only to Erickson's unit on the west side. In reversing Erickson's conviction, the Supreme Court concluded that "the issue is not whether the warrant is defective, but whether the search conducted exceeded the scope of the warrant. On this question, we agree with Erickson that it did."[59]

Searches Made without a Warrant

John Manning was a suspect in a hit-and-run auto accident in which a boy was struck and killed. Officers, suspecting that Manning was involved, conducted a search of his home and garage without a warrant and took pictures of his car.

---

[54] Supra note 46, p. 406.

[55] State v. Rangeloff, 580 N.W.2d 593, 600 (1998).

[56] Id.

[57] State v. Schmitz, 474 N.W.2d 249, 250 (1991).

[58] Id., p. 252.

[59] State v. Erickson, 496 N.W.2d 555, 560 (1993).

Based on the evidence obtained during the search, Manning was arrested, tried, and convicted of leaving the scene of an accident. The Supreme Court, however, reversed and granted a new trial. Writing for the Court, Justice Alvin C. Strutz declared: "There are numerous decisions of both the State and Federal courts . . . to the effect that evidence seized during an unlawful search cannot constitute proof against the victim of the search."[60]

If officers have time to secure a warrant, but do not do so, the evidence seized will not be admissible against the defendant. The Court reached that conclusion in a case where officers had learned that a package containing marijuana had arrived at a bus depot, but waited 22 hours before opening it. "There was ample time to obtain a warrant;" Justice Robert Vogel wrote, "the package was, in effect, in the custody of the police, since they had made arrangements to hold it until they authorized delivery; and no other legitimate excuse for not obtaining a warrant is shown."[61]

There are some situations in which officers may make a valid search without a warrant. One of those situations is when the search is incident to a lawful arrest. In order that such searches be legal, however, the arrest and the search must be done at the same time. For example, when officers smelled burning marijuana near a house trailer, they entered over the protest of the occupants. While waiting for a search warrant, the officers searched the trailer and found drug paraphernalia.

When the warrant did not arrive, the officers arrested one of the occupants, Darrin R. Ackerman, for possessing drug paraphernalia.

Ackerman was convicted but his conviction was reversed by the Supreme Court. Chief Justice Gerald VandeWalle wrote the Court's opinion, and pointed out: "Here, . . . the officers did not arrest for an offense committed in their presence and then enter and search. . . . The drug paraphernalia was not in plain view until after the officers entered the trailer without a warrant and the search was not incident to an arrest because no arrests were made until more than an hour after the search."[62]

Courts, including the North Dakota Supreme Court, have generally permitted officers considerable leeway in making searches pursuant to the arrest of a person in, or near, an automobile. This was the situation when the police arrested Kimberly K. Wanzek for driving with a suspended driver's license and driving under the influence of alcohol. The officers had followed Wanzek to an apartment building where she was arrested after she had gotten out of the car and was standing at the rear door on the driver's side.

---

[60] State v. Manning, 134 N.W.2d 91, 98 (1965).

[61] State v. Matthews, 216 N.W.2d 91, 104 (1974).

[62] State v. Ackerman, 499 N.W.2d 882, 885 (1993).

After placing Wanzek in their patrol car, Officer Thomas Nagel searched the interior of the car and found a bag of marijuana in the glove compartment.

Subsequently, Wanzek was found guilty of possessing a controlled substance and she appealed to the Supreme Court. She argued that because she was no longer in the vehicle at the time of her arrest, it was illegal for the officer to search it.

In response, the Court pointed out that courts throughout the country have answered the question differently; some courts holding that the search is proper only if the person arrested is in the car at the time of the search.

In deciding that the search was proper in this case the Court said: "We are not persuaded by the line of cases which hold an arrestee is an occupant only when arrested inside the vehicle or where the police initiate contact with the arrestee before the arrestee exits the vehicle."[63]

Inventory searches in which officers find contraband are permitted under some circumstances. For example, John J. Klodt had left his pickup parked on private property for several days when the owner of the property called Sheriff Ted Cornell about it. Sheriff Cornell moved the pickup to a spot near his own garage and began to inventory the pickup's contents. There was some equipment generally used in the oil well drilling industry in plain view in the back of the pickup. Upon contacting the State Crime Bureau, Cornell was told to take the property and store it in a vault so no one could steal it, which he did.

When it was determined that the equipment was stolen, Klodt was arrested and charged with theft. At his trial, Klodt argued that the search was invalid and that therefore the equipment could not be used against him. The trial court disagreed and so did the Supreme Court. "We reject that argument because the property was in plain view and was removed from the pickup for the purpose of securing the property from theft. There was no reason for the sheriff to obtain a search warrant under these circumstances."[64]

Sometimes officers may find themselves in an emergency situation, and a search under such conditions may be legal even though made without a warrant. For example, after Kevin Ternes drove through a stop sign and collided with another car, he continued on, eventually stopping at his home in a trailer park. A witness to the accident followed Ternes to the trailer park and called the police, who arrived shortly thereafter. When no one responded to the officers' knocking and calling out, they entered the trailer and found Ternes in the bathroom holding a towel to a bleeding gash in his neck. After questioning him for a short while, the officers arrested him for driving under the influence, with a suspended driver's license and without liability insurance.

---

[63] State v. Wanzek, 598 N.W.2d 811, 815 (1999).

[64] State v. Klodt, 298 N.W.2d 783, 787 (1980).

Upon being convicted for these offenses, Ternes appealed to the Supreme Court. He argued that because the officers did not have a warrant to enter the trailer, his arrest and the search of the trailer were illegal. The Supreme Court disagreed, and held: "The emergency doctrine allows police to enter a dwelling without a warrant to render emergency aid and assistance to a person whom they reasonably believe to be in distress."[65]

The fact that the officers found Ternes bleeding and administered first aid to him constituted an emergency for the purposes of determining that the search was lawful.

The *Ternes* case indicates, however, that there must be a real emergency before the police are permitted to enter, search, and arrest. The Court did not find such an emergency when officers responded to a call at 4:20 A.M. that there was a loud party at the Alpha Tau Omega fraternity house in Fargo. When the officers arrived on the scene, they heard loud music and saw beer bottles being thrown out a window. When they shined their flashlights at the windows, the music stopped and no more bottles were thrown out.

The officers tried the door bell but it was not working, so they knocked on the door but no one responded. After pounding on the door, it came open and the officers saw several intoxicated minors and cans and bottles of beer in the hallway. The officers charged several individuals with loud party violations, and minors in possession and consumption of alcohol.

At their trials, the defendants moved to suppress the evidence arguing that entry into the fraternity house was unlawful. Judge Norman J. Backes agreed and suppressed the evidence and the city appealed.

The issue before the Supreme Court was whether there had been exigent circumstances to permit the officers to enter the fraternity house, thus making the seizure of the evidence permissible. The Court said there was not and affirmed Judge Backes' decision.

The Court pointed out: "The government has the burden to demonstrate exigent circumstances existed in order to overcome the presumption a warrantless search is unreasonable."[66] They did not do so in this case.

The Court said: "Exigent circumstances 'has been defined as an emergency situation requiring swift action to prevent imminent danger to life or serious damage to property, or to forestall the imminent escape of a suspect or destruction of evidence.'"[67]

Another situation in which officers are permitted to make a search without a warrant is when they search garbage cans. The Court upheld that such a search of Teresa R. Rydberg's garbage could be made by officers acting on information

[65] City of Fargo v. Ternes, 522 N.W.2d 176, 178 (1994).

[66] City of Fargo v. Lee, 580 N.W.2d 580, 582 (1998).

[67] Id. See also: State v. DeCoteau, 592 N.W.2d 579 (1999).

given by an informant that Rydberg was a supplier of cocaine. During the search, the officers found evidence of cocaine which was confirmed by the State Laboratory. On the basis of this information, a search warrant was obtained to search Rydberg's residence where they found cocaine and drug paraphernalia.

Rydberg was tried and convicted of possessing a controlled substance and she appealed. She argued that the search of her garbage violated her right of privacy, and that therefore the search of her home was unlawful. The Supreme Court disagreed. "Based on the public location of Rydberg's garbage, we conclude the garbage searches, in this case, did not violate Article I, Section 8 of the North Dakota Constitution. By placing her garbage on or against the public alley, where it was exposed to the general public, and with the express purpose of abandoning it to the trash collector, Rydberg waived any privacy interest she may have had in the garbage."[68]

When making an arrest, an officer may pat down the suspect. If, during the pat down, the officer feels what appears to be a weapon, he or she may continue the search and whatever evidence the officer finds may be used against the defendant. That was the situation when officers were searching a house with a warrant looking for drugs.

Officer Maxiner was confronted by Jeffrey Zearley and a pushing match occurred. When officer Maxiner pushed Zearley against a wall, he made a pat-down search and, feeling something he thought was a knife, he reached into Zearley's pocket and extracted a drug pipe and packets of methamphetamine.

Officer Maxiner then arrested Zearley. Zearley was convicted and appealed to the Supreme Court arguing that the patdown and seizure of the pipe and drugs violated his right to be free from unreasonable searches. The Court disagreed. "In a tense situation like this confrontation," Justice Herbert L. Meschke declared, "the officer may not be able to adequately and quickly access the hazards before a patdown. That is why we conclude that the patdown was reasonable."[69]

The Court, however, was not sure that the pocket search was reasonable, and therefore sent the case back to the trial court. That court held that the pocket search was reasonable under the circumstances and the Supreme Court upheld that decision. "We believe," the Court said, "there was sufficient evidence to support the trial court's determination that the officer had an articulable and reasonable suspicion that Zearley was armed."[70]

Arrests Made with or without a Warrant

Before a magistrate can issue a warrant for an arrest, the magistrate must have probable cause to do so. The Court did not find that the magistrate had probable

[68] State v. Rydberg, 519 N.W.2d. 306, 310 (1994).

[69] State v. Zearley, 444 N.W.2d 353, 359 (1989).

[70] State v. Zearley, 468 N.W.2d 391, 392 (1991).

cause when he issued a warrant for the arrest of Russell Kulisich for allegedly breaking into a drug store. At the time of the search of Kulisich's room, the officers searched William Erdman who happened to be there at the time. Finding drugs on Erdman, the officers arrested him for possessing narcotics.

At his trial, Erdman argued that the seizure was illegal because the warrant had not been issued on a finding of probable cause. The Supreme Court agreed.

In discussing the warrant, the Court said: "The record discloses, without contradiction, that the warrant of arrest was issued by the magistrate without any inquiry as to whether the complainant, or any other witness, had reasonable grounds to believe that an offense had been committed and that Kulisich had committed it."[71] Furthermore, the Court wrote, the complainant "gave absolutely no facts or particulars to support the blank allegation as set out in the complaint, nor did he give the magistrate any information or facts as to how he, the complaining witness, knew that Kulisich had broken into and entered the drug store."[72]

Many times officers are called upon to make an arrest based upon the actions of the person they arrest. That was true when Deputy Sheriff Bradley Kapp received a call that a person appearing to be under the influence of alcohol was driving on the interstate highway.

As Kapp entered the interstate, he observed the described vehicle stopped on an exit ramp. He immediately turned back through the median and pulled up behind the stopped vehicle. After waiting for a short time, Kapp turned on the flashing lights, got out of his car, and approached the other car. As the driver of the other vehicle (Dallas Guthmiller) got out of his car, it appeared to Kapp that he was having difficulty standing. When Kapp approached Guthmiller, he could smell the odor of alcohol and noted that Guthmiller's speech was slurred.

When asked to do so, Guthmiller refused to take a sobriety test, claiming that he was not driving because he was stopped. Kapp arrested Guthmiller for driving under the influence. He was convicted and appealed.

Guthmiller argued that Kapp had no reason to stop him because he, Kapp, had not seen him driving erratically and therefore had no reason to make an investigation. The Supreme Court disagreed, being of the opinion that Kapp's knowledge of the color, direction, and license number of Guthmiller's car plus the somewhat prolonged stop at the stop sign justified Kapp's investigation and Guthmiller's arrest.[73]

While the Court held in Guthmiller's case, that Officer Kapp was justified in arresting Guthmiller, the Court has also pointed out: "An officer must have an articulable and reasonable suspicion that a motorist is violating the law in order

---

[71] State v. Erdman, 170 N.W.2d 872, 875 (1969).

[72] Id.

[73] State v. Guthmiller, 499 N.W.2d 590 (1993).

to legally stop a vehicle. . . . This standard requires less than probable cause but more than a mere hunch."[74]

Sobriety and Game Checkpoints

While Dale Uhden was riding his motorcycle, he was stopped at a sobriety checkpoint conducted by the Bismarck Police Department. When the checkpoint officer noticed that Uhden had bloodshot eyes, an odor of alcohol, and poor balance, he arrested Uhden for driving under the influence. Uhden was tried and convicted, and appealed to the Supreme Court.

Among the issues before the Court was whether sobriety checkpoints violated Article I, Section 8. The Court held that such checkpoints did not violate that section.

Writing for the Court, Chief Justice VandeWalle declared: "We believe the record supports the county court's finding of constitutionality, as the strictures of the guidelines and briefing [prepared by the City] adequately advance the public interests and limit interference with individual liberty, and Uhden does not draw our attention to any countervailing evidence in the record."[75]

In *State v. Albaugh*,[76] the Court had before it the legality of a game and fish checkpoint. When Harold Albaugh was forced to stop at such a checkpoint, Game Warden Supervisor Floyd Chrest saw two open cans of beer in the center console of Albaugh's car. Chrest summoned Police Chief Dean Danzeisen who, after conducting a field sobriety test, arrested Albaugh for driving under suspension and while being impaired. Albough was convicted but appealed, arguing that the checkpoint violated Section 8. The Supreme Court disagreed and responded: "To assess the reasonableness of a checkpoint stop under both the federal and state constitutions, we employ a three-part analysis, balancing the State's interest in the checkpoint's purpose against the degree that the checkpoint advances that interest and the severity of the intrusion upon the individual's liberty."[77]

ALL COURTS SHALL BE OPEN

> **Section 9.** All courts shall be open, and every man for any injury done him in his lands, goods, person or reputation shall have remedy by due process of law, and right and justice administered without sale, denial or delay. Suits may be brought against the state in such manner, in such courts, and in such cases, as the legislative assembly may, by law, direct.

---

[74] State v. Brown, 509 N.W.2d 69, 71 (1993).

[75] City of Bismarck v. Uhden, 513 N.W.2d. 373, 379 (1994).

[76] 571 N.W.2d 345 (1997).

[77] Id., p. 347.

In construing the phrase "all courts shall be open," the Supreme Court has said: "Our research shows that the portion of Section 9 relied upon by the plaintiffs has been repeatedly construed as a guarantee of *access* to our State system of justice."[78] "But," the Court continued, "even if a more broad interpretation of this clause was warranted, Section 9 never has been construed as an absolute right; indeed, this court once stated that the provision must be interpreted in light of the 'superior rights of the public and the necessities of the occasion.'"[79]

The Court, therefore, has upheld a statutory requirement that controversies arising out of the construction and repair of highways be submitted to arbitration. Writing for the Court, Justice Ralph J. Erickstad said: "(W)e see nothing in the provisions of the state or federal constitutions referred to us prohibiting the arbitration statues in question, which require the determination by arbitration of disputes arising out of highway construction and repair contracts between the State and a prime contractor."[80]

The Court has also upheld the Skiing Responsibility Act of 1979 which limits the liability of ski resort operators if they are in compliance with certain statutory requirements.[81]

When the Skiing Responsibility Act was challenged as a violation of Section 9, the Supreme Court held that because the section does not give an "absolute" right of access to the courts, and because the Skiing Responsibility Act does not bar all legal action against resort operators, Section 9 was not violated.[82]

An example of when courts must be open is found in the Supreme Court's response to State's Attorney Cynthia Rothe's closure of a state's attorney's inquiry into a criminal act causing death. Upon learning that the inquiry would be closed, KFGO Radio, Inc., brought an action in the District Court challenging that decision. The trial judge granted an injunction requiring the inquiry to be open, which the Supreme Court sustained on appeal.

Justice William L. Paulson wrote the Court's opinion. He acknowledged that Section 9 required courts to be open and that the trial judge was correct to require it to be open in this case. Justice Paulson pointed out, however: "In the interest of fairness, a court may exclude from the courtroom members of the public who are creating physical disturbances or causing potentially dangerous situations. The limitations imposed are required to effectuate the essential dignity and integrity of the judicial process."[83] Furthermore, the Justice declared: "A literal interpretation of... [Section 9] would wreak havoc with established judicial practices in that it would allow public access to all phases of the administration of

---

[78] Andrews v. O'Hearn, 387 N.W.2d 716, 723 (1986).

[79] Id.

[80] Hjelle v. Sornsin Construction Company, 173 N.W.2d 431, 437 (1969).

[81] NDCC Section 53-09-01 through 11.

[82] Bouchard v. Johnson, 555 N.W.2d 81, 89 (1996).

[83] KFGO Radio, Inc. v. Rothe, 298 N.W.2d 505, 513 (1980).

justice, including chambers' conferences, plea bargaining and settlement conferences, adoption proceedings, those juvenile proceedings presently closed, grand jury proceedings and appellate court conferences."[84]

Suits May Be Brought against the State

The idea that government should not be subject to legal action is traceable back to medieval England where it was thought that the "king can do no wrong."[85]

When the Supreme Court confronted the question concerning the meaning of this part of Section 9, it responded: "The right to maintain a suit against the state, . . . exists only as provided by statute."[86]

This was the Court's approach to the question of sovereign immunity for many years.[87]

In 1974, however, the Court had before it a case brought by the parents of Jeffrey Kitto, age 12, who drowned in a pond near Minot, North Dakota. The parents sued the Minot Park District, asserting that the District had been negligent in not fencing the pond. In allowing the case to proceed, the Court drew a distinction between *state sovereignty*, which protects the state from legal action, and *governmental immunity*, which protects other branches of government.

In examining Section 9, the Court declared: "We are persuaded that a reconsideration of the constitutional basis for governmental immunity establishes that this doctrine, . . . is not constitutionally mandated."[88]

In 1968, the Supreme Court said that governmental immunity was "preserved on the basis of three general classifications: (1) The sovereign is immune from suit; . . .(2) The curious philosophy that it is more expedient that isolated individuals should suffer than that society in general be inconvenienced; and (3) That from a practical view of public policy, governments . . . will perform their duties more efficiently . . . if not jeopardized by the threat of tort liability."[89]

Following the *Kitto* case, individual justices began to question the validity of sovereign immunity. For example, Justice Herbert L. Meschke wrote: "Since our forefathers fought a Revolution to repudiate an unresponsive sovereign, it is antithetical to our heritage to immunize any government from accountability for its actions."[90] And when the Court dismissed Mary Leadbetter's suit against the

---

[84] Id.

[85] *Sovereign Immunity: An Outdated Doctrine Faces Demise in a Changing Judicial Arena*, 69 North Dakota Law Review 401 (1993).

[86] Wirtz v. Nestos, 200 N.W. 524, 534 (1924).

[87] Watland v. North Dakota Workmen's Comp. Bureau, 225 N.W. 812 (1929); Henderson v. Scott, 10 N.W.2d 490 (1943); Senger v. Hulstrand Const., Inc., 320 N.W.2d 507 (1982).

[88] Kitto v. Minot Park District, 224 N.W.2d 795, 801 (1974).

[89] Shermoen v. Lindsay, 163 N.W.2d 738, 742 (1968).

[90] Dickinson Public School Dist. v. Sanstead, 425 N.W.2d 906, 911 (1988).

University of North Dakota and one of its professors for sexual assault, Justice Meschke and Justice Beryl J. Levine dissented. "When government," Justice Meschke asserted, "is not governed by the same laws as its citizens and private institutions, it is troubling. Sovereign immunity is a hallmark of a totalitarian form of government, not of a constitutional democracy, as recent events in eastern Europe tend to evidence."[91]

By 1994, when Judy Ann Bulman's case reached the Court, the membership of the Court had changed. Chief Justice Ralph J. Erickstad and Justice H. F. Gierke III had left the Court and Justices William A. Neumann and Dale V. Sandstrom had become justices.

Bulman had sued a construction contractor and the State of North Dakota for negligently maintaining a roadway upon which her husband Lloyd was killed. District Judge Donald L. Jorgensen dismissed the case against the state on the grounds of sovereign immunity and Bulman appealed. Four justices voted to reverse. In doing so they said: "We conclude that the State's sovereign immunity for tort liability is outdated and no longer warranted."[92]

In referring to Section 9, Justice Levine wrote: "Nothing in that provision elevates the common-law doctrine of sovereign immunity to constitutional status, or precludes this Court from abolishing that common-law doctrine. To the extent our prior decisions hold otherwise, we believe they were wrong, and we explicitly overrule them."[93]

Chief Justice Gerald W. VandeWalle dissented. He wrote: "Sovereign immunity may have its roots in the common law. Nothing ordains that a constitution must be a brand new theory. Except as an excuse for judges to ignore constitutional provisions they find personally unacceptable, it makes little difference that the provisions had its roots in common law. Once it is embedded in our Constitution, its status is the same as any other provision of the North Dakota State Constitution."[94]

NO PERSON SHALL, FOR A FELONY, BE PROCEEDED AGAINST CRIMINALLY, OTHERWISE THAN BY INDICTMENT

Section 10. Until otherwise provided by law, no person shall, for a felony, be proceeded against criminally, otherwise than by indictment, except in cases arising in the land or naval forces, or in the militia when in actual service in time of war or public

---

[91] Leadbetter v. Rose, 467 N.W.2d 431, 437 (1991).

[92] Bulman v. Hulstrand Const. Co., Inc., 521 N.W.2d 632, 639 (1994). See: *Sovereign Immunity—Judicial Abrogation of North Dakota's Soveriegn Immunity Results in Its Possible Legislative Reassertion and Legislation to Provide Injured Parties a Remedy for the Torts Committed by the State or Its Agents,* 71 North Dakota Law Review 761 (1995).

[93] Id., p. 637.

[94] Id., p. 641.

danger. In all other cases, offenses shall be prosecuted criminally by indictment or information. The legislative assembly may change, regulate or abolish the grand jury system.

At the time North Dakota became a state, the Territory of Dakota Code of Criminal Procedure, which the new state adopted, contained a provision whereby a person accused of a crime could be prosecuted either by information or indictment.[95]

The North Dakota Supreme Court, therefore, has held that even if a defendant is prosecuted by a criminal complaint, which is in essence the same as an information, that is not grounds for dismissal.[96]

The Legislature has not abolished the grand jury system in North Dakota.[97]

ALL PERSONS SHALL BE BAILABLE BY SUFFICIENT SURETIES, UNLESS FOR CAPITAL OFFENSES

Section 11. All persons shall be bailable by sufficient sureties, unless for capital offenses when the proof is evident or the presumption great. Excessive bail shall not be required, nor excessive fines imposed, nor shall cruel or unusual punishments be inflicted. Witnesses shall not be unreasonably detained, nor be confined in any room where criminals are actually imprisoned.

When the Court was considering the petition of William E. West, an accused murderer, for bail, it took note of the fact that: "On the one hand, the constitution itself does not give the right to bail in the class of cases last mentioned; and, on the other hand, the constitution does not inhibit the legislature from doing so."[98]

The Court then examined the circumstances under which bail had been denied to West, and concluded: "In performing this duty all members of this court have given the evidence and the law applicable thereto a careful consideration, and the conclusion has been reached that the petitioner is not entitled to bail as a matter of strict legal right."[99]

When presented with the question of whether persons who have been convicted of a crime are entitled to bail pending appeal, the Court responded that such persons were not entitled to bail.[100]

---

[95] NDCC Section 29-01-01. See: NDCC Section 29-01-13(2) and (4) for definitions of indictment and information.

[96] State v. Buehler, 125 N.W.2d 155 (1963).

[97] NDCC Chapter 29-10.1.

[98] In re West, 88 N.W. 88, 89 (1901).

[99] Id., p. 90.

[100] State v. Tucker, 222 N.W. 651 (1928).

The Court has also held that this section does not apply to "persons who are held in custody under executive warrants of rendition in extradition proceedings."[101]

Excessive Bail Shall Not Be Required, Nor Excessive Fines Imposed

When a jury awarded Robert L. Stoner $25,200 as compensatory damages and $200,000 as punitive damages in an action against Nash Finch, Inc., for abuse of process, Nash Finch appealed to the Supreme Court. One of the arguments Nash Finch used in urging the Court to set aside the punitive damages award was that it was an excessive fine and prohibited by Section 11.

Writing for the Court, Justice H. F. Gierke III disagreed, and pointed out that the U.S. Supreme Court had held that the excessive fines clause of the Eighth Amendment did not apply to punitive damages. Justice Gierke then wrote: "The excessive fines clauses of the federal and state constitutions are virtually identical, and Nash Finch has posited no reasons for interpreting the state excessive fines clause differently from its federal counterpart. Accordingly, we conclude that the punitive damage award in this case does not violate the Eighth Amendment or Article I, Section 11 of the State Constitution."[102]

Nor Shall Cruel or Unusual Punishments Be Inflicted

When Leo Jochim was convicted of stealing some turkeys and sentenced to three years in the penitentiary, he appealed arguing that the sentence was cruel and unusual, in violation of Section 11. The Supreme Court disagreed and wrote:

> It is neither "cruel" nor "unusual" to sentence a man to the penitentiary for grand larceny. To come within this prohibition, it must be both cruel and unusual. To revive some of the old penalties, such as amputation of the hand that seized the turkey, burning at the stake, boiling in oil, or the placing of the defendant in the stocks or pillory, might be considered "cruel" or "unusual" punishment, but the penalty imposed in this case is the usual and ordinary one.[103]

The Court has also held that Section 11 is not violated when a defendant is sentenced to the penitentiary for the crime of petit larceny.[104]

---

[101] In re Amundson, 19 N.W.2d 918, Headnote 3 (1945).

[102] Stoner v. Nash Finch, Inc., 446 N.W.2d 747, 755 (1989).

[103] State v. Jochim, 213 N.W. 484, 488 (1927). The Court has upheld the following sentences as not being cruel and unusual: 1–3 years for assault with a deadly weapon with intent to do bodily harm but not with the intent to kill, State v. Turner, 229 N.W. 7 (1930); 15 years for kidnapping, State v. Taylor, 293 N.W. 219 (1940); and 3 years for indecent liberties with a female under 18 years of age, State v. Holte, 87 N.W.2d 47 (1957).

[104] State v. Kingen, 226 N.W. 505 (1929).

THE PARTY ACCUSED SHALL HAVE THE RIGHT TO A SPEEDY AND PUBLIC TRIAL

Section 12. In criminal prosecutions in any court whatever, the party accused shall have the right to a speedy and public trial; to have the process of the court to compel the attendance of witnesses in his behalf; and to appear and defend in person and with counsel. No person shall be twice put in jeopardy for the same offense, nor be compelled in any criminal case to be a witness against himself, nor be deprived of life, liberty or property without due process of law.

The Court has discussed the question of whether a delay in arresting a person denies that person a speedy trial in violation of this section.

On January 3, 1983, an informant told officers that Dan Joe Denny was selling marijuana. The officers did not arrest Denny at the time but continued their investigation until they arrested him on August 22, 1983.

In response to Denny's argument that he was denied a speedy trial, the Court responded: "The right to a speedy trial is guaranteed by the Sixth Amendment to the United States Constitution and Article I, Section 12 of the North Dakota Constitution. That right, however, does not attach until a defendant 'in some way becomes an accused.'"[105]

In discussing the question of possible prejudice to a defendant in the delay, the Court pointed out: "Possible prejudice, however, is not itself sufficient to establish a due process claim. . . . Case law suggests that the amount of pre-accusation delay does not establish prejudice per se."[106]

While this section guarantees the defendant a public trial, there are times when justice is best served when the trial is closed. In such situations, however, the party seeking closure must "make a threshold showing that there is an overriding interest that can best be protected only by closure."[107] And "before the trial court may exclude the public, it must articulate its reasons on the record and those reasons must be expressed in findings that enable a reviewing court to exercise its function."[108]

The Supreme Court was presented with that kind of situation in the trial of Barry Caesar Garcia for murder. One of the persons who was with Garcia at the time of the alleged murder was called to testify, but when put on the stand and asked his name he responded: "'I an not going to say nothing.'"[109] At this point, the trial judge excused the jury. During the proceedings that followed, the judge learned that the witness, a juvenile, had not been granted immunity from

---

[105] State v. Denny, 350 N.W.2d 25, 27 (1984).

[106] Id. See also: State v. Weisz, 356 N.W.2d 462 (1984) where the Court upheld a 10-month delay in arrest and prosecution.

[107] State v. Klem, 438 N.W.2d 798, 800 (1989).

[108] Id., p. 801.

[109] State v. Garcia, 561 N.W.2d 599, 602 (1997).

prosecution and was concerned about testifying with the media and others present. The trial judge, over the objections of defendant's counsel, ordered the trial to continue without the media and those not directly involved in the case.

Garcia was convicted and appealed. One of the issues his counsel raised on appeal was Garcia's constitutional right to a public trial. The Supreme Court responded to that issue: "A trial court may exclude members of the public from a trial if a witness will be inhibited or embarrassed to testify in the presence of an audience from his tender age or the nature of his testimony, from actual threats, or from the possibility of reprisals by others if the witness testifies."[110]

To Have the Process of the Court to Compel the Attendance of Witnesses in His Behalf

The cases in which the Court has considered this part of Section 12 have dealt with the assertion by a defendant that the state must grant immunity to a potential witness so that person can testify for the defense without fear of prosecution. In response, the Supreme Court has written: "We conclude that neither the Sixth Amendment to the United States Constitution nor Article I, Section 12 of the Constitution of North Dakota requires that the State grant immunity to defense witnesses."[111]

To Appear and Defend in Person

This part of Section 12 entitles the defendant to be present at all times during his or her trial. It is, therefore, a violation of this section when a trial court conducts any part of the trial without the presence of the defendant. Such was the situation in Fred Schasker's case.

Schasker had been tried for grand larceny. While he was in jail awaiting the verdict, the jury requested that part of the testimony of a witness be read back to them. In response to that request, and without the defendant or his attorney being present, the trial judge had the court reporter read that part of the testimony to the jury.

The jury found Schasker guilty, but the Supreme Court reversed. "The defendant," Justice John Burke declared, "had the constitutional right to be present and defend in person and with counsel during the whole of the trial."[112]

Sometimes a trial judge may have communication with a jury without the presence of the defendant. For example, when Leland Thomas Ash was being tried for murder, the jury sent several notes to the judge. One note requested a list of the exhibits, and two sought a clarification of testimony. The judge had an

---

[110] Id. at 606.

[111] State v. Dachtler, 318 N.W.2d 769, 773 (1982).

[112] State v. Schasker, 235 N.W. 345, 346 (1931).

exhibit list prepared and given to the jury, but with regard to the testimony, the judge responded: "'You should rely upon your recollection of all testimony of all witnesses.'"[113] Defendant's counsel was aware of these communications but did not object to them.

Ash was convicted and on appeal argued that the communication between the judge and the jury without the defendant being present was unconstitutional under Section 12. The Supreme Court agreed that this was a violation of the defendant's rights but concluded that it was harmless error. "We discern no possibility of prejudice to Ash," Justice Herbert L. Meschke wrote for the Court, "from these communications by the court with the jury outside Ash's presence, particularly when his counsel repeatedly waived the defendant's absence."[114]

Sometimes the trial judge's contact with a prospective juror without the prosecutor, defense counsel, or the defendant being present may result in the Supreme Court granting a new trial. One such situation occurred at the beginning of the trial of Richard B. Baer for driving under the influence.

During the jury selection process, "the district court asked, '[h]ave any of you lost the right to vote for any reason?'" When one of the jurors raised his hand, the court asked: "You've lost your right to vote?" The juror responded: "I don't know if that is still the case."[115]

Later, during a brief recess and out of the presence of the defendant, the trial judge dismissed the prospective juror. After Baer was convicted, he appealed to the Supreme Court which reversed.

Chief Justice VandeWalle explained the Court's decision: "We reverse in this case because the district court violated the defendant's constitutional right to be present when a prospective juror was removed from the venire and the State has not persuaded us that the violation was harmless beyond a reasonable doubt."[116]

To Appear and Defend . . . with Counsel

"Originally, in England, a person charged with treason or felony was denied aid of counsel, except in respect of legal questions which the accused himself might suggest."[117] The situation was different, however, in the American colonies. Writing in 1932, the U.S. Supreme Court pointed out: "It thus appears that in at least twelve of the thirteen colonies the rule of the English common law, . . . had

---

[113] State v. Ash, 526 N.W.2d 473, 481 (1995).

[114] Id. For a similar result, see: State v. Smuda, 419 N.W.2d 166 (1988) and State v. Zimmerman, 524 N.W.2d 111 (1994).

[115] City of Mandan v. Baer, 578 N.W.2d 559, 560 (1998).

[116] Id., p. 563.

[117] Powell v. Alabama, 287 U.S. 45, 60 (1932).

been definitely rejected and the right to counsel fully recognized in all criminal prosecutions, save that in one or two instances the right was limited to capital offenses or to the more serious crimes."[118]

Very early in North Dakota's history, the Supreme Court held that this clause in Section 12 did not require the appointment of counsel for indigents. This clause, the Court said, "guarantees to all accused persons the right to have counsel appear for them. As to compensation of such counsel, that provision determines nothing."[119]

It was, therefore, through legislation that North Dakota indigent defendants were provided counsel at government expense. For example, Section 10,216 of the Revised Code of 1905 provided that when a person "is unable to employ counsel, the court shall appoint and assign counsel for his defense and allow and direct to be paid by the county in which such trial is had."[120]

The Supreme Court has pointed out: "There is no arbitrary point in time at which the right to be represented by counsel or, if indigent, the right to be represented by court-appointed counsel, attaches in pre-trial proceedings."[121] Also, the person seeking the appointment of counsel has the burden of proving indigency, and even if the defendant proves indigency, neither he nor she has the right to choose the lawyer to be appointed.[122]

The Supreme Court has also written: "One can be indigent even though he is not a pauper."[123]

Indigency, however, in this context does not have the same meaning as used in determining the eligibility for welfare services. For example, the Court said in *State v. Jensen*[124] that it could not, however, "hold that one who has a tax-free income of $1,065 per month, no dependents, and a moderate equity in three rental properties, and who is paying $100 per month on his attorney's fees, is 'indigent' within the meaning of . . . our prior holdings."[125]

While the right to be represented by counsel is guaranteed by Section 12, a defendant by his or her words and actions may waive that right. Whether a defendant has waived his or her right to counsel, however, depends upon the facts surrounding the alleged waiver. "A defendant," the Court has said, "may competently and intelligently waive his right to the assistance of counsel. Whether there has been such a waiver is to be determined by the facts of each case. The burden

[118] Id., pp. 64–65.

[119] Harris v. Rolette County, 112 N.W. 971, 972 (1907).

[120] See: NDCC Section 29-07-01.1 and Rule 44 of the Rules of Criminal Procedure.

[121] State v. Starratt, 153 N.W.2d 311, 312, Syllabus by the Court No. 3 (1967).

[122] State v. DuPaul, 527 N.W.2d 238 (1995).

[123] State v. Jensen, 241 N.W.2d 557, 560 (1976).

[124] 241 N.W.2d 557 (1976).

[125] Id., p. 561.

of proof [that there was no waiver] is upon the defendant to establish the facts upon which he relies."[126]

A finding of no waiver occurred in the case of Oscar Whiteman, Jr., the Court noted:

> The defendant is an Indian citizen, 25 years of age, with only a grade school education. He was confronted by the most serious crime under our law. He had no one with whom to counsel or from whom to seek advice to protect his legal rights. He had been detained in an atmosphere of hostility of which the trial court was not aware. He had been subjected to intimidations, threats and even violence, and the evidence bears out that he felt there was nothing he could do except to plead guilty to the information charging him with murder in the first degree. He felt that he had no alternative. It was a waiver compelled by a lack of choice, arising out of the necessities of the circumstances.... A waiver of counsel based on these conditions cannot be said to be freely and understandingly made."[127]

When a defendant waives the right to counsel, he/she cannot later complain that counsel was denied in violation of this section. Such was the case of Bronson J. Rockwell, who was charged with driving under the influence of alcohol.

At Rockwell's request, the trial court appointed counsel for him. Later, however, Rockwell told the court that he had lost confidence in the attorney, and desired the court to appoint a new attorney for him. The court refused to do so, pointing out that Rockwell had "no right to pick and choose who that counsel would be."[128]

At Rockwell's request, the trial court allowed the counsel to be available for consultation with him during the trial. Rockwell was convicted and appealed to the Supreme Court.

On appeal, Rockwell argued that he had not waived counsel, and therefore had been denied his rights under Section 12. The Court disagreed and pointed out first, "there is no federal or state constitutional right to standby counsel."[129] "Further," Justice Carol Ronning Kapsner wrote for the Court, "Rockwell represented himself throughout the remainder of the proceedings without expressing any desire to relinquish his right to self-representation or to reassert his right to counsel."[130]

The Court has said: "A corollary to a defendant's right to counsel is a defendant's constitutional right to self-representation if the defendant knowingly and

---

[126] State v. Whiteman, 67 N.W.2d 599, 611 (1954).

[127] Id., p. 610.

[128] City of Fargo v. Rockwell, 597 N.W.2d 406, 407 (1999).

[129] Id., p. 411.

[130] Id., p. 412.

intelligently waives the right to counsel."[131] But the Court has also said: "Self-representation may be a defendant's right, but it is 'not a license to abuse the dignity of the courtroom, nor to ignore rules of procedure.'"[132]

Writing for the Court, Chief Justice VandeWalle has cautioned: "A defendant need not have the skill and experience of a lawyer to competently and intelligently choose self-representation, but the defendant should be aware of the dangers and disadvantages of self-representation so the record establishes the choice is made with eyes open."[133]

If a defendant wants to conduct his or her own defense, the trial court may, but is not required to appoint counsel to standby and offer whatever assistance the defendant requires. Of this procedure, the Court has pointed out: "As a practical matter, standby counsel does not represent the defendant; the defendant represents himself and may or may not chose to consult with his standby counsel during the course of the proceedings."[134]

If a defendant can convince the Supreme Court that his or her counsel was ineffective, the defendant will be given a new trial. That was true in Ed Keller's case. Keller was tried and convicted for engaging in liquor traffic. On appeal to the Supreme Court, he pointed out in a long affidavit that during his trial his "attorney was then intoxicated to such an extent that he did not know what was transpiring at all times in the courtroom, and was unable to properly defend the action."[135] The Supreme Court, accepting the affidavit as factual, reversed and granted Keller a new trial. Justice William L. Nuessle, writing for the Court, declared: "Under such circumstances, the defendant was clearly prejudiced without apparent fault on his part. It is inconceivable why the trial of the cause was permitted to continue when his attorney was in such a condition of intoxication as the showing of the defendant established. . . . Every defendant is entitled to . . . a [fair] trial, and the requirement is not satisfied with one which is a farce and a travesty on justice."[136]

When a defendant raises questions concerning the actions or nonactions of his or her counsel at the trial, the reviewing court is presented with having to second-guess the decisions made by counsel. This the Supreme Court has said "would require this Court to do exactly that which we refuse to do, scrutinize defense counsel's trial judgment and strategy with the benefit of perfect 20/20 hindsight."[137] Defendants, therefore, have generally not been successful on appeal in raising the issue of ineffective counsel.[138]

---

[131] State v. Poitra, 578 N.W.2d 121, 123 (1998).

[132] Supra note 126, p. 409.

[133] State v. Dvorak, 604 N.W.2d 445, 448 (2000).

[134] Supra note 126, p. 412.

[135] State v. Keller, 223 N.W. 698, 699 (1929).

[136] Id., pp. 699–700.

[137] State v. Micko, 393 N.W.2d 741, 747, Note 4 (1986).

[138] State v. Ricehill, 415 N.W.2d 481, 484 (1987); State v. Woehlhoff, 473 N.W.2d 446, 449 (1991); State v. McDonnell, 550 N.W.2d 62, 65 (1996).

No Person Shall Be Twice Put in Jeopardy for the Same Offense

In discussing the Double Jeopardy Clause of the Fifth Amendment to the U.S. Constitution, the U.S. Supreme Court has written: "Jeopardy denotes risk. In the constitutional sense, jeopardy describes the risk that is traditionally associated with a criminal prosecution."[139]

The North Dakota Supreme Court has explained "that a person is put in jeopardy when his trial commences, which in a jury case occurs when the jury is impaneled and sworn, and in a non-jury trial when the court begins to hear evidence."[140]

When a defendant has been acquitted, Section 12 prohibits the government from trying the defendant again. Such was the case of Elden A. Kraft, a bar owner in Dickinson, North Dakota, who was charged with dispensing alcoholic beverages to a minor. Kraft was being tried in the Stark County (ND) court. At the close of the City's case, Kraft moved for an acquittal arguing that the city had failed to prove that he was the owner of the liquor license at the time of the alleged offense. The judge entered a verdict of acquittal and the City of Dickinson appealed.

In dismissing the appeal, the Supreme Court declared: "Acquittal by the trial court for lack of evidence also bars retrial, even when the acquittal is based on erroneous evidentiary rulings."[141]

When a defendant appeals from a conviction claiming errors were made during the trial, and the Supreme Court agrees and reverses the conviction, the state is free to try the defendant again. That is not considered double jeopardy. That was the situation that Paul Kranz found himself in when he was convicted of menacing.

At the beginning of the trial, the judge told Kranz that if he "requested" a jury one would be called. Because Kranz did not respond, the trial proceeded without a jury. Upon being convicted, Kranz appealed to the Supreme Court arguing that he was denied his right to a jury trial and the Supreme Court agreed and reversed. The Court said, however: "[A defendant waives double jeopardy protection after a verdict or judgment against him is set aside at his own instance, either by motion in a trial court or by a successful appeal.]"[142]

Another situation in which double jeopardy does not apply is when a person has been arrested, prosecuted, and convicted for driving under the influence of alcohol and his or her driver's license has been suspended after an administrative hearing.

---

[139] Breed v. Jones, 421 U.S. 519, 528 (1975).

[140] State v. Berger, 235 N.W.2d 254, 257 (1975).

[141] City of Dickinson v. Kraft, 472 N.W.2d 441, 443 (1991). See also: State v. Meyer, 494 N.W.2d 364, 366 (1992); State v. Hammond, 498 N.W.2d 126 (1993).

[142] State v. Kranz, 353 N.W.2d 748, 753 (1984).

Edwin Zimmerman and Albert E. Knutson raised the double jeopardy issue after their licenses had been suspended and they were charged and convicted of driving under the influence of alcohol. In upholding their convictions, the Supreme Court responded: "We conclude the administrative suspension of Zimmerman's and Knutson's driver's licenses do not constitute punishment for double jeopardy analysis."[143]

Nor Be Compelled . . . to Be a Witness against Himself

The privilege not to incriminate oneself came into the judicial system early in English history. It was a reaction to the inquisitorial system used in the ecclesiastic courts where a witness was required to take an oath to tell the truth.

"The privilege against self-incrimination is one of the chief concepts that make the Anglo-American system of criminal justice an 'accusatorial' rather than an 'inquisitorial' process. . . . The privilege against self-incrimination was part of the common law of England before the American Revolution and was generally recognized in the colonies."[144]

When Anton Beer was called to testify against Edward G. Patterson, who was charged with violating the state's prohibition laws, Beer refused to answer any questions, claiming that he was protected by the self-incrimination clause of Article I, Section 12. Beer argued "that the constitutional provision would be infringed if any answer given by him would lead to other evidence against him, if such evidence could be used against him, although his answers could not."[145]

The trial judge disagreed and held Beer in contempt. The Supreme Court reversed Beer's conviction. The Court wrote: "If the witness is subject to criminal prosecution after his answers have been given, where the privilege has been rightfully and in good faith claimed by him, it needs no more than the statement of the fact that the constitutional guaranty has been violated."[146]

A witness who does not want to respond to a question on the grounds that the answer may tend to incriminate himself or herself must personally raise the objection. The witness' counsel cannot invoke the privilege for the client.[147] The witness, however, may waive his or her right not to testify, provided that such a waiver is knowingly and intelligently given.[148]

---

[143] State v. Zimmerman, 539 N.W.2d 49, 56 (1995). See also: State v. Jacobson, 545 N.W.2d 152, 153 (1996).

[144] *The Encyclopedia Americana*, Int. ed., "Fifth Amendment" (Danbury, CT: Grolier, 1996), Vol. 11, p. 187.

[145] In re Beer, 115 N.W. 672, 673 (1908).

[146] Id.

[147] State v. Manning, 134 N.W.2d 91, 100 (1965).

[148] State v. Gross, 351 N.W.2d 428, 432 (1984).

However, a witness, testifying under the compulsion of a subpoena, need not be told that he or she has a right not to answer incriminating questions.[149]

The privilege not to testify against oneself can be invoked in a state's attorney's inquiry,[150] before a Grand Jury,[151] and in any criminal or civil proceeding.[152] Furthermore, the Court has said: "A fundamental principle of constitutional law is the prosecutor may not comment on a defendant's failure to testify in a criminal case."[153]

When a witness is granted immunity from prosecution, he or she must then respond to questioning. However, the immunity must be "broad enough to remove any danger of incrimination, . . . [and must leave] 'the witness . . . in substantially the same position as if the witness had claimed his privilege.'"[154]

In North Dakota, grants of immunity are to be made by the state attorney general, except that in a state's attorney inquiry, application must be made to the district judge.[155]

Nor Be Deprived of Life, Liberty, or Property without Due Process of Law

In commenting on this clause the North Dakota Supreme Court has said: "Due process of law means 'the law of the land'; that which 'secures the individual from the arbitrary exercise of the powers of government, unrestrained by the established principles of private rights and distributive justice.'"[156]

The "arbitrary exercise of the powers of government" occurs when the government enacts laws that are so vague that those subject to the laws are uncertain as to their meaning; and when the government does not provide adequate notice and opportunity to be heard when it takes actions that affect people's lives or property. Furthermore, the procedure by which people's lives and property are affected must be fair.

In addressing the question of whether a statute is void for vagueness, the Court, quoting from an opinion of the U.S. Supreme Court, notes: "'Void for vagueness simply means that criminal responsibility should not attach where one could not reasonably understand that his contemplated conduct is proscribed.'"[157]

---

[149] State v. Iverson, 187 N.W.2d 1, 17–18 (1971).

[150] Matter of Contempt of Grajedas, 515 N.W.2d 444 (1994).

[151] In re Beer, 115 N.W. 672 (1908).

[152] State v. Gross, 351 N.W.2d 428 (1984).

[153] State v. His Chase, 531 N.W.2d 271, 273 (1995).

[154] Supra note 148, 515 N.W.2d, p. 450.

[155] NDCC Section 31-01-09.

[156] State v. Cromwell, 9 N.W.2d 914, 919 (1943).

[157] State v. Henderson, 156 N.W.2d 700, 706 (1968).

Applying that test, the Court has upheld the termination of parental rights where the trial court found that the child was "'without proper parental care or control;'"[158] a statute requiring the driving of a car be done "'in a careful and prudent manner, having due regard to the traffic, surface, and width of the highway and other conditions then existing;'"[159] and the word "dancing" as used in a cabaret licensing ordinance prohibiting "'any form of dancing.'"[160] The Court has also said that a statute which prohibits a person from driving any vehicle while not "'in actual physical control of . . . (the) vehicle,'"[161] does not violate due process.

In *State v. Beyer*,[162] County Judge Gary A. Holum was presented with the question of the validity of a law which required motor vehicles to have "'a muffler . . . to prevent excessive or unusual noise.'"[163] Judge Holum concluded that these words were "'too broad and subject to too many interpretations to be fairly administrated.'"[164] He therefore dismissed the case. The Supreme Court, however, disagreed and reversed. Writing for the Court, Justice Levine said: "We have found no cases concluding that this statutory language is unconstitutionally vague or indefinite, and neither the parties nor the county court have cited such a case."[165]

In discussing the requirement of notice and an opportunity to be heard, the Court has said: "There must . . . be notice of some kind, and it must be a notice of such a character that it will have a tendency, in a reasonable degree, to convey information to interested parties that the action affects their rights."[166]

The Court has held that in some instances, notice meets the constitutional requirement even if only given by publication in a newspaper. For example, when the city of Minot created a special improvement district to construct a downtown parking lot, it gave notice by publication in the newspaper. Property owners who were the potential taxpayers for the project brought an action asserting a violation of due process. The trial court upheld the procedure, and the Supreme Court affirmed. It said: "In this jurisdiction an opportunity to be heard with right of review upon the question of assessments for benefits is all that is required to satisfy the due process provisions of the Constitutions of the United States and North Dakota."[167] "(T)here is no requirement," the Court has said, "that actual notice be received by all interested persons."[168]

---

[158] In re J. Z., 190 N.W.2d 27, 36 (1971).

[159] State v. Hagge, 211 N.W.2d 395, 396 (1973).

[160] Olson v. City of West Fargo, 305 N.W.2d 821, 822 (1981).

[161] State v. Schwalk, 430 N.W.2d 317 (1988).

[162] 441 N.W.2d 919 (1989).

[163] Id., p. 920.

[164] Id., p. 921.

[165] Id.

[166] Fenton v. Minnesota Title Ins. & Trust Co., 109 N.W. 363, 366 (1906).

[167] Fisher v. City of Minot, 188 N.W.2d 745, 747 Syllabus No. 3. (1971).

[168] So. Valley Grain Dealers v. Bd. of Cty. Com'rs., 257 N.W.2d 425, 430 (1977).

As noted above, notice is required when municipalities create special assessment districts. Other interests that require notice and an opportunity to be heard, before the government takes negative action, are holders of state licenses to engage in a profession or occupation,[169] and automobile driver's licenses.[170]

Parents also have rights that are protected by due process. The Supreme Court has said: "The fundamental natural right of a parent to the custody and society of his child and to provide for his moral, mental and physical welfare has been recognized to be of constitutional dimension."[171] The Court has pointed out, however, that: "A parent's relationship with a biological child is entitled to constitutional protection, but that relationship is neither absolute nor unconditional. . . . The due process clause affords parents certain procedural protections before their relationship with a biological child can be irrevocably severed."[172]

Government-created rights are also protected by due process. One of those government-created rights is worker's compensation. When the Workers Compensation Bureau terminated Troy Beckler's benefits, the Court reversed because the "Bureau's procedures did not give Beckler a pretermination notice that his disability benefits would be terminated, a summary of the medical evidence supporting termination and an opportunity to respond."[173]

THE RIGHT OF TRIAL BY JURY (IN CIVIL CASES)

Section 13. The right of trial by jury shall be secured to all, and remain inviolate. A person accused of a crime for which he may be confined for a period of more than one year has the right of trial by a jury of twelve. The legislative assembly may determine the size of the jury for all other cases, provided that the jury consists of at least six members. All verdicts must be unanimous.

In referring to the right to a jury trial in civil cases, the Supreme Court has said that this section "preserve[s] the right to a trial by jury in those cases which historically were subject to trial by jury."[174]

Historically, cases equitable in nature were triable without a jury. These include cases in which a plaintiff sought (1) a declaratory judgment,[175] (2) specific

---

[169] Matter of Ellis, 504 N.W.2d 559 (1993) license to practice law; Comn. on Medical Competency v. Racek, 527 N.W.2d 262 (1995) license to practice medicine.

[170] Kosmatka v. Safety Responsibility Div., etc., 196 N.W.2d 402 (1972).

[171] In re J. Z., 190 N.W.2d 27, 29 (1971). See also: McGurren v. S. T., 241 N.W.2d 690, 695 (1976).

[172] Matter of Adoption of J.W.M., 532 N.W.2d 372, 375 (1995).

[173] Beckler v. N. D. Workers Comp. Bureau, 418 N.W.2d 770, 775 (1988).

[174] Landers v. Goetz, 264 N.W.2d 459, 462 (1978). There was no right to a trial by jury in cases which were "equitable in nature." Id., p. 462.

[175] Eck v. City of Bismarck, 302 N.W.2d 739 (1981).

performance of a contract,[176] (3) foreclosure of a mortgage,[177] partition of land,[178] to quiet title to land,[179] or in divorce proceedings.[180]

Among the types of cases historically subject to trial by a jury are cases where money damages are sought by one of the parties,[181] when a claim of ownership and possession of property are made,[182] and when one person sues another for conversion of the first person's property.[183]

Because this section gives the Legislature the right to "determine the size of the jury in all other cases," it has provided that "(i)n all civil actions when a jury is impaneled, a jury must consist of six qualified jurors unless any party makes a timely written demand for a jury of nine."[184]

When District Judge James H. O'Keefe declared a moratorium on civil jury trials because of lack of funds, the Supreme Court held that the moratorium was a violation of Bernhard Odden's right to a civil jury trial.[185]

The Right of Trial by Jury in (Criminal Cases)

When Ed Norton was convicted of engaging in liquor traffic he appealed to the Supreme Court. Among the arguments Norton made for reversal of his conviction was that the constitution at that time required that the "'jury . . . may consist of less than twelve men,'"[186] and the jury that convicted him consisted of nine men and three women. The Supreme Court disagreed, being of the opinion that although only men were qualified to vote and be jurors when the constitution was adopted, the change which allowed women to vote also made them eligible to be jurors.

When the Legislature set the number of jurors at six in felony cases unless the defendant made a demand for 12, the Supreme Court declared the law to be a violation of this section. Writing for the Court, Justice Meschke said: "By requiring a felony defendant to either affirmatively demand a jury of twelve or accept a

---

[176] Northwestern Bell Tel. Co. v. Cowger, 303 N.W.2d 791 (1981).

[177] Midwest Fed. S. & L. Ass'n. of Minot v. Kouba, 335 N.W.2d 780 (1983) real estate mortgage; General Elec. Credit Corp. v. Richman, 338 N.W.2d 814 (1983) chattel mortgage.

[178] Murphy v. Murphy, 595 N.W.2d 571 (1999).

[179] Id.

[180] Martian v. Martian, 328 N.W.2d 844 (1983).

[181] Moses v. Burleigh County, 438 N.W.2d 186 (1989). See also: Rivinius v. Huber, 24 N.W.2d 911 (1946).

[182] First National Bank of Dickinson v. Kling, 257 N.W. 631 (1934). See also: Zimmer v. Bellon, 153 N.W.2d 757 (1967).

[183] Cook v. Hansen, 499 N.W.2d 94 (1993).

[184] NDCC Section 28-14-03.1.

[185] Odden v. O'Keefe, 450 N.W.2d 707 (1990).

[186] State v. Norton, 255 N.W. 787, 792 (1934).

legislatively designated alternative, the statute impinges upon the defendant's unconditional right to have a jury of twelve."[187]

A felony defendant may, however, waive his or her right to a 12-person jury providing that the waiver is clear and certain. It cannot be inferred from a silent record.[188]

While this section requires a jury representing a fair cross section of the community, the burden is on the defendant to show that the jury he or she had was not representative of the community. For example, the Court has held: "A mere observation that there are no Native Americans on a jury panel that was drawn from a population containing Native Americans 'simply is not sufficient to demonstrate any systematic exclusion.'"[189] Furthermore, "in order to exercise the right to a jury trial in municipal court, the legislature may require a defendant who violates a city ordinance to demand a jury trial. Requiring a defendant to request a jury trial . . . thus does not stray from the boundaries of our constitution."[190] The Supreme Court has also held that this section permits six-person juries in misdemeanor cases.[191]

When R. Y., Jr., was adjudicated a juvenile delinquent by a district judge, he appealed to the Supreme Court arguing that his constitutional right to a jury trial had been violated. The Supreme Court disagreed and pointed out: "The juvenile court did not exist prior to the adoption of the North Dakota Constitution in 1889. . . . The first juvenile court was established in North Dakota in 1911. . . . Prior to that time children over the age of seven years were tried as adults."[192]

THE PRIVILEGE OF THE WRIT OF HABEAS CORPUS SHALL NOT BE SUSPENDED

Section 14. The privilege of the writ of habeas corpus shall not be suspended unless, when in case of rebellion or invasion, the public safety may require.

"The primary function of the writ [of habeas corpus] is to release from unlawful imprisonment. . . . The office of the writ is not to determine prisoner's guilt or innocence, and only issue which it presents is whether prisoner is restrained of his liberty by due process."[193]

---

187 State v. Hegg, 410 N.W.2d 152, 154 (1987).

188 Id. See also: State v. Gates, 496 N.W.2d 553 (1993).

189 State v. Fredericks, 507 N.W.2d 61, 65 (1993).

190 City of Bismarck v. Fettig, 601 N.W.2d 247, 251–252 (1999).

191 State v. Benson, 376 N.W.2d 36, 39–40 (1985).

192 In re R. Y., 189 N.W.2d 644, 651 (1971).

193 Henry Campbell Black, *Black's Law Dictionary* (St. Paul, MN: West Publishing Co., 1990), p. 709.

One author has written: "This is the most famous writ in the law; and, having for many centuries been employed to remove illegal restraint upon personal liberty, no matter by what power imposed, it is often called the great writ of liberty."[194]

Very early in the state's history, the Supreme Court pointed out: "A defendant in a criminal case can never secure his release on habeas corpus by showing that there was no evidence of his guilt to sustain the judgment of conviction."[195] Basically, habeas corpus tests the jurisdiction of the court in which a defendant has been convicted. If a defendant wants to challenge the evidence of guilt or the correctness of the proceedings in which he or she was convicted, that person's recourse is to appeal.

An example of the operation of the writ of habeas corpus is the case of Ann Davis, who was convicted of assignation, that is, keeping a bawdy house. The trial judge sentenced Davis to one year in the state penitentiary, although the statute making it a crime to keep a bawdy house did not specify that the sentence be served there. Davis petitioned the Supreme Court for a writ of habeas corpus arguing that she should not have been sentenced to the penitentiary but to the county jail, and the Supreme Court agreed.

Writing for the Court, Justice Obert C. Teigen said: "Generally where the statute does not state a crime is a felony or misdemeanor, or classify it by fixing the place of imprisonment, . . . the defendant will be given the benefit of the doubt and the offense will be deemed a misdemeanor, punishable by confinement in the county jail."[196]

Another example of the use of the writ is the case of Alice Solberg, age 17, who was sentenced to the State Training School at Mandan, North Dakota, when a judge declared her to be a delinquent because she had become pregnant. Under the law existing at the time, before a minor could be committed to the Training School, the judge was obligated to find that "'the parents . . . are unfit . . . to care for, protect, educate or discipline such child.'"[197] Because Judge John C. Lowe did not make such findings in this case, the Supreme Court granted the writ releasing Alice Solberg from the School. "We are satisfied," the Supreme Court said, "that the Legislature intended . . . [that] the court . . . find as a jurisdictional prerequisite to the power to transfer the custody of a delinquent child to the state and to commit the same to a public institution, that the parents are unfit custodians of the child."[198]

---

[194] John Bouvier, *Bouvier's Law Dictionary* (Kansas City, MO: Vernon Law Book Company, 1914), Vol. I, p. 1400.

[195] State v. Barnes, 65 N.W. 688, 689 (1895).

[196] Davis v. Riedman, 114 N.W.2d 881, 883 (1962).

[197] Ex parte Solberg, 203 N.W. 898 (1925).

[198] Id., p. 902.

NO PERSON SHALL BE IMPRISONED FOR DEBT

Section 15. No person shall be imprisoned for debt unless upon refusal to deliver up his estate for the benefit of his creditors, in such manner as shall be prescribed by law; or in cases of tort; or where there is strong presumption of fraud.

The legal encyclopedia *Corpus Juris Secundum* has this to say about the constitutional guarantees against imprisonment for debt.

> In general, such constitutional provisions were adopted to protect the poor but honest debtor who is unable to pay his debts, and were not intended to shield a dishonest man who takes an unconscionable advantage of another. . . . Accordingly, no one should be imprisoned for a failure to pay money unless the evidence clearly shows that the party charged has the money within his power to pay, or that he had the money and wrongfully disposed of it.[199]

When A. E. Sunderhauf, acting as a guardian *ad litem*, was ordered to pay court costs in a lawsuit brought on behalf of his ward N. O. Granholm, he responded that he had no funds belonging to his ward, and therefore was unable to pay the costs. Because he did not pay the costs, the court ordered Sunderhauf committed to the county jail until such time as the costs were paid. Sunderhauf appealed from the order, arguing that his incarceration was a violation of this section and the Supreme Court agreed. The Court held that because the refusal was not a tortuous or fraudulent act, Sunderhauf was "protected from arrest and imprisonment by . . . [this section] of the state constitution."[200]

The Supreme Court has held that this section does not prevent imprisonment for refusing to pay alimony or support.[201] Nor does it protect a person who has issued a check without an account or with insufficient funds in an account.[202]

When Dennis Hatch was convicted of theft for receiving unemployment compensation for a week during which he was working, he argued that he was being imprisoned for a debt. The Court responded: "The penalty of imprisonment Hatch received, . . . is not for failing to make refund . . . but for knowingly obtaining property of another by deception with intent to deprive the owner thereof. This does not constitute imprisonment for debt."[203]

---

[199] 16A. Corpus Juris Secumdom, *Constitutional Law*, Section 487, pp. 552–553.

[200] Granholm v. Sweigle, 57 N.W. 509, 510 (1893),

[201] Gross v. Gross, 206 N.W. 793, 795 (1925).

[202] State v. McDowell, 312 N.W.2d 301, 307 (1981).

[203] State v. Hatch, 346 N.W.2d 268, 275 (1984).

PRIVATE PROPERTY SHALL NOT BE TAKEN . . . FOR PUBLIC USE WITHOUT JUST COMPENSATION

> **Section 16.** Private property shall not be taken or damaged for public use without just compensation having been first made to, or paid into court for the owner, unless the owner chooses to accept annual payments as may be provided for by law. No right of way shall be appropriated to the use of any corporation until full compensation therefor be first made in money or ascertained and paid into court for the owner, unless the owner chooses annual payments as may be provided by law, irrespective of any benefit from any improvement proposed by such corporation. Compensation shall be ascertained by a jury, unless a jury be waived. When the state or any of its departments, agencies or political subdivisions seek to acquire right of way, it may take possession upon making an offer to purchase and by depositing the amount of such offer with the clerk of the district court of the county wherein the right of way is located. The clerk shall immediately notify the owner of such deposit. The owner may thereupon appeal to the court in the manner provided by law, and may have a jury trial, unless a jury be waived, to determine the damages, which damages the owner may choose to accept in annual payments as may be provided by law. Annual payments shall not be subject to escalator clauses but may be supplemented by interest earned.

In discussing this section in 1902, the North Dakota Supreme Court, quoting a South Dakota case, pointed out: "'The constitutional provision is unquestionably a wise and just one, and well calculated to protect property owners from injustice and wrong on the part of municipal or other corporations or individuals invested with the privilege of taking private property for public use."[204]

The Supreme Court has made a distinction between the determination that there is a public need and whether the taking of the particular property being taken is necessary to solve that need.

For example, when the Oakes Municipal Airport Authority sought to take some property owned by Raymond Wiese, the Court pointed out that "courts cannot review or disturb an airport authority's determination that a new airport facility is necessary."[205] What the courts can review, however, is "whether the taking of the particular property sought to be condemned is reasonably suitable and usable for the authorized public use."[206]

Public use is defined by statute to include almost any purpose for which government wants to take private property.[207] Public use also permits the taking

---

[204] Donovan v. Allert, 91 N.W. 441, 446 (1902).

[205] Oakes Municipal Airport Auth. v. Wiese, 265 N.W.2d 697, 700 (1978).

[206] Id.

[207] NDCC Section 32-15-02.

of property for railroads, street railways, power lines, and telephone lines even though the taker is a private organization.[208]

North Dakota courts have upheld the taking of property for highways, streets, bridges, power and telephone lines, construction of a pedestrian mall, a gravel pit, an airport, railroad tracks, and for commercial growth and removal of stagnation.[209]

There does not have to be an actual taking of property before a landowner is entitled to compensation for actions taken which cause damage. For example, the Court has said, "the rights of an abutting owner to ingress and egress are private rights which cannot be destroyed or impaired without just compensation."[210] The Court found such an impairment of ingress and egress when the state constructed a new highway bypass near Minot, North Dakota, causing the property owner to "travel approximately six blocks east . . . or west"[211] in order to reach the bypass.

Other examples of when compensation may be required include street improvements that cause water to flow under the front door of a business and flood the premises; the placing of power lines in such a way as to interfere with aerial spraying, thus reducing the value of farm land; construction of a highway causing a circuity of travel to reach a business, causing loss of patronage, diminution of value of property, and leaving owner no direct access to highway; the placing of telephone poles two feet from the sidewalk leading to the entrance to residence; and the creation of a dump which polluted the air over plaintiff's property.[212]

The Supreme Court has held that some actions by government which result in damage to property owners are not compensable. Examples of such cases are the elimination of parking in front of a grocery store, damage from overflow of a sewer, and damage caused by flooding of farmland near bridges constructed

---

[208] Id. See also: Gram Const. Co. v. Minneapolis, St. P. & S. S. M. Ry., 161 N.W. 732 (1917); Donovan v. Allert, 91 N.W. 441 (1902); Otter Tail Power Co. v. Von Bank, 8 N.W.2d 599 (1943).

[209] Highways—Chandler v. Hjelle, 126 N.W.2d 141 (1964); streets—Jamestown Plbg. & Heat. Co. v. City of Jamestown, 164 N.W.2d 355 (1969); bridges—Cummings v. City of Minot, 271 N.W. 421 (1937); power lines—Otter Tail Power Co. v. Von Bank, 8 N.W.2d 599 (1943); telephone lines—Donovan v. Allert, 91 N.W. 441 (1902); pedestrian mall—City of Fargo v. Fahrlander, 199 N.W.2d 30 (1972); gravel pit—Becker County Sand & Gravel Co. v. Wosick, 245 N.W. 454 (1932); airport—Oakes Mun. Airport Auth. v. Wiese, 265 N.W.2d 697 (1978); railroads—Gram Const. Co. v. Minneapolis, St. P. & S. S. M. Ry., 161 N.W. 732 (1917); commercial growth—City of Jamestown v. Leevers, 552 N.W.2d 365 (1996).

[210] Chandler v. Hjelle, 126 N.W.2d 141, 146 (1964).

[211] Cady v. North Dakota Dept. of Transportation, 472 N.W.2d 467, 470 (1991).

[212] Jamestown Plbg. & Heat. Co. v. City of Jamestown, 164 N.W.2d 355 (1968); United Power Ass'n. v. Heley, 277 N.W.2d 262 (1979); Filler v. City of Minot, 281 N.W.2d 237, 243 (1979); Donovan v. Allert, 91 N.W. 441 (1902); Donaldson v. City of Bismarck, 3 N.W.2d 808 (1942). For a list of other cases in which compensation was required see: Eck v. City of Bismarck, 283 N.W.2d 193 (1979).

by the county where rainfall was twice the maximum expected in a hundred years of rainfall.[213]

TREASON AGAINST THE STATE SHALL CONSIST ONLY IN LEVYING WAR AGAINST IT

Section 17. Treason against the state shall consist only in levying war against it, adhering to its enemies or giving them aid and comfort. No person shall be convicted of treason unless on the evidence of two witnesses to the same overt act, or confession in open court.

The Supreme Court has not decided any cases involving this section.

NO BILL OF ATTAINDER . . . SHALL EVER BE PASSED

Section 18. No bill of attainder, ex post facto law, or law impairing the obligations of contract shall ever be passed.

"Bills of attainder are legislative acts that apply either to named individuals or to easily ascertainable members of a group in such a way as to inflict punishment on them without a judicial trial."[214] The prohibition of bills of attainder is part of the separation of powers of government, federal and state. U.S. Chief Justice Earl Warren, in discussing bills of attainder, pointed out: "Thus the Bill of Attainder Clause not only was intended as one implementation of the general principle of fractionalized power, but also reflected the Framers' belief that the Legislative Branch is not so well suited as politically independent judges and juries to the task of ruling upon the blameworthiness of, and levying appropriate punishment upon, specific persons."[215]

The Supreme Court has not decided any cases involving bills of attainder.

No . . . Ex Post Facto Law . . . Shall Ever Be Passed

When called upon to define ex post facto laws, the North Dakota Supreme Court adopted the definition given by U.S. Supreme Court Justice Samuel Chase in 1798. Justice Chase explained ex post facto laws:

"1. Every law that makes an action done before the passing of the law, and which was innocent when done, criminal; and punishes such action. 2. Every law that aggravates a crime, or makes it greater than it was, when committed. 3. Every law that changes

---

[213] Yegen v. City of Bismarck, 291 N.W.2d 422 (1980); Hamilton v. City of Bismarck, 300 N.W. 631 (1941); Frank v. County of Mercer, 186 N.W.2d 439 (1971).

[214] *American Jurisprudence*, 2nd ed., "Constitutional Law" (Danvers, MA: West Group, 1998), Vol. 16B, Section 671, pp. 160–161.

[215] United States v. Brown, 381 U.S. 437, 445 (1965).

> the punishment, and inflicts a greater punishment, than the law annexed to the crime, when committed. 4. Every law that alters the legal rules of evidence, and receives less, or different, testimony, than the law required at the time of the commission of the offense, in order to convict the offender."[216]

The case in which the above quotation appears concerned David J. Pleason, who allegedly imported liquor illegally into the state in 1924. At that time, the law required the state to start proceedings against suspects within two years of the alleged commission of a misdemeanor. In 1925, the Legislature provided that the two-year period would not run while a suspect was out of state.

Because Pleason had left the state, the charges were not filed against him until he returned in February 1927. Pleason was convicted but on appeal argued that changing the time for filing charges was an ex post facto law. The Supreme Court disagreed and affirmed his conviction.

The Court declared: "The facts brought out in the case are exactly the same as they were before the amendment and have the same effect; the rules of evidence, method of prosecution, and the penalty are not changed."[217]

In January 1927, the Legislature, with the intent to cure defects in deeds and mortgages executed prior to that date, adopted a statute validating such instruments. Shortly thereafter, the First National Bank of Mott sought to foreclose a mortgage executed by W. A. Acklin and Mary A. Acklin. At the time the Acklins signed the mortgage, the law required that a mortgage on a homestead must be executed and acknowledged by both husband and wife.

In response to the foreclosure, the Acklins asserted that the mortgage was not valid because Mary A. Acklin's signature had not been acknowledged. When the bank responded that the defect was cured by the 1927 law, the Supreme Court disagreed and said, "we fail to see how a subsequent act of the Legislature can endow with life that which never had an existence, and which could not exist primarily because of lack of essential elements."[218]

At the time that James Burr plead guilty to gross sexual imposition, he was not required to register as a sexual offender. Several years thereafter, however, the Legislature enacted legislation requiring registration of offenders like Burr. Burr registered, as required, but was later charged with failing to notify authorities of a change of residence. In defense, Burr argued that, as applied to him, the registration requirement was an ex post facto law and unconstitutional. The Supreme Court disagreed and pointed out that the "purpose of the registration requirement is protection of a legitimate public interest, which imposes a collateral consequence upon conviction, not added punishment."[219]

---

[216] State v. Pleason, 218 N.W. 154, 155 (1928).

[217] Id.

[218] Acklin v. First Nat. Bank, 254 N.W. 769, 774 (1934).

[219] State v. Burr, 598 N.W.2d 147, 159 (1999).

No . . . Law Impairing the Obligations of Contract Shall Ever Be Passed

Because of the depression existing in the country in the early 1930s, the North Dakota Legislature enacted legislation temporarily extending the period of redemption from mortgage foreclosures for two years. When Harry C. Cleveringa foreclosed a mortgage in February 1932, Sheriff E. M. Klein of Emmons County refused to issue a certificate of sale, arguing that the period in which the owners could redeem the property having been extended, the purchaser at the foreclosure sale was not entitled to title until the time for redemption had passed.

The Supreme Court disagreed, pointing out that the statutory period for redemption was part of the mortgage contract and that the law extending the period was a violation of this section. The Court declared: "It is clear that this law, so far as it is attempted to be applied to mortgages executed prior to its passage, does impair the obligations of the contract."[220]

The Supreme Court did not find an impairment of the obligations of a contract when the Legislature provided for a resale at a mortgage foreclosure when "'it appears upon due examination that the sale price is unreasonable and unfairly inadequate, or that justice has otherwise not been done.'"[221] The Court said: "Not only does the statute [requiring a resale] relate to remedial processes, but it is an assertion by the state of its protective power to safeguard the vital interests of the people."[222]

In 1955, the Legislature enacted comprehensive legislation regulating the dairy industry. The law sought to prevent certain unfair trade practices such as giving retailers certain discounts, furnishing advertising material, paying for storage of dairy products, making loans to retailers to purchase refrigeration equipment, furnishing to or making repairs to dealers' equipment, and extending credit longer than 30 days.

Fairmont Foods Company brought an action against the attorney general seeking a judgment that the law was unconstitutional. Among the constitutional questions raised was whether the law was an impairment of the contracts which Fairmont Foods had with the retailers with which it did business.

District Judge George Thom, Jr., found the law to be unconstitutional and the Supreme Court agreed and said that "the enforcement . . . [of the law] would

---

[220] State v. Klein, 249 N.W. 118, 122 (1933). See also: First Federal Savings and Loan Ass'n. v. Haley, 357 N.W.2d 492 (1984) where the Supreme Court held that a law changing the time when the period of redemption would start could not be applied to a mortgage executed prior to the date of the change in the law.

[221] First Nat'l. Bank of Waseca v. Paulson, 288 N.W. 465, 469 (1939).

[222] Id., p. 471.

result in the impairment of... [Fairmont Foods'] right of contract and property rights."[223]

THE MILITIA SHALL BE SUBORDINATE TO THE CIVIL POWER

Section 19. The military shall be subordinate to the civil power. No standing army shall be maintained by this state in time of peace, and no soldiers shall, in time of peace, be quartered in any house without the consent of the owner; nor in time of war, except in the manner prescribed by law.

The North Dakota Supreme Court has not decided any cases dealing with a standing army.

TO GUARD AGAINST TRANSGRESSIONS OF THE HIGHER POWERS

Section 20. To guard against transgressions of the high powers which we have delegated, we declare that everything in this article is excepted out of the general powers of government and shall forever remain inviolate.

The Supreme Court has construed this section as placing a limitation on the ability of the legislature to enact legislation that restricts the rights protected under Article I. However, this section does not "hamper the people in amending the constitution whenever they deem it necessary for the public good, and thus they may amend even article I."[224]

NO SPECIAL PRIVILEGES OR IMMUNITIES SHALL EVER BE GRANTED WHICH MAY NOT BE ALTERED

Section 21. No special privileges or immunities shall ever be granted which may not be altered, revoked or repealed by the legislative assembly; nor shall any citizen or class of citizens be granted privileges or immunities which upon the same terms shall not be granted to all citizens.

Section 22. All laws of a general nature shall have a uniform operation.

Because the above two sections both require laws to apply equally to all, lawyers often cite both sections in cases where the Legislature has exempted some parties from the application of a law. For example, an 1890 law prohibited

---

[223] Fairmont Foods Company v. Burgum, 81 N.W.2d 639, 647 (1957).

[224] Larkin v. Gronna, 285 N.W. 59, 62–63 (1939).

lending institutions from charging more than 12 percent per annum interest. The law, however, did not apply to building and loan associations.

When the question arose whether the law violated these sections, the Supreme Court held that it did not. The Court wrote:

> We hold, . . . [that the] act, excepting building and loan associations . . . from the operation of the act, was not intended to include, . . . the transactions of any such association with any parties other than its own stockholders; and that, as thus limited, the legislature had the power to make the exception; and that, said chapter is uniform in its operation upon all classes upon which it does operate, it is not vulnerable to any of the constitutional objections urged.[225]

Because not all classifications made by the Legislature are contrary to the requirements of these sections, the Supreme Court has developed several methods of determining which classifications are permissible and which are not. For example, in 1919 the Legislature enacted workers' compensation legislation to protect employees engaged in hazardous employment. Henry Amerland brought an action seeking to have the law declared unconstitutional arguing that his two clerk employees were not engaged in hazardous work, and therefore classifying them as such was unconstitutional. The Court disagreed, and declared: "What trades and occupations may be regulated is ordinarily a matter for the Legislature, in the absence of a distinctive showing of an unreasonable and arbitrary discrimination or classification."[226]

Although the state has had a long history of Sunday Closing Laws, the Supreme Court has consistently upheld these laws against charges that they violate these sections. For example, when C. W. Temple and Clara Wright were arrested and convicted for operating a theater on Sunday they argued to the Supreme Court that the statute was unconstitutional as a violation of these sections. The Court, however, disagreed and declared: "[T]he books are replete with authorities passing upon the constitutionality of similar statutes, and almost without exception, holding them valid as against these identical, and similar, objections."[227]

Since the Court decided the above case, it has upheld a statute prohibiting the sale of "'any commodity on the first day of the week.'"[228] In this case, the statute permitted the sale of "'drugs, medicines, surgical appliances, milk, ice cream and soda fountain dispensations, fruits, candy and confectionery, tobacco, and cigars, newspapers and magazines'"[229] at any time of the day.

---

[225] Vermont Loan & Trust Co. v. Whited, 49 N.W. 318, 323 (1891).

[226] State v. Hagan, 175 N.W. 372, 379 (1919).

[227] State v. Barnes, 132 N.W. 215, 219 (1911).

[228] State v. Diamond, 219 N.W. 830, 832 (1928).

[229] Id.

Subsequently, the Court upheld an ordinance of the City of Bismarck which prohibited conducting business or labor for profit on Sunday, but permitted owner-managed grocery stores employing not more than three employees to remain open. A majority of the Court was of the opinion that the ordinance was reasonable and not an invidious discrimination.[230]

The Court has upheld a number of other classifications which it concluded were reasonable and not arbitrary and thus were not violations of Sections 21 and 22. These include a big game hunting license law which exempted owners and operators of farms and ranches;[231] a law limiting a veteran's bonus to those individuals who had served in the armed forces for a period of 15 years prior to 8/5/1964 and had been a resident of North Dakota on 3/29/1971;[232] a law prohibiting the establishment of a commercial apiary within two miles of another commercial apiary. This was reasonable, the Court said, in order to prevent honey raiding and spreading of bee diseases.[233]

The Court has, however, found a number of laws to be arbitrary and unreasonable, and therefore unconstitutional under these sections. One such law prohibited legislators from doing more than $10,000 per year business with the state or any subdivision thereof. The Court was of the opinion that the dollar limitation was an arbitrary classification.[234] Other classifications held to be unconstitutional include a statute prohibiting illegitimate children from inheriting from legitimate children of their mother;[235] a statute preventing a guest in an automobile from recovering damages for the ordinary negligence of the driver;[236] and a statute which required a son to pay costs of treatment of his mother at the state hospital. In this case, the Court wrote: "We believe that the classification . . . [in the statute] is arbitrary and oppressive, that there exists no reasonable relationship between the legislative purpose . . . [of saving the state money] and the selection of the class of 'responsible relatives'" forced to pay these costs.[237]

As the above cases indicate, most of the classifications which the government makes are reasonable and not arbitrary and therefore are upheld by the courts. There are, however, some classifications which the courts will scrutinize more carefully, and in most cases will be found to violate the constitution. An example of such a classification is one in which the government treats individuals differently because of their gender. One such situation involved the transfer of female

[230] City of Bismarck v. Materi, 177 N.W.2d 530 (1970). NDCC Chapter 12.1-30 now permits most businesses to operate Sundays from noon until midnight.

[231] State v. Miller, 129 N.W.2d 356 (1964).

[232] Horst v. Guy, 211 N.W.2d 723 (1973).

[233] State v. Knoefler, 279 N.W.2d 658, 664 (1979).

[234] Melland v. Johanneson, 160 N.W.2d 107 (1968).

[235] In re Estate of Jensen, 162 N.W.2d 861 (1968).

[236] Johnson v. Hassett, 217 N.W.2d 771 (1974).

[237] Hospital Services v. Brooks, 229 N.W.2d 69, 72 (1975).

prisoners out of state but the incarceration of male prisoners in the state. This procedure made it difficult for female prisoners to get access to the parole system and the courts. Three justices of the Supreme Court concluded that this procedure was a violation of these sections. Justice Robert Vogel pointed out that there are some classifications that are "'inherently suspect.'"[238]

"Included within the 'inherently suspect' category are classifications based upon such criteria as race, sex, illegitimacy, and immutable characteristics determined solely by accident of birth."[239] Applying that test, three justices concluded that the law violated these sections. Two justices agreed with the result, but did not believe that the constitutionality of the law was properly before the Court.

In *Hanson v. Williams County*,[240] the Court considered a state law which required that legal action for damages occurring as a result of a defective product be brought within 10 years of the initial purchase of the product. Plaintiff Bonny Hanson brought an action seeking damages for the death of her son when a piece of road machinery jumped backwards as it was being started. The accident occurred on August 24, 1983, almost 20 years after the machine was originally sold. The trial court dismissed the case, but the Supreme Court reversed, holding that the statute unconstitutionally classified the times when actions could be brought because of defective products.

The Court examined the reasons for the 10-year limitation for product liability cases and noted that the legislature had found that high insurance costs to defend such cases had an adverse effect upon manufacturers of such products. Nevertheless, the Court concluded that for such legislation to stand the classification must bear a "close correspondence" to the goals sought by the legislation, and there was no such relationship in this case.

CONSTITUTION OF THE UNITED STATES IS THE SUPREME LAW OF THE LAND

Section 23. The state of North Dakota is an inseparable part of the American union and the Constitution of the United States is the supreme law of the land.

Although this section states that it is the U.S. Constitution that is the supreme law of the land and must be respected, the North Dakota Supreme Court has extended the same consideration to federal law. For example, when the Court had to determine whether the commissioner of the United States Land Department had the authority to cancel patents issued by local land office

[238] State ex rel. Olson v. Maxwell, 259 N.W.2d 621, 627 (1977).

[239] Id.

[240] 389 N.W.2d 319 (1986). For a similar result see: Dickie v. Farmers Union Oil Co. of La Moure, 611 N.W.2d 168 (2000).

employees, the Court noted: "The commissioner having power to investigate . . . [fraudulent claims] and to reach a conclusion upon them, his decision is final, unless the case is taken out of the ordinary rule by what are characterized as its exceptional features. It is one of the elements of the law that the decision of the land department on a question of fact is ordinarily binding on the courts."[241]

The Court has deferred to federal law even when doing so results in adverse consequences to those dealing with the federal government. That occurred when Angus Stewart, his wife Phoebe, and brother John were forced to pay a deficiency judgment in an action the government brought against them on a promissory note secured by a chattel mortgage on their property.

During negotiations for settlement of the matter, counsel for the government told the Stewarts that "he had no authority to cancel and surrender the notes upon completion of the sale nor to waive any deficiency judgment."[242] Apparently being of the opinion, however, that no deficiency judgment would be sought against them, the Stewarts cooperated in the sale of their property. When the sale did not produce enough funds to satisfy the note, the government brought an action against them for the deficiency.

Although the Stewarts admitted that they had been told by government counsel he had no authority to waive the deficiency, they defended on the grounds that they were of the opinion that "'the plaintiff [government] would accept the proceeds of sale in full of the debt evidenced by the note.'"[243]

In upholding the deficiency judgment, the Supreme Court said: "[W]henever an agency or instrumentality of the United States is lawfully operating in this State under a law of Congress, the court takes judicial notice of the law itself and its scope."[244] On that basis, the Court affirmed the lower court's granting the government a deficiency judgment against the Stewarts.

THIS CONSTITUTION . . . [IS] MANDATORY AND PROHIBITORY

Section 24. The provisions of this constitution are mandatory and prohibitory unless, by express words, they are declared otherwise.

This section requires courts to strictly apply the provisions of the constitution. The Supreme Court did just that when it nullified a state law relating to the boundaries of Stark County. The Legislature provided that several unorganized

---

[241] Parsons v. Wenzke, 61 N.W. 1036, 1038 (1894). This case was appealed to the U.S. Supreme Court which affirmed the finding of the commissioner that the patent had been obtained by fraud. Parsons v. Wenzke, 164 U.S. 89 (1896).

[242] Regional Agricultural Credit Corp. v. Stewart, 289 N.W. 801, 802 (1940).

[243] Id.

[244] Id., p. 803.

counties could be added to Stark County if "a majority of the aggregate voters cast"[245] at an election voted to accept the change.

When the vote was taken, a majority of those voting did approve the addition. The Supreme Court held, however, that because the law did not conform to the constitution, the election was of no effect. The constitution, the Court said, required a "'majority of all legal votes cast in each county at such election'"[246] and that did not happen in this case. The Court found that in one of the unorganized counties, which was to be added to Stark County, a majority of one had voted against the change.

In its discussion, the Court declared: "It is obvious that, if the Legislature had no power to authorize a change of boundaries of Stark county in the manner or on the conditions provided in this statute, then the act was a nullity from the beginning, and all proceedings under it were likewise nullities."[247]

Another example of the Court's insistence that the constitution be strictly followed is the case of *Johnson v. Grand Forks County*.[248] This case involved the section of the constitution which set forth the qualifications for voters "at any election" but which said nothing about candidates paying fees.

In 1905, the Legislature provided that candidates for certain county offices pay a fee of 2 percent of the annual salary of the office to have their names printed on the ballot. A candidate for treasurer and one for clerk of court in the June primary election paid the fee but after the election brought an action seeking return of the sums paid.

The county's defense was that because primary elections did not come into being until after the constitution in 1889, that section did not apply to such elections. The Supreme Court disagreed. "The Constitution," the Court declared, "requires no fee. If we once admit the power of the Legislature to make even the smallest additions not contemplated by the Constitution to the qualifications required to entitle one to vote, there is no limit to the requirements which may be added."[249]

Even though a constitutional provision does not so specify, it may still be subject to another constitutional provision. For example, although Article XI, section 11 provides for the removal of certain elected officials for "misconduct, malfeasance, crime or misdemeanor in office," the Supreme Court has held that such removal proceedings must still provide due process of law, that is, "'the right of the accused to a hearing, to be confronted with his accusers, and to the right of defense.'"[250]

---

[245] State v. Stark County, 103 N.W. 913 (1905).

[246] Id.

[247] Id., p. 915.

[248] 113 N.W. 1071 (1907).

[249] Id., p. 1074.

[250] State v. District Court, 291 N.W. 620, 627 (1940).

Article II

Elective Franchise

THE GENERAL ELECTION OF THE STATE SHALL BE HELD BIENNIALLY

Section 1. The general election of the state shall be held biennially as provided by law.

Every citizen of the United States, who has attained the age of eighteen years and who is a North Dakota resident, shall be a qualified elector. When an elector moves within the state, he shall be entitled to vote in the precinct from which he moves until he establishes voting residence in another precinct. The legislative assembly shall provide by law for the determination of residence for voting eligibility, other than physical presence. No elector shall lose his residency for voting eligibility solely by reason of his absence from the state.

The legislative assembly shall provide by law for secrecy in voting, for absentee voting, for administration of elections and for the nomination of candidates.

The sections of the constitution relating to the Elective Franchise are the end product of a number of amendments to similar sections in the original constitution. The discussion that follows, therefore, relates to the Supreme Court's interpretation of the original and subsequent amendments that are applicable today.

Acting pursuant to the last paragraph of Section 1, the Legislature has enacted legislation setting forth in detail the procedures to be followed in holding primary and general elections.

As originally adopted, Article II contained sections defining qualified electors, one of which read: "Third. Civilized persons of Indian descent who shall have severed their tribal relations two years next preceding such election."

In an early case dealing with the right to vote, the Court held that Indians living on a reservation who owned their own land were qualified voters. The Court based its decision on that part of section 1 which "defines who shall be deemed qualified electors, and the first class is 'Citizens of the United States.'"[251] The Court pointed out that under federal law, Indians had been declared to be citizens of the United States.

The extent to which the Legislature has authority to regulate voting came before the Court in a case wherein 41 of the ballots cast for county auditor had not been stamped and initialed as required by law. In arguing that these ballots should be counted, counsel pointed out that the constitution did not require stamping and initialing of ballots, and not to count them would be disenfranchising those voters. The Court responded by pointing out: "There are many regulative provisions in election statutes the enforcement of which will and do operate to deprive voters of their privilege, and yet their constitutionality cannot be successfully challenged."[252] Furthermore, the Court wrote: "The capital purpose of these statutes, manifestly, is to provide the voter with an official ballot, and to enable him to make sure that he gets such ballot."[253]

Although the constitution did not provide for primary elections, the Legislature created them in 1905. Under that legislation, candidates were required to pay a fee of 2 percent of the annual salary of the office in order to have their names printed on the primary ballot. Several candidates paid the fee and later action was brought to recover those fees.

In response, the county argued that because primary elections were not mentioned in the constitution, it was not a constitutional election and that therefore the Legislature could do as it pleased in setting up the system. The Supreme Court disagreed. "The Constitution," Justice B. F. Spalding wrote, "requires no fee. If we once admit the power of the Legislature to make even the smallest additions not contemplated by the Constitution to the qualifications required to entitle one to vote, there is no limit to the requirements which may be added."[254]

---

[251] State v. Denoyer, 72 N.W. 1014, 1019 (1897). See also: Swift v. Leach, 178 N.W. 437, 440 (1920).

[252] Miller v. Schallern, 79 N.W. 865, 866–867 (1899).

[253] Id., p. 867.

[254] Johnson v. Grand Forks County, 113 N.W. 1071, 1074 (1907). See also: Johnson v. Grand Forks County, 135 N.W. 179 (1912) for a similar result.

In 1907, the Legislature prohibited candidates from running in the general election unless the candidate had received at least 30 percent as many votes in the primary as his party's choice for secretary of state had received during the previous general election. When challenged, the Supreme Court declared this law to be unconstitutional. Being of the opinion that the choice of 30 percent was purely arbitrary and no real criteria of a party's strength, the Court said: "We believe that a proper regard for the constitutional guaranties and safeguards of our citizens requires that this feature of the primary law should be held inoperative."[255]

NO PERSON CONVICTED OF A FELONY SHALL BE QUALIFIED TO VOTE

> **Section 2.** No person who has been declared mentally incompetent by order of a court or other authority having jurisdiction, which order has not been rescinded, shall be qualified to vote. No person convicted of a felony shall be qualified to vote until his or her civil rights are restored.

Although the right to vote was not at issue, the Court discussed the effect of a felony conviction on that right in a case involving the removal of Governor William Langer from office. Langer, together with several other persons, was convicted in federal court of conspiracy to defraud the U.S. Government.

While Langer's conviction was on appeal, Lieutenant Governor Ole H. Olson brought an action seeking to remove Langer from office. In his defense, Langer argued that he was entitled to remain governor until his conviction had been upheld on appeal. The Court disagreed. Justice John Burke, writing for the Court, declared: "We . . . conclude from a review of the authorities that, when a defendant is convicted of a felony in this state, his disqualification as an elector attaches immediately, and that this disqualification is not suspended by his appeal and the furnishing of a supersedeas bond."[256]

---

[255] State v. Hamilton, 129 N.W. 916, 921 (1910). See also: State v. Flaherty, 169 N.W. 93 (1918).

[256] State v. Langer, 256 N.W. 377, 391 (1934).

Article III

Powers Reserved to the People

THE PEOPLE RESERVE THE POWER TO PROPOSE AND ENACT LAWS

> **Section 1.** While the legislative power of this state shall be vested in a legislative assembly consisting of a senate and a house of representatives, the people reserve the power to propose and enact laws by the initiative, including the call for a constitutional convention; to approve or reject legislative Acts, or parts thereof, by the referendum; to propose and adopt constitutional amendments by the initiative; and to recall certain elected officials. This article is self-executing and all of its provisions are mandatory. Laws may be enacted to facilitate and safeguard, but not to hamper, restrict, or impair these powers.

In discussing the relationship between the legislative power and the initiative and referendum the Court has explained:

> By the initiative, the people have provided against nonaction by their duly constituted representatives in the legislative branch; and by the referendum, an appeal may be taken directly to the people from affirmative action by these representatives. In the one case affirmative legislation results, the people, without the intervention of representatives, declare what shall be law; in the other case, the people veto affirmative

> action by their agents; in the one instance we have a constructive exercise of legislative power; in the other, merely negation.[257]

Furthermore, the Court has said: "The initiative and referendum are both phases of legislative processes, but they are wholly separate and independent powers. The constitution declares them as separate powers."[258]

The referendum process does not apply to actions of the Legislature in ratifying an amendment to the U.S. Constitution. The North Dakota Supreme Court has pointed out "that the act of ratification by the State derives its authority from the Federal Constitution; and that a State has no authority to require the submission of the ratification to a referendum under the State Constitution."[259]

The Court has also held that Article III does not apply to municipal ordinances. The Court reached this conclusion when it upheld the refusal of the Fargo City Commission to allow city residents to vote on an increase in the sales and use tax for the construction of a multipurpose dome facility.[260]

A PETITION TO INITIATE OR REFER A MEASURE SHALL BE PRESENTED TO THE SECRETARY OF STATE FOR APPROVAL

> **Section 2.** A petition to initiate or to refer a measure shall be presented to the secretary of state for approval as to form. A request for approval shall be presented over the names and signatures of twenty-five or more electors as sponsors, one of whom shall be designated as chairman of the sponsoring committee. The secretary of state shall approve the petition for circulation if it is in proper form and contains the names and addresses of the sponsors and the full text of the measure.

When ascertaining whether the petition for an initiative or referendi is in proper form, the secretary of state must not be concerned with the merits of the petition. The secretary's duty is to prepare a "ballot title," and ascertain whether the measure contains "impermissible, extraneous statements."[261]

A "full text of the measure" means exactly that, and a petition that incorporates by reference statutes affected by the initiative is not sufficient.[262]

Insofar as improper, extraneous statements are concerned, the Court has examined such situations to see if the condemned matter was really improper or extraneous. For example, in the referral of a bill to rename Minot State

---

[257] Baird v. Burke County, 205 N.W. 17, 20 (1925).

[258] Dawson v. Tobin, 24 N.W.2d 737, 749 (1946).

[259] State ex rel. Askew v. Meier, 231 N.W.2d 821, 823 (1975).

[260] Pelkey v. City of Fargo, 453 N.W.2d 801 (1990).

[261] Municipal Services Corp. v. Kusler, 490 N.W.2d 700 (1992). As originally written, this section required the petition to have a "ballot title." That requirement is now in NDCC Section 16.1-01-09.

[262] Dyer v. Hall, 199 N.W. 754, 756 (1924).

College to Dakota Northwestern University, the petition contained the following statement:

> "House Bill No. 1500 would rename Minot State College to Dakota Northwestern University. This would increase the number of universities in the state from two to three, with commensurate increases in state funding responsibilities."[263]

The Court found this to be an impermissible statement and set aside the secretary of state's approval of the petition.

This petition came back before the Court again when another challenge was made that it contained extraneous matter. The petition was challenged because the secretary of state's statement describing the petition said that it would be voted on "'at the next general election.'"[264] It was argued that this was extraneous because Section 5 requires that the measure be "voted upon at a statewide election or at a special election called by the governor."

The Court, however, held that the statement in the petition referring to "the next general election" would be interpreted to be "the next statewide election" and therefore was not extraneous.

If the ballot title is consistent with the contents of the proposed initiative, it satisfies this section, even though those opposing the initiative argue that the title is misleading. That was the Court's decision when it upheld a ballot title for an initiative establishing an environmental fund and imposing a fee on disposal of waste material. Opponents argued that the secretary's use of the word "fee" in the ballot title was misleading because the "fee" was actually a "tax" and the title should have so stated. The Court disagreed because the initiative itself used the word "fee." "In reviewing a petition for form," the Court declared, "the Secretary must not be concerned with the merits of the petition or with the substance of the text."[265]

THE PETITION SHALL BE CIRCULATED ONLY BY ELECTORS

> **Section 3.** The petition shall be circulated only by electors. They shall swear thereon that the electors who have signed the petition did so in their presence. Each elector signing a petition shall also write in the date of signing and his post-office address. No law shall be enacted limiting the number of copies of a petition. The copies shall become part of the original petition when filed.

In order to fulfill the requirement that the elector circulating the petition swear that the signers signed in his/her presence, the Legislature enacted legislation requiring each copy of the petition to contain an affidavit executed by the

[263] Haugland v. Meier, 335 N.W.2d 809, 811 (1983).

[264] Haugland v. Meier, 339 N.W.2d 100, 102 (1983).

[265] Municipal Services Corp. v. Kusler, 490 N.W.2d 700, 706 (1992).

circulator, reciting those facts. The Court upheld that requirement in *Wood v. Byrne*.[266] "Any person," Chief Justice John Burke wrote, "who circulates a copy of a petition in any neighborhood, or any person who has information upon which he can form a belief, can make such an affidavit in compliance with the statute as we construe it, and, as so construed, it is a reasonable constitutional regulation and a valid statute."[267]

This section requires the signor to "write in the date of signing and his post-office address," the Legislature has interpreted this to mean "Residential Address or Complete Rural Route or General Delivery Address."[268]

In upholding this statute, the Court has said that the post office address and the residential address are not the same. "The post office address of a person," the Court has written, "is the place to which his mail is directed in order that it may be delivered to him by the post office. . . . His residence is the place where he remains when not called elsewhere for labor or a special or temporary purpose and to which he returns in seasons of repose."[269]

The Court, however, has approved those signatures which include a post office address but give the precinct number of the signor in place of the signor's residence address.[270] Giving the precinct number indicates that the signor is an elector living in the state.

The Court has also approved the signatures of those who gave the name of the county as their place of residence.[271] And post office addresses which only indicate the city in which the signor lives is sufficient because generally, if the secretary of state needs to do so, he/she can locate those signors to determine whether they had signed the petition.[272]

THE PETITION . . . [MUST] BE . . . SIGNED BY ELECTORS EQUAL IN NUMBER TO TWO PERCENT OF THE RESIDENT POPULATION

Section 4. The petition may be submitted to the secretary of state if signed by electors equal in number to two percent of the resident population of the state at the last federal decennial census.

Prior to being amended in 1978, this section required referendum petitions to contain 7,000 valid signatures. In *Moses v. Thorson*,[273] a district court found that

[266] 232 N.W. 303 (1930).
[267] Id., p. 306.
[268] NDCC Section 16.1-01-09.
[269] Dawson v. Meier, 78 N.W.2d 420, 428 (1956).
[270] Id., p. 427.
[271] Hernett v. Meier, 173 N.W.2d 907, 911 (1970).
[272] McCarney v. Meier, 286 N.W.2d 780, 786 (1979).
[273] 299 N.W. 309 (1941).

of the 7,077 signatures on a referral petition, 172 were by persons who had not signed the petition, and 105 were signatures added after the affidavit as to the validity of the signatures had been signed. In concluding that the petition did not contain the required number of signatures, the Supreme Court declared: "When such spurious and invalid signatures are deducted there are not more than 6,800 signatures on the petition."[274]

AN INITIATIVE PETITION SHALL BE SUBMITTED NOT LESS THAN NINETY DAYS BEFORE THE STATEWIDE ELECTION

> **Section 5.** An initiative petition shall be submitted not less than ninety days before the statewide election at which the measure is to be voted upon. A referendum petition may be submitted only within ninety days after the filing of the measure with the secretary of state. The submission of a petition shall suspend the operation of any measure enacted by the legislative assembly except emergency measures and appropriation measures for the support and maintenance of state departments and institutions. The submission of a petition against one or more items or parts of any measure shall not prevent the remainder from going into effect. A referred measure may be voted upon at a statewide election or at a special election called by the governor.

Jeff Husebye, seeking to refer a measure adopted by the Legislature, delivered petitions to Secretary of State Al Jaeger shortly before 5:00 P.M. on the ninetieth day. Husebye informed Jaeger that more petitions were coming. The secretary responded that no petitions would be accepted after 5:00 P.M. After Husebye had made several unsuccessful attempts to deliver additional petitions to Jaeger, he mailed them before midnight and they were delivered to the secretary's office the next morning. Jaeger, however, refused to accept the petitions and returned them unopened to Husebye.

When the signatures were counted on the petitions which Husebye had delivered to the secretary, they did not contain enough signatures to refer the measure.[275]

Husebye brought an action against the secretary, arguing that the law was in conflict with this section, and therefore unconstitutional. The Supreme Court agreed. Writing for the Court, Chief Justice VandeWalle said: "We conclude that the statute relied upon by... [the Secretary of State] is unconstitutional and that the State Constitution requires the Secretary of State to accept referral petitions until midnight of the 90th day after the date the referred measure was filed with the Secretary of State."[276]

---

[274] Id., p. 310.

[275] Husebye v. Jaeger, 534 N.W.2d. 811, 813 (1995).

[276] Id., p. 812. The Legislature has amended the statute (NDCC Section 16.1-01-09(7) to make it consistent with this case.

The case of *Haugland v. Meier*,[277] brought to the Court two constitutional questions relating to this section. One of the questions was whether the words "at the next general election" in the referral's ballot title was consistent with this section's requirement that the referral be "voted upon at a statewide election." The Court held that it was.

The other question required the Court to determine whether the law being referred was "suspended" at the time of the submission of the petitions in view of the fact that the law had already taken effect. The Court's response was: "The petitioner's argument that the measure had gone into effect and consequently could not be suspended is not in conformity with the aforementioned constitutional provision."[278]

Sometimes petitions for referral will call for striking only a part of a law leaving the question of whether the part not stricken can stand alone. In such a case, the Supreme Court has written: "We conclude that if the result of striking from a law an item, a part, clause, or section, . . . and to leave a portion which, standing alone, is in reality a fundamental perversion of the purpose the . . . [Legislature] intended to effect when the whole was enacted, the effect of such a referendum is to nullify the whole act as if the statute had been disapproved in its entirety."[279]

When a referral is successful, that is, the referred law is rejected by the voters, any law which the referred law had repealed is revived.[280]

THE SECRETARY OF STATE SHALL PASS UPON EACH PETITION

Section 6. The secretary of state shall pass upon each petition, and if he finds it insufficient, he shall notify the "committee for the petitioners" and allow twenty days for correction or amendment. All decisions of the secretary of state in regard to any such petition shall be subject to review by the supreme court. But if the sufficiency of such petition is being reviewed at the time the ballot is prepared, the secretary of state shall place the measure on the ballot and no subsequent decision shall invalidate such measure if it is at such election approved by a majority of the votes cast thereon. If proceedings are brought against any petition upon any ground, the burden of proof shall be upon the party attacking it.

Section 7. All decisions of the secretary of state in the petition process are subject to review by the supreme court in the exercise of original jurisdiction. If his decision is being reviewed at the time the ballot is prepared, he shall place the measure on the

---

[277] 339 N.W.2d 100 1983).

[278] Id., p. 108.

[279] Baird v. Burke County, 205 N.W. 17, 24 (1925).

[280] Dawson v. Tobin, 24 N.W.2d 737, 750 (1946). See also: State v. Sathre, 113 N.W.2d 679 (1962).

ballot and no court action shall invalidate the measure if it is approved at the election by a majority of the votes cast thereon.

These two sections give the Supreme Court the power to review decisions of the secretary of state in refusing or accepting initiative or referral petitions. In commenting on its obligation, the Court has said: "The question we must decide is, is the petition sufficient under the Constitution, and the Constitution makes it our duty to decide it."[281]

As discussed above in Sections 2 and 3, many of the cases brought to the Court relate to correctness of the petition such as number of signatures, sufficient address of the signors, complete ballot title, a full text of the measure being proposed or referred, and whether the petition contains "extraneous material."

The Court has also been called upon to examine the text to see if a word or words sufficiently describe what the initiative is really all about. That was the situation in *Municipal Services Corp. v. Kusler*.[282] One of the questions before the Court was whether the use of the word "fee" accurately described the funds to be collected from those engaged in the business of waste disposal. Those businesses argued that the so-called fee was really a tax and therefore the ballot measure was inaccurate.

In responding to this argument, Justice Beryl J. Levine declared for the Court: "If the applicants believe that the measure is actually a tax, rather than a fee, their argument should be directed to the political arena of debate among the electorate where the merits of that point can be argued. The Secretary's use of the term fee in the ballot title, as it was used in the proposed measure, itself, is neither misleading nor inaccurate."[283]

When the Court is asked to examine the constitutionality of an initiated measure, it will refuse to do so. "Until the issue of constitutionality arises in an actual, litigated controversy," Justice Levine wrote, "a determination of the constitutional question would be an advisory opinion."[284]

Both of these sections provide that once the ballot is prepared no subsequent decision of the Court shall invalidate the measure if it is approved by the voters. The Court considered those provisions in *Shore v. Meier*.[285] In this case, the secretary of state had prepared the ballot on June 13, 1963, but the petition for review was not filed until July 1, 1963. In dismissing the case, Justice Thomas J. Burke declared: "Once the ballot is prepared the election must go on, no matter to what extent the petitions to place the measure on the ballot may be insufficient."[286]

---

[281] Preckel v. Byrne, 243 N.W. 823, 825 (1932).

[282] 490 N.W.2d 700 (1992).

[283] Id., p. 703.

[284] Id., p. 706.

[285] 122 N.W.2d 566 (1963).

[286] Id., p. 568.

In discussing its authority under these sections to review decisions of the secretary of state with regard to initiative or referral petitions, the Court has pointed out: "These provisions are self-executing and mandatory, . . . and our authority to review the Secretary of State's decisions on these matters is without limitation."[287] This contrasts with the Court's discretionary jurisdiction in other cases discussed hereafter under Article VI.

IF A MAJORITY OF VOTES CAST UPON [A] . . . MEASURE ARE AFFIRMATIVE, IT SHALL BE DEEMED ENACTED

Section 8. If a majority of votes cast upon an initiated or a referred measure are affirmative, it shall be deemed enacted. An initiated or referred measure which is approved shall become law thirty days after the election, and a referred measure which is rejected shall be void immediately. If conflicting measures are approved, the one receiving the highest number of affirmative votes shall be law. A measure approved by the electors may not be repealed or amended by the legislative assembly for seven years from its effective date, except by a two-thirds vote of the members elected to each house.

The question before the Supreme Court in *State ex rel. Wefald v. Meier,*[288] concerned the wording of the question on a referral ballot which the voters were required to answer. The ballot prepared by the secretary of state contained the statement:

"Shall said referred measure be approved:

Yes ______

No ______"[289]

Attorney General Robert Wefald brought an action against Secretary of State Ben Meier asserting that "an affirmative vote should be considered as a vote to repeal the bill; and a negative vote would be construed not to repeal the bill. The practical effect of the Attorney general's position in this case would be that a 'Yes' vote would be a vote against the proposed . . . [bill] and a 'No' vote would be in favor of . . . [the bill]."[290]

The Court responded:

The language of Article III, Section 8 of the Constitution of North Dakota, clearly states that a referred measure shall be deemed enacted if a majority of the votes cast

---

[287] Husebye v. Jaeger, 534 N.W.2d 811, 813 (1995). See also: Municipal Services Corp. v. Kusler, 490 N.W.2d 700, 701–702 (1992).

[288] 347 N.W.2d 562 (1984).

[289] Id., p. 563.

[290] Id., p. 565.

> are affirmative and that a referred measure which is rejected shall immediately become void. It is clearly the intent of the Constitution that the voters cast their ballots to approve or reject the referred measure, not to repeal or reject the action of the Legislature. Our prior cases are in accord.[291]

Sometimes the Legislature enacts a law that repeals and replaces a law then existing. If the new law is referred to the voters and they vote to reject it, the law repealed by the referred law is revived. In commenting upon this the Court declared: "It necessarily follows that from the time such rejection became effective the whole . . . measure, including the repealing provision therein, was recalled and destroyed, and that the law that had been replaced and superseded by the rejected . . . measure was revived."[292]

The Court has had an opportunity, in two cases, to apply the part of this section which requires a "two-thirds vote of the members elected to each house" to amend or repeal an initiated measure previously approved by the electors. In each case, the Court held that the legislative attempt to change the initiated law failed because a two-thirds vote was not obtained.[293]

In an article titled "Judicial Review of Direct Democracy," author Julian N. Eule comments on state constitutions that require a two-thirds vote of the legslature to change an initiated measure.

> Such state constitutions must fairly be read at least to give parity to direct democracy. Indeed, to the extent that voter initiatives and referenda are free to undo legislative decisions, while state legislatures often are constitutionally limited in the amendment or repeal of voter action, a strong case may be made for the preferred position of citizen lawmaking.[294]

A CONSTITUTIONAL AMENDMENT MAY BE PROPOSED BY INITIATIVE PETITION

> **Section 9.** A constitutional amendment may be proposed by initiative petition. If signed by electors equal to four percent of the resident population of the state at the last federal decennial census, the petition may be submitted to the secretary of state. All other provisions relating to initiative measures apply hereto.

This section requires persons wishing to initiate a proposed amendment to the state constitution to present a petition to the secretary of state for approval as required by Section 2. Those signing the petition must be electors, and the date of their signing and their post office address must be given as required by Section 3.

---

[291] Id., p. 565–566.
[292] Dawson v. Tobin, 24 N.W.2d 737, 750 (1946).
[293] State v. Smart, 184 N.W. 623, 624 (1921); State v. Baker, 299 N.W. 574, 580 (1941).
[294] Julian N. Eule, *Judicial Review of Direct Democracy*, 99 Yale Law Journal 1503, 1545 (1990).

In order for the petition to be placed on the ballot, the petition must be submitted "not less than ninety days before the statewide election at which the . . . [proposed amendment] is to be voted upon" as specified in Section 5.

The obligations of the secretary of state, and the authority of the Supreme Court to review his/her decisions, for initiated measures contained in Sections 6 and 7 are the same for initiated constitutional amendments.

The effective date of an approved initiated measures is "thirty days after the election." Under this section, an approved initiated constitutional amendment would also take effect 30 days after the election.

ANY ELECTED OFFICIAL . . . SHALL BE SUBJECT TO RECALL BY PETITION OF ELECTORS

Section 10. Any elected official of the state, of any county or of any legislative or county commissioner district shall be subject to recall by petition of electors equal in number to twenty-five percent of those who voted at the preceding general election for the office of governor in the state, county, or district in which the official is to be recalled.

The petition shall be filed with the official with whom a petition for nomination to the office in question is filed, who shall call a special election if he finds the petition valid and sufficient. No elector may remove his name from a recall petition.

The name of the official to be recalled shall be placed on the ballot unless he resigns within ten days after the filing of the petition. Other candidates for the office may be nominated in a manner provided by law. When the election results have been officially declared, the candidate receiving the highest number of votes shall be deemed elected for the remainder of the term. No official shall be subject twice to recall during the term for which he was elected.

In a case involving the recall of an elected state official, the secretary of state is the person with whom the petition must to be filed. In commenting upon the secretary's duties, the Court has said:

> It will be noted that this recall amendment does not provide any machinery, except in a very limited way, concerning the circulation of petitions, the determination of their sufficiency, or concerning the special election to be held thereunder. . . . The mandatory nature of the amendment, under its very terms, specifying by whom the petitions must be signed, the percentage of electors required, and the duty thereupon imposed upon the officer to call a special election, requires an exercise of a discretion by such officer.[295]

Although this section now provides that no "elector may remove his name from a recall petition," that was not always true. For example, in a 1932 case, the

[295] State ex rel. Laird v. Hall, 186 N.W. 284, 285 (1921).

Court had before it a petition recalling State Senator Jones. When the petition was filed it contained more than enough valid signatures to fulfill the statutory requirement. However, before the recall election was set, two petitions were filed requesting a number of names be stricken from the petition. Because the total number seeking to have their names stricken was sufficient to bring the number below the requisite amount necessary for a recall, the county auditor refused to call a special election.

County Judge Thomas H. Pugh, therefore, issued an order for the election to be held and the Supreme Court affirmed that decision. The Court declared: "When a petition is filed, it is in fact either good or bad, either sufficient or insufficient. If it is good and sufficient, the officer has no discretion thereafter. . . . He 'shall' call the election. If the petition is insufficient and bad then, though the petition has been filed, he must refuse to call the election."[296]

When the Court was asked to clarify who is an elector qualified to sign a petition to recall State Senator Fred J. Aandahl, the Court responded that electors were qualified even though they had not voted for governor at the last general election. The Court wrote: "Since the Constitution defines a qualified elector, and states specifically that the qualified electors shall sign the petition, it would seem clear that it is the intent of the Constitution to make any qualified elector eligible to sign the petition, . . . [and that the percentage requirement] is not a limitation upon the qualifications, but is intended, rather, to prescribe a number of signatures sufficient to show the necessity for a recall."[297]

---

[296] Coghlan v. Cuskelly, 244 N.W. 39, 41 (1932).

[297] State ex rel. Riedman v. Baillie, 245 N.W. 466, 468 (1932).

Article IV

Legislative Branch

THESE HOUSES ARE JOINTLY DESIGNATED AS THE LEGISLATIVE ASSEMBLY OF THE STATE OF NORTH DAKOTA

Section 1. The senate must be composed of not less than forty nor more than fifty-four members, and the house of representatives must be composed of not less than eighty nor more than one hundred eight members. These houses are jointly designated as the legislative assembly of the state of North Dakota.

The place that the legislative assembly plays in the government of the state was expressed by the Supreme Court early in the state's history. Justice Alfred Wallin wrote in 1893: "As to this it will suffice to say that all governmental sovereign power is vested in the legislature, except such as is granted to the other departments of the government, or expressly withheld from the legislature by constitutional restrictions."[298]

Because this sovereign power is invested in both houses of the Legislature, the Supreme Court has said: "This legislative power, to evidence its expression, requires the independent and concurrent action of each house. . . . Each house must act independently as a separate body."[299] This "independent and concurrent action" is necessary, the Court has pointed out: "Otherwise one branch of the

[298] State v. Boucher, 56 N.W. 142, 145 (1893).

[299] State v. Poindexter, 183 N.W. 852, 853–854 (1921).

Legislative Assembly might override through its independent action constitutional provisions . . . in a valid legislative enactment."[300]

THE LEGISLATIVE ASSEMBLY SHALL FIX THE NUMBER OF SENATORS AND REPRESENTATIVES

> **Section 2.** The legislative assembly shall fix the number of senators and representatives and divide the state into as many senatorial districts of compact and contiguous territory as there are senators. The districts thus ascertained and determined after the 1990 federal decennial census shall continue until the adjournment of the first regular session after each federal decennial census, or until changed by law.
>
> The legislative assembly shall guarantee, as nearly as is practicable, that every elector is equal to every other elector in the state in the power to cast ballots for legislative candidates. A senator and at least two representatives must be apportioned to each senatorial district and be elected at large or from subdistricts from those districts. The legislative assembly may combine two senatorial districts only when a single member senatorial district includes a federal facility or federal installation, containing over two-thirds of the population of a single member senatorial district, and may provide for the election of senators at large and representatives at large or from subdistricts from those districts.

In 1964, the U.S. Supreme Court wrote: "The right to vote freely for the candidate of one's choice is of the essence of a democratic society, and any restrictions on that right strike at the heart of representative government."[301]

That philosophy has been part of the North Dakota State Constitution from the beginning and is now embodied in this section, which requires reapportionment every ten years. Reapportionment of state legislative districts, however, is fraught with politics because such reapportionment will substantially affect which political party has control of one or both houses of the legislature. And that is true for North Dakota.

Writing in 1981, one author pointed out: "The problem of reapportioning the state legislature has troubled North Dakota for the past eight decades. The longevity of the problem may be explained, in part, by the array of issues which must be considered whenever a reapportionment plan is devised."[302]

Because apportionment must also meet the requirements of the Fourteenth Amendment Equal Protection Clause of the U.S. Constitution, much of the

---

[300] Id., p. 855.

[301] Reynolds v. Sims, 377 U.S. 533, 555 (1964).

[302] Sandra L. Tabor, *Apportionment in North Dakota: The Saga of Continuing Controversy*, 57 North Dakota Law Review 447 (1981).

litigation concerning the validity of some reapportionment plans for the North Dakota Legislature has been in the federal courts.[303]

When the North Dakota Supreme Court has been called on to consider the apportionment of the State Legislature, it has pointed out that the goal of reapportionment is to create legislative districts having equal population. The Court has acknowledged, however, that this is impossible. "The authorities," Justice James Morris noted, "generally recognize that this situation, of necessity, vests in the Legislature or other apportioning body a discretion to make an apportionment that varies to some extent from absolute equality of representation. Our problem is to determine whether or not the action of the group falls within the limits of that discretion."[304]

When the Court has struck down a reapportionment plan because it does not meet the requirements of either the Equal Protection Clause of the Fourteenth Amendment or this section, it has held that the last apportionment shall remain in effect and that the Legislature has a continuing duty to reapportion.[305]

ONE-HALF OF THE MEMBERS OF . . . [EACH HOUSE] AS NEARLY AS IS PRACTICABLE, ARE ELECTED BIENNIALLY

Section 3. The legislative assembly shall establish by law a procedure whereby one-half of the members of the senate and one-half of the house of representatives, as nearly as is practicable, are elected biennially.

Originally, the constitution provided for two classes of senators, one-half of which were to be elected for two-year terms and one-half for four-year terms. In contrast, all members of the house were to be elected every two years. In commenting on this, the Supreme Court has pointed out: "The House of Representatives is a new body every two years. After each general election the old house ceases to exist as a body, and the new membership becomes the new house. Not so with the Senate. It is a continuous body. It never goes out of existence. . . . [this] was to maintain a Senate which should at all times have one-half of its member, as nearly as practicable, experienced men."[306]

The term of the members of the House and the times when they are to be elected were changed when the present section was adopted at the general election held in November 1996.

In carrying out the mandate of this section, the Legislature has provided that one-half of the members of each body be elected from even-numbered districts

---

303 Id., pp. 454–478.

304 State v. Sathre, 113 N.W.2d 679, 684 (1962).

305 Id., p. 687.

306 State v. Meyer, 127 N.W. 834, 836 (1910).

at one biennial election and one-half from odd-numbered districts at the next biennial election.[307]

SENATORS AND REPRESENTATIVES . . . [ARE] ELECTED FOR . . . FOUR YEARS

Section 4. Senators and representatives must be elected for terms of four years.

The terms of representatives was set at four years by an amendment to the constitution adopted at the general election in November 1996.

EACH PERSON ELECTED TO THE LEGISLATIVE ASSEMBLY MUST BE . . . A QUALIFIED ELECTOR

Section 5. Each person elected to the legislative assembly must be, on the day of the election, a qualified elector in the district from which the member was chosen and must have been a resident of the state for one year immediately prior to that election.

When asked to give a definition of "elector," the Court responded: "We . . . conclude that the word 'electors' . . . means all persons who, by the terms of the Constitution, have the qualifications necessary to entitle them to vote. Persons qualified to vote, but who do not vote, are still electors."[308] Persons entitled to vote in North Dakota are citizens of the United States, 18 years of age, and who are residents of the state.[309]

Originally, women were not considered electors, even though they met the constitutional qualifications. The constitution did, however, give them the right to "'vote for all school officers, and upon all questions pertaining solely to school matters, and be eligible to any school office.'"[310]

NO MEMBER MAY HOLD ANY FULL-TIME APPOINTIVE STATE OFFICE ESTABLISHED BY THIS CONSTITUTION

Section 6. While serving in the legislative assembly, no member may hold any full-time appointive state office established by this constitution or designated by law. During the term for which elected, no member of the legislative assembly may be appointed to any full-time office which has been created, or to any office for which the compensation has been increased, by the legislative assembly during that term.

---

[307] NDCC Section 54-03-01.10, staggering of terms of representatives; NDCC Section 03-01.8, staggering of the terms of senators.

[308] State v. Blaisdell, 119 N.W. 360, 362 (1909).

[309] Article II, Section 1. Elective Franchise.

[310] Wagar v. Prendeville, 130 N.W. 224, 225 (1911).

One constitutional scholar has written:

> The reasons for excluding persons from offices who have been concerned in creating them, or increasing their emoluments, are to take away, as far as possible, any improper bias in the vote of the representative, and to secure to the constituents some solemn pledge of his disinterestedness.[311]

This section originally prohibited any member of the Legislature from being "elected" to any office "'the emoluments of which shall have been increased, during the term for which he was elected.'"[312]

That section was before the Court when William L. Guy was elected governor in 1960. Guy was a member of the Legislature in 1959 when it appropriated $4,500.00 to purchase a new car for the governor. Shortly after Guy took office as governor in January 1961, an action was brought against him claiming that he was ineligible for the office because the emoluments of the office (the car) had been increased by the 1959 Legislature in which he was then serving as a member.

The Supreme Court disagreed and pointed out that the car was owned by the state and the governor would not be entitled to mileage when he used it.

Furthermore, the Court wrote: "The purchase of the automobile merely changed the mode of transportation available to the Governor. It did not increase the emoluments of his office."[313]

TERMS OF MEMBERS OF THE LEGISLATIVE ASSEMBLY BEGIN ON THE FIRST DAY OF DECEMBER FOLLOWING THEIR ELECTION

> **Section 7.** The terms of members of the legislative assembly begin on the first day of December following their election.
>
> The legislative assembly shall meet at the seat of government in the month of December following the election of the members thereof for organizational and orientation purposes as provided by law and shall thereafter recess until twelve noon on the first Tuesday after the third day of January or as such other time as may be prescribed by law but not later than the eleventh day of January.
>
> No regular session of the legislative assembly may exceed eighty natural days during the biennium. The organizational meeting of the legislative assembly may not be counted as part of those eighty natural days, nor may days spent in session at the call of the governor or while engaged in impeachment proceedings, be counted. Days spent in regular session need not be consecutive, and the legislative assembly may

---

[311] State v. Guy, 107 N.W.2d 211, 218 (1961).

[312] Id., p. 215.

[313] Id., p. 216.

authorize its committees to meet at any time during the biennium. As used in this section, a "natural day" means a period of twenty-four consecutive hours.

Neither house may recess nor adjourn for more than three days without consent of the other house.

Section 54-03-02 of the North Dakota Century Code implements this section.

THE HOUSE OF REPRESENTATIVES SHALL ELECT ONE OF ITS MEMBERS TO ACT AS PRESIDING OFFICER

Section 8. The house of representatives shall elect one of its members to act as presiding officer at the beginning of each organizational session.

The presiding officer elected by the House pursuant to this section is referred to as Speaker.[314]

[MEMBER] . . . OF THE LEGISLATIVE ASSEMBLY SHALL [NOT] OFFER OR PROMISE TO GIVE HIS VOTE OR INFLUENCE

Section 9. If any person elected to either house of the legislative assembly shall offer or promise to give his vote or influence, in favor of, or against any measure or proposition pending or proposed to be introduced into the legislative assembly, in consideration, or upon conditions, that any other person elected to the same legislative assembly will give, or will promise or assent to give, his vote or influence in favor of or against any other measure or proposition, pending or proposed to be introduced into such legislative assembly, the person making such an offer or promise shall be deemed guilty of solicitation of bribery. If any member of the legislative assembly, shall give his vote or influence for or against any measure, proposition, pending or proposed to be introduced into such legislative assembly, or offer, promise or assent so to do upon condition that any other member will give, promise or assent to give his vote or influence in favor of or against any other such measure or proposition pending or proposed to be introduced into such legislative assembly, or in consideration that any other member hath given his vote or influence, for or against any other measure or proposition in such legislative assembly, he shall be deemed guilty of bribery. And any person, member of the legislative assembly or person elected thereto, who shall be guilty of either such offenses, shall be expelled, and shall not thereafter be eligible to the legislative assembly, and, on the conviction thereof in the civil courts, shall be liable to such further penalty as may be prescribed by law.

[314] NDCC Section 54-03-08.

The legislative assembly has implemented this section by adopting NDCC Chapter 12.1-12 titled BRIBERY—UNLAWFUL INFLUENCE OF PUBLIC SERVANTS. This chapter makes bribery a Class C felony, the maximum penalty for which is five years' imprisonment and/or a fine of two thousand dollars.

NO PERSON CONVICTED OF BRIBERY, . . . OR OTHER INFAMOUS CRIME SHALL BE ELIGIBLE TO THE LEGISLATIVE ASSEMBLY

Section 10. No member of the legislative assembly, expelled for corruption, and no person convicted of bribery, perjury or other infamous crime shall be eligible to the legislative assembly, or to any office in either branch thereof.

This section concerns the eligibility of a person to serve in the legislative assembly and does not provide a method of contesting an election because of alleged corrupt election practices. When confronted with a contest of an election for alleged corrupt election practices, the Court responded: "Art. IV, Section 10, N. D. Const., is in harmony with our interpretation that a corrupt practices act violation is not grounds for an election contest because that constitutional provision contemplates a conviction of 'bribery, perjury or other infamous crime' before a person is ineligible for the legislative assembly."[315]

GOVERNOR SHALL ISSUE WRITS OF ELECTION TO FILL SUCH VACANCIES AS MAY OCCUR IN EITHER HOUSE

Section 11. The governor shall issue writs of election to fill such vacancies as may occur in either house of the legislative assembly.

When the governor has issued a writ of election to fill a vacancy in the legislative assembly, the courts are reluctant to intervene. The reason for the reluctance was discussed by the Supreme Court in *State v. Quam*.[316] In that case, Justice A. G. Burr wrote: "Among the powers granted to and the duties imposed upon the governor under the constitution, is that of issuing a writ of election to fill a vacancy which may exist in either house of the legislative assembly. This power is vested solely in the governor and neither of the other departments may interfere with him in this respect."[317] The Court, therefore, refused to intervene when the governor issued a writ on December 17, 1942, for an election to be held January 14, 1943, although an argument was made that the time between the issuance of the writ and the election did not give ample time for persons to file petitions for nomination.

---

[315] Republican Com. v. Democrat Com., 466 N.W.2d 820, 828 (1991).

[316] 7 N.W.2d 738 (1943).

[317] Id., p. 739.

EACH HOUSE IS THE JUDGE OF THE QUALIFICATIONS OF ITS MEMBERS

Section 12. A majority of the members elected to each house constitutes a quorum. A smaller number may adjourn from day to day and may compel attendance of absent members in a manner, and under a penalty, as may be provided by law.

Each house is the judge of the qualifications of its members, but election contests are subject to judicial review as provided by law. If two or more candidates for the same office receive an equal and highest number of votes, the secretary of state shall choose one of them by the toss of a coin.

Each house shall determine its rules of procedure, and may punish its members or other persons for contempt or disorderly behavior in its presence. With the concurrence of two-thirds of its elected members, either house may expel a member.

Early in the state's history, the Supreme Court held that this section does not apply to an election contest arising out of a primary election. The Court said: "But a primary election is not an election within the meaning of such constitutional provision, nor within the common acceptation of the term."[318] A person wishing to contest a primary election, therefore, must look to the courts for relief.

Although this section gives each house control over election contests, the Legislature has provided that: "Legislative election contests must be determined in court as provided . . . for other contests. No legislative election may be contested before either house of the legislative assembly."[319]

NO LAW MAY BE ENACTED EXCEPT BY A BILL PASSED BY BOTH HOUSES

Section 13. Each house shall keep a journal of its proceedings, and a recorded vote on any question shall be taken at the request of one-sixth of those members present. No bill may become law except by a recorded vote of a majority of the members elected to each house, and the lieutenant governor is considered a member-elect of the senate when the lieutenant governor votes.

No law may be enacted except by a bill passed by both houses, and no bill may be amended on its passage through either house in a manner which changes its general subject matter. No bill may embrace more than one subject, which must be expressed in its title; but a law violating this provision is invalid only to the extent the subject is not so expressed.

---

318 Leu v. Montgomery, 148 N.W. 662, 663 (1914). See also: Walton v. Olson, 170 N.W. 107 (1918).

319 Section 16.1-16-10 Legislative Contest of Election. See also: Republican Com. v. Democrat Com., 466 N.W.2d 820, Note 2, p. 824 (1991).

Every bill must be read on two separate natural days, and the readings may be by title only unless a reading at length is demanded by one-fifth of the members present.

No bill may be amended, extended, or incorporated in any other bill by reference to its title only, except in the case of definitions and procedural provisions.

The presiding officer of each house shall sign all bills passed and resolutions adopted by the legislative assembly, and the fact of signing shall be entered at once in the journal.

Every law, except as otherwise provided in this section, enacted by the legislative assembly during its eighty natural meeting days takes effect on August first after its filing with the secretary of state, or if filed on or after August first and before January first of the following year ninety days after its filing, or on a subsequent date if specified in the law unless, by a vote of two-thirds of the members elected to each house, the legislative assembly declares it an emergency measure and includes the declaration in the Act. Every appropriation measure for support and maintenance of state departments and institutions and every tax measure that changes tax rates enacted by the legislative assembly take effect on July first after its filing with the secretary of state or on a subsequent date if specified in the law unless, by a vote of two-thirds of the members elected to each house, the legislative assembly declares it an emergency measure and includes the declaration in the Act. An emergency measure takes effect upon its filing with the secretary of state or on a date specified in the measure. Every law enacted by a special session of the legislative assembly takes effect on a date specified in the Act.

The legislative assembly shall enact all laws necessary to carry into effect the provisions of this constitution. Except as otherwise provided in this constitution, no local or special laws may be enacted, nor may the legislative assembly indirectly enact special or local laws by the partial repeal of a general law but laws repealing local or special laws my be enacted.

In January 1921, the House of Representatives created a committee to audit the state bank and empowered the committee to secure legal and business assistance. When vouchers were presented for payment for such services and expenses, the state auditor refused to honor them because the action by the House had not been submitted to the Senate for approval.

The District Court refused to order payment and the Supreme Court affirmed that decision. The Court asked: "To what extent is the power of one branch of the Legislative Assembly, when acting alone and without concurrence of the other, restricted by the Constitution, or subservient to legislative enactment?"[320]

The Court responded: "The Legislative Assembly neither authorized the appointment nor the expenses of such investigating committee. It follows

[320] State v. Poindexter, 183 N.W. 852, 853 (1921).

therefore, . . . that there exists no legislative appropriation and no legislative authority for the disbursement out of the balance of funds appropriated of moneys for the petitioners."[321]

Although this section does not address the question of whether the Legislature may delegate its authority to legislate to other governmental bodies, courts have generally held that such delegation of power is unconstitutional. And early in the state's history the Supreme Court wrote: "It is well established that the exercise of the power thus intrusted to the Legislature cannot be delegated by that body."[322]

Quoting from another case, the Court pointed out however: "'The Legislature cannot delegate its power to make a law, but it can make a law to delegate a power to determine some fact or state of things upon which the law makes, or intends to make, its own action depend. To deny this would be to stop the wheels of government.'"[323]

Trying to draw the line between an unconstitutional delegation of Legislature power and a constitutional grant of power to some other governmental body has been difficult for courts. For example, in a 1904 case the Court considered a law which allowed "'boards of county commissioners to institute proceedings to enforce payment of taxes on real property sold to the state or county for taxes.'"[324] The Court concluded that this was not a delegation of legislative power, but rather a grant of discretionary authority to county boards to determine whether to proceed to enforce back taxes.

Cases wherein the Court has found an unconstitutional delegation of power include: (1) a law creating a Board of Capitol Commissioners to remodel the state capital and build a governor's residence, where the law did not specify what funds should be used on the capitol remodeling nor on the governor's residence;[325] (2) the establishment of a State Bonding Department where the commissioner had the power to allocate funds between payment of losses and payment of salaries and expenses of the Department and there was no limitation on the amount expended for each;[326] and (3) the grant of authority to the State Board of Higher Education to construct buildings where the grant did not specify where the buildings were to be built nor limit the cost thereof.[327]

In examining the history of legislative nondelegation, Chief Justice Ralph Erickstad recently wrote for the Court: "We have recently noted a gradual change in our approach to the nondelegation doctrine, and we now follow the modern

---

321 Id., p. 856.

322 Picton v. Cass County, 100 N.W. 711, 712 (1904).

323 Id., p. 713.

324 Id., p. 711.

325 State v. Budge, 105 N.W. 724 (1905).

326 State v. Taylor, 145 N.W. 425 (1913).

327 Nord v. Guy, 141 N.W.2d 395 (1966).

view which recognizes that, in a complex area, it may be necessary and appropriate to delegate in broad and general terms, as long as there are adequate standards and procedural safeguards."[328]

Having reached that position, the Court upheld legislation giving the director of the Office of Management and Budget the authority to reduce agencies' budgets by 2 percent.[329] And the Court also found no unconstitutional delegation of power when the Legislature granted the North Dakota Board of Nursing the authority to establish standards for all nursing educational programs.[330]

No Bill May Embrace More Than One Subject, Which Must Be Expressed in Its Title

In explaining the purpose for this constitutional requirement, the Court has written: "This provision is intended to forestall what Judge Cooley denominates 'log-rolling' legislation, and prevent legislation not fully understood by members of the legislature, as well as to prevent surprises or misapprehensions on the part of the public."[331]

In explaining how the judicial system will approach claims that a law violates this part of Section 13, the Court stated:

> Accordingly, the principles that will be followed as guides in the construction of . . . [this section] of the state Constitution are as follows: (1) The law will not be declared unconstitutional on account of the defect pointed out in the title, unless it is clearly so. (2) The title will be liberally construed, and not in a strict or technical manner. (3) If the provisions of the act are germane to the expressions of the title, the law will be upheld. (4) Conflict with the constitutional provision must be clear and palpable, and, in case of doubt as to whether the subject is expressed in the title, the law will be upheld.[332]

The Supreme Court applied the above test in a case wherein Thomas H. Poole, who had held the position of adjutant general of the National Guard, was replaced at the end of two years when the newly elected governor appointed Amasa P. Peake to the position.

Poole argued that a statute setting two years as the term of the adjutant general violated the title of the Act which provided for appointment of officers of the National Guard. That title was: "'An act providing that all appointments to

---

[328] N. D. Council of School Adm'rs. v. Sinner, 458 N.W.2d 280, 285 (1990).

[329] Id., p. 286.

[330] Trinity Med. Center v. N. D. Board of Nursing, 399 N.W.2d 835 (1987).

[331] State v. Woodmanse, 46 N.W. 970, 971 (1890).

[332] State v. Peake, 120 N.W. 47, 49 (1909). See also: Sunbehm Gas, Inc. v. Conrad, 310 N.W.2d 766, 772 (1981).

the various departments of the National Guard of the state of North Dakota shall be made from officers of the field and line.'"[333]

In concluding that the term limit statute fell within that title, the Court said: "As the very essence of the right and privilege conferred by an appointment to public office consists in its duration, or, in other words, its term or tenure, it follows that the subject of term of office is fairly included in a broad signification of the word 'appointment.'"[334]

A review of the cases indicates that the assertion that this part of Section 13 has been violated is often made as a last resort. For example, when John Haas appealed his conviction for illegally selling intoxicating liquor, he claimed that the title of the act under which he was convicted related only to "'*penalties* [emphasis added] for the unlawful manufacture, sale and keeping for sale intoxicating liquors'" but did not make "the . . . *sale* . . . of liquors as a beverage unlawful."[335] Section 13 was therefore violated, he argued, because the title did not cover the unlawful *sale* of liquor.

The Supreme Court disagreed and pointed out that "the constitution had already made . . . [the] declaration . . . [that the sale of intoxicating liquor was unlawful] and all that was needed to supplement the fundamental law was a legislative enactment prescribing the penalties for such unlawful conduct."[336]

Another example is *State v. Brown*[337] where the Supreme Court held: "The title, 'An act to provide for the punishment of any person carrying concealed any dangerous weapons or explosives' . . . is sufficiently comprehensive to cover a provision in the act . . . which makes the carrying of concealed revolvers and other dangerous weapons unlawful . . . is not in violation of . . . [Section 13] of the Constitution . . . which provides that 'no bill may embrace more than one subject, which shall be expressed in its title.'"[338]

A case wherein the Court did find a violation of Section 13 is *State v. Nomland*.[339] In this case, the Court considered whether the title "'An act creating the office of the state board of auditors and prescribing the duties thereof'" sufficiently identified the subject of the act. In concluding that the subject matter was not evident from the title, the Court asked: "Was the act passed for

---

[333] Id., p. 48.

[334] Id., p. 49.

[335] State v. Haas, 50 N.W. 254, 255 (1891). Italics supplied.

[336] Id. Other cases in which the Supreme Court found no violation of Section 13 include: Martin v. Tyler, 60 N.W. 392 (1894); In re Kol, 88 N.W. 273 (1901); Erickson v. Cass County, 92 N.W. 841 (1902); Powers Elevator Co. v. Pottner, 113 N.W. 703 (1907); State v. Minneapolis & Northern Elevator Co., 114 N.W. 482 (1908); State v. Brandner, 130 N.W. 941 (1911); Klein v. Hutton, 191 N.W. 485 (1922); Sunbehm Gas, Inc. v. Conrad, 310 N.W.2d 766 (1981).

[337] 165 N.W. 520, Syllabus (1917).

[338] Id.

[339] 57 N.W. 85 (1893).

the purpose of creating that board? Was that the subject—the object—of the act? Clearly not. The board was simply an instrumentality for the accomplishment of some purpose, but what purpose no human foresight could determine from the title."[340]

Every Law . . . Takes Effect on August First after Its Filing with the Secretary of State

In *State v. Olson*,[341] the Supreme Court pointed out that there were four methods by which a law becomes effective. Those methods are:

> (1) By an emergency clause to make the act effective as a law upon passage and approval by the necessary two-thirds affirmative vote required by the constitutional provision.
> (2) By permitting an act not stated or adopted as an emergency act to become effective . . . [August] 1st, after the close of the session, pursuant to the constitutional provision.
> (3) By a specific provision in the act providing that such acts shall become effective as a law at a time subsequent to . . . [August] 1st after the close of the session.
> (4) Possibly by the referendum of an act not an emergency measure to the people, and through adoption of the same at an election, whereupon, pursuant to the Constitution concerning the referendum [Article III], such act becomes effective as a law 30 days after such election.[342]

In the *Olson* case, the Court also held that these rules apply to laws enacted at a special session of the Legislature.

Two-Thirds of the Members Elected to Each House . . . [May Declare] . . . an Emergency Measure

If a proposed law is declared to be an emergency measure and is approved by two-thirds of the members elected to each house, the declaration of an emergency is conclusive on the courts.[343] Furthermore, when an emergency measure makes a change in or repeals existing law but the emergency law is later repealed, the prior laws which were changed or repealed by the emergency law are revived.[344] And the Supreme Court has said: "Even if that emergency clause is

---

[340] Id., p. 86. See also: Dornacker v. Strutz, 1 N.W.2d 614 (1942).

[341] 176 N.W. 528, 532 (1920). Article III, Section 8 provides that: "An initiative . . . which is approved shall become law thirty days after the election."

[342] Id., p. 532.

[343] Cuthbert v. Smitz, 282 N.W. 494 (1938).

[344] Dawson v. Tobin, 24 N.W.2d 737, 750 (1946).

attached to a law granting special privilege that does not affect the act but only the validity of the emergency clause."[345]

No Local or Special Laws May Be Enacted

When the Legislature enacted legislation regulating the location of county-seats, it prohibited (1) the relocation of any county-seat to any place not located on a railroad, and (2) the removal of a county-seat from a county where the value of the courthouse and jail exceeded $35,000. In concluding that this legislation violated the prohibition against special laws, the Court wrote:

> This section of the constitution must have a reasonable construction. To say that no classification can be made under such an article would make it one of the most pernicious provisions ever embodied in the fundamental law of a state. It would paralyze the legislative will. . . . On the other hand, the classification may not be arbitrary. The legislature cannot finally settle the boundaries to be drawn. Such a view of the organic law would bring upon this court the just reproach that it had suffered the legislature to disregard a constitutional barrier by relegating to it the question where that barrier should be set up.[346]

The Supreme Court upheld comprehensive laws creating a procedure for liquidating insolvent banks against a charge that such laws violated this part of Section 13. In referring to the law, the Court pointed out: "The statutory provision under consideration here is neither special nor local; it is general. It operates equally upon all persons and things within the scope of the statute. . . . All insolvent banking corporations and all persons in any manner affected are treated alike under like circumstances and conditions."[347]

In 1979, the Legislature enacted the Skiing Responsibility Act[348] which, for the most part, protected ski operators from liability for accidents involving skiers. In upholding the Act against a claim that it was a special law, the Court declared: "In our view, . . . [the law] operates alike to all similarly situated persons. The statute applies to all persons operating a skiing facility within the state. This is a permissible class and does not create a special law."[349]

---

[345] Ferch v. Housing Authority of Cass County, 59 N.W.2d 849, 869 (1953).

[346] Edmonds v. Herbrandson, 50 N.W. 970, 971 (1891).

[347] State v. First State Bank, 202 N.W. 391, 399 (1924).

[348] NDCC Chapter 53-09.

[349] Bouchard v. Johnson, 555 N.W.2d 81, 88 (1996).

ALL SESSIONS OF THE LEGISLATIVE ASSEMBLY . . . MUST BE OPEN AND PUBLIC

Section 14. All sessions of the legislative assembly, including the committee of the whole and meetings of legislative committees, must be open and public.

This section has undergone several changes since it was adopted as part of the original constitution in 1889. The provision in that document read: "The sessions of each house and of the committee of the whole shall be open unless the business is such as ought to be kept secret."[350]

An amendment to the constitution in 1974 changed the section to read: "All sessions of the legislative assembly, including the committee of the whole and meetings of the legislative committees, shall be open to the public."[351] This section was amended in 1983 to read in its present form.

The Supreme Court has not decided any cases involving this section.

MEMBERS OF THE LEGISLATIVE ASSEMBLY ARE IMMUNE FROM ARREST DURING THEIR ATTENDANCE AT THE SESSIONS

Section 15. Members of the legislative assembly are immune from arrest during their attendance at the sessions, and in going to or returning from the sessions, except in cases of felony. Members of the legislative assembly may not be questioned in any other place for any words used in any speech or debate in legislative proceedings.

In commenting upon a similar provision in the U.S. Constitution, James Wilson, a delegate to the Constitutional Convention of 1787, declared:

> In order to enable and encourage a representative of the public to discharge his public trust with firmness and success, it is indispensably necessary, that he should enjoy the fullest liberty of speech, and that he should be protected from the resentment of every one, however powerful, to whom the exercise of that liberty may occasion offence.[352]

Referring specifically to legislators, the U.S. Supreme Court has written: "Legislators are immune from deterrents to the uninhibited discharge of their legislative duty, not for their private indulgence but for the public good."[353]

The Supreme Court has not decided any cases involving this section.

---

[350] Daniel Guy and Jack McDonald, *Government in the Sunshine*, 53 North Dakota Law Review 51, 52 (1976).

[351] See notes 76-82 to Article I, Section 9 re: "courts shall be open," Constitution of North Dakota.

[352] Tenny v. Brandhove, 341 U.S. 367, 373 (1951). See: Article I, Section 6, Clause 1 of the U.S. Constitution.

[353] Id., p. 377.

ANY AMENDMENT TO THIS CONSTITUTION MAY BE PROPOSED IN EITHER HOUSE OF THE LEGISLATIVE ASSEMBLY

Section 16. Any amendment to this constitution may be proposed in either house of the legislative assembly, and if agreed to upon a roll call by a majority of the members elected to each house, must be submitted to the electors and if a majority of the votes cast thereon are in the affirmative, the amendment is a part of this constitution.

In addition to this method of amending the constitution, the Supreme Court has held that the Legislature has the power to submit to the people the question of whether a constitutional convention should be held. Writing for the Court, Justice Guy C. H. Corliss declared: "The decided weight of authority and the more numerous precedents are arrayed on the side of the doctrine which supports the existence of this inherent legislative power to call a constitutional convention, notwithstanding the fact that the instrument itself points out how it may be amended."[354]

[354] State v. Dahl, 68 N.W. 418, 420 (1896).

Article V

Executive Branch

THE EXECUTIVE POWER IS VESTED IN THE GOVERNOR

> **Section 1.** The executive power is vested in the governor, who shall reside in the state capital and shall hold the office for the term of four years beginning in the year 2000, and until a successor is elected and qualified.

Although the constitution does not specify when the term of the governor begins, the Legislature has provided that the term of all state officers begin on January 1 next succeeding the election.[355]

The Court discussed the question of when the governor's term begins when Governor Allen I. Olson claimed he was entitled to remain in office until January 5, 1985.

Governor Olson was elected in November 1980 and took the oath of office January 6, 1981. George Sinner was elected governor in November 1984 and took the oath of office December 31, 1984. Governor Olson argued that because he had not taken the oath until January 6, 1981, his four-year term of office did not expire until January 5, 1985. The Supreme Court disagreed and pointed out: "The term of Governor begins on January 1 and terminates on December 31 in the fourth year thereafter. . . . Although a Governor may serve less than four years

[355] NDCC Section 44-01-03.

if, upon his own choosing, he does not take office until subsequent to January 1 next succeeding his election, his tenure, but not his term of office, is thereby affected."[356]

ELECTORS . . . SHALL CHOOSE A GOVERNOR, LIEUTENANT GOVERNOR, . . . (AND OTHER STATE OFFICERS)

Section 2. The qualified electors of the state at the times and places of choosing members of the legislative assembly shall choose a governor, lieutenant governor, agriculture commissioner, attorney general, auditor, insurance commissioner, three public service commissioners, secretary of state, superintendent of public instruction, tax commissioner, and treasurer. The legislative assembly may by law provide for a department of labor to be administered by a public official who may be either elected or appointed.

The powers and duties of the agriculture commissioner, attorney general, auditor, insurance commissioner, public service commissioners, secretary of state, superintendent of public instruction, tax commissioner, and treasurer must be prescribed by law. If the legislative assembly establishes a labor department, the powers and duties of the officer administering that department must be prescribed by law.

In implementing this section, the Legislature has created a Department of Labor,[357] and has provided that a Superintendent of Public Instruction be created and elected on a no-party ballot.[358] The Legislature has also prescribed the powers and duties of each of the offices created by this section.[359]

GOVERNOR AND THE LIEUTENANT GOVERNOR MUST BE ELECTED ON A JOINT BALLOT

Section 3. The governor and the lieutenant governor must be elected on a joint ballot. Each vote cast for a candidate for governor is deemed cast also for the candidate for lieutenant governor running jointly with the candidate for governor. The joint candidates having the highest number of votes must be declared elected. If two or more joint candidates have an equal and highest number of votes for governor and lieutenant governor, the legislative assembly in joint session at its next regular session shall

[356] State v. Olson, 359 N.W.2d 876, 882 (1985).

[357] NDCC Chapter 34-05.

[358] NDCC Section 16.1-11-08.

[359] NDCC Chapter 54-09 SECRETARY OF STATE; NDCC Chapter 54-10 STATE AUDITOR; NDCC Chapter 54-11 STATE TREASURER; NDCC Chapter 54-12 ATTORNEY GENERAL; NDCC Chapter 4-01 COMMISSIONER OF AGRICULTURE; NDCC Chapter 49-01 PUBLIC SERVICE COMMISSION; NDCC Chapter 26.1-01 COMMISSIONER OF INSURANCE; NDCC Chapter 57-01 TAX COMMISSIONER.

choose one pair of joint candidates for the offices. The returns of the election for governor and lieutenant governor must be made in the manner prescribed by law.

The Supreme Court has not decided any cases involving this section.

TO HOLD AN ELECTIVE OFFICE . . . A PERSON MUST BE A QUALIFIED ELECTOR OF THIS STATE

Section 4. To be eligible to hold an elective office established by this article, a person must be a qualified elector of this state, must be at least twenty-five years of age on the day of the election, and must have been a resident of this state for the five years preceding election to office. To be eligible to hold the office of governor or lieutenant governor, a person must be at least thirty years old on the day of the election. The attorney general must be licensed to practice law in this state.

This section requires the governor to be "a qualified elector of the state." Article II, Section 2 of the constitution provides that: "No person convicted of a felony shall be qualified to vote." The Supreme Court, applying both these sections, held that Governor William Langer, who had been convicted of conspiracy to defraud the federal government, was no longer qualified to be governor even though his case was on appeal.

The Court asked: "Is the Governor temporarily disqualified, and do the powers and duties of the Governor devolve upon the Lieutenant Governor during the period of such disability?"[360] In response to that question, Justice John Burke wrote: "We therefore conclude from a review of the authorities that, when a defendant is convicted of a felony in this state, his disqualification as an elector attaches immediately, and that this disqualification is not suspended by his appeal and the furnishing of a supersedeas bond."[361]

The question of what it means to be "a resident of this state for the five years preceding election," was before the Court in the case of Thomas H. Moodie who was elected governor in November 1934. Although Moodie had been a resident of North Dakota, he moved to Minneapolis, Minnesota, in July 1929. While in Minneapolis, he voted in both a primary and general election, filed a federal income tax return giving his Minneapolis address, and took out a resident fishing license. When Moodie returned to North Dakota in 1931, he filed a North Dakota income tax return and stated that he had not filed one for the prior year because he had not been a resident then.

Early in 1935, Walter Welford, who had been elected lieutenant governor in 1934, brought legal action claiming that Moodie had not been a resident of the state for five years preceding the election and therefore was not qualified to hold

[360] State v. Langer, 256 N.W. 377, 381 (1934).

[361] Id., p. 391.

that office. The Supreme Court agreed. "The lack of residential qualifications on the part of the Governor is a legal disability. The Constitution does not differentiate between a disability existing before election and one occurring after election in regard to the right of the Lieutenant Governor to assume the powers and duties of the office of Governor."[362]

A rather unusual situation arose relating to the qualification to be a candidate for governor when Alvin C. Strutz was defeated in the 1944 primary as a candidate for that office. After the primary election, Strutz filed a petition with the secretary of state to have his name placed on the ballot as a candidate for governor in the 1944 general election. Immediately thereafter, a petition was filed with the Supreme Court to prevent the secretary of state from certifying Strutz as a gubernatorial candidate because to do so would be a violation of a state law prohibiting a candidate who was defeated in the primary from being a candidate in the ensuing general election.

In denying the petition, the Supreme Court held that the statute prohibiting losers in primary elections from being candidates in the general election violated this section. "In principle there is no difference between a legislative enactment which seeks to add qualifications to those specified in the Constitution," the Court declared, "and a legislative enactment which seeks to create a disqualification. The 'legislature cannot enlarge nor diminish constitutional provisions prescribing eligibility and qualifications to hold office created by Constitution.'"[363]

QUALIFIED ELECTORS SHALL CHOOSE THE ELECTED STATE OFFICIALS

Section 5. The qualified electors shall choose the elected state officials at a time designated by the legislative assembly. The elected state officials shall serve until their successors are duly qualified. Terms of office are four years, except that terms of the public service commissioners are six years, so arranged that one of them is elected every two years. The terms of the governor and lieutenant governor begin on December fifteenth following their election.

If two or more candidates for any executive office other than for governor and lieutenant governor receive an equal and highest number of votes, the legislative assembly in joint session shall choose one of them for the office.

The Supreme Court has not considered any cases involving this section.

---

362 State v. Moodie, 258 N.W. 558, 567 (1935).

363 State v. Hall, 15 N.W.2d 736, 741 (1944). For a similar result see: State v. Thorson, 6 N.W.2d 89 (1942).

ELECTED OFFICIALS . . . SHALL HOLD OFFICE IN THE STATE CAPITOL

Section 6. The elected officials and the chief executive officers of the principal departments shall hold office in the state capitol.

The Supreme Court has not considered any cases involving this section.

THE GOVERNOR IS COMMANDER-IN-CHIEF OF THE STATE'S MILITARY FORCES

Section 7. The governor is the chief executive of the state. The governor shall have the responsibility to see that the state's business is well administered and that its laws are faithfully executed.

The governor is commander-in-chief of the state's military forces, except when they are called into the service of the United States, and the governor may mobilize them to execute the laws and maintain order.

The governor shall prescribe the duties of the lieutenant governor in addition to those prescribed in this article.

The governor may call special sessions of the legislative assembly.

The governor shall present information on the condition of the state, together with any recommended legislation, to every regular and special session of the legislative assembly.

The governor shall transact and supervise all necessary business of the state with the United States, the other states, and the officers and officials of this state.

The governor may grant reprieves, commutations, and pardons. The governor may delegate this power in a manner provided by law.

The Legislature has implemented the governor's constitutional authority over the National Guard by legislation providing:

> In case of insurrection, invasion, tumult, riot, breach of the peace, or imminent danger thereof, to provide a presence at state ceremonial events, or to provide assistance to political entities in search and rescue efforts or to respond to a potential natural or environmental hazard or nuisance, the governor may order into active service of this state any part of the national guard that the governor may deem proper.[364]

The Governor Shall Prescribe the Duties of the Lieutenant Governor

During its 1979 session, the Legislature created the Federal Aid Coordinator Office and provided that the lieutenant governor should be the coordinator.

---

[364] NDCC Section 37-01-04.

Governor Arthur A. Link vetoed this part of the law on the grounds that under this section of the constitution only the governor had authority to prescribe duties for the lieutenant governor. In an action brought in the Supreme Court, that Court agreed with Governor Link. The Court declared: "To uphold this enactment would be to allow the legislature to seriously modify a constitutionally created office and would be ignoring an express provision in our constitution that the *governor* shall prescribe additional duties to the lieutenant governor."[365]

The extent to which the governor may assign additional duties to the lieutenant governor was before the Supreme Court in the case of *State ex rel. Peterson v. Olson*.[366]

In this case, Governor Allen I. Olson assigned additional duties to Lieutenant Governor Ernest M. Sands, including "assisting in intergovernmental affairs; acting as a liaison between state, county, and city governments; assisting in ceremonial functions; and assisting in economic development programs."[367]

The state auditor and state treasurer, after refusing to approve additional funds for the lieutenant governor for his performance of these additional duties, sought approval of their actions by the Supreme Court. The auditor and treasurer argued that the governor, in assigning these additional duties to the lieutenant governor, converted that position into to a full-time one in violation of the constitution. The Supreme Court disagreed.

"Apart from those duties explicitly reserved to the Governor under the Constitution," Justice William L. Paulson wrote for the Court, "the Governor has the authority to delegate duties to the Lieutenant Governor. . . . Because the duties which the Governor delegated to the Lieutenant Governor were not duties expressly reserved to the Governor, the Governor did not violate the provisions of Article V. Section 7 when he delegated additional duties to the Lieutenant Governor."[368]

The Governor May Grant Reprieves, Commutations, and Pardons

The Legislature has given the governor the authority to create a Pardon Advisory Board, which the governor has done.[369] This Board consists of the attorney general, two members of the parole board, and two citizens of the state. The governor, however, retains "the power to remit fines and grant commutations, reprieves, pardons, and conditional pardons after judgement of conviction."[370]

---

[365] State ex rel. Link v. Olson, 286 N.W.2d 262, 274 (1979).

[366] 307 N.W.2d 528 (1981).

[367] Id., p. 530.

[368] Id., p. 533.

[369] NDCC Chapter 12-55.1. The granting of parole from the penitentiary is within the power of the Parole Board created by NDCC Chapter 12-59.

[370] NDCC Section 12-55.1-04.

THE GOVERNOR MAY FILL A VACANCY IN ANY OFFICE

Section 8. The governor may fill a vacancy in any office by appointment if no other method is provided by this constitution or by law. If, while the senate is recessed or adjourned, a vacancy occurs in any office that is filled by appointment with senate confirmation, the governor shall make a temporary appointment to the office. When the senate reconvenes the governor shall make a nomination to fill the office. Except on request of the senate, no nominee rejected by the senate may again be nominated for that office at the same session, nor may the nominee be appointed to that office during a recess or adjournment of the senate.

In addition to the power of appointment granted by this section, the Legislature has given the governor the power to remove certain public officers who have been "guilty of misconduct, malfeasance, crime in office, neglect of duty in office, or habitual drunkenness or gross incompetency."[371]

The Supreme Court has not decided any cases involving this section.

THE GOVERNOR MAY VETO A BILL PASSED BY THE LEGISLATIVE ASSEMBLY

Section 9. Every bill passed by the legislative assembly must be presented to the governor for the governor's signature. If the governor signs the bill, it becomes law.

The governor may veto a bill passed by the legislative assembly. The governor may veto items in an appropriation bill. Portions of the bill not vetoed become law.

The governor shall return for reconsideration any vetoed item or bill, with a written statement of the governor's objections, to the house in which it originated. That house shall immediately enter the governor's objections upon its journal. If, by a recorded vote, two-thirds of the members elected to that house pass a vetoed item or bill, it, along with the statement of the governor's objections, must immediately be delivered to the other house. If, by a recorded vote, two-thirds of the members elected to the other house also pass it, the vetoed item or bill becomes law.

While the legislative assembly is in session, a bill becomes law if the governor neither signs nor vetoes it within three legislative days after its delivery to the governor. If the legislative assembly is not in session, a bill becomes law if the governor neither signs nor vetoes it within fifteen days, Saturdays and Sundays excepted, after its delivery to the governor.

Because the governor's veto power does not extend to initiated measures, the Supreme Court struck down the governor's veto of a legislative appropriation for the salary of the director of the state laboratories because that veto would

---

[371] NDCC Section 44-11-01.

have had the effect of destroying the department which was created by an initiated measure.[372]

This section gives the Legislature the opportunity to override a veto if the governor acts within three days and the Legislature is still in session. If the governor exercises his power of veto, however, after the Legislature has adjourned, that will end the matter.[373]

In commenting on the governor's authority to "veto items in an appropriation bill," the Court has written that if the governor did not have this power he "would be placed in the position of vetoing a bill which contains many items which to him seem necessary and proper, and items which may be clearly obnoxious. He is not compelled to balance the good against the evil for in the provision of [this] section . . . he may disapprove the evil and permit the good to stand."[374]

The Court has, however, limited the governor's line-item veto power to those parts of bills that specifically appropriate funds. "We hold that the governor, in exercising his partial veto power," Justice Vernon R. Pederson declared, "may only veto items or parts in appropriation bills that are related to the vetoed appropriation and are so separate and distinct that, after removing them, the bill can stand as workable legislation which comports with the fundamental purpose the legislature intended to effect when the whole was enacted."[375]

A GOVERNOR WHO ASKS, [OR] RECEIVES, . . . ANY BRIBE . . . THEREOF FORFEITS ALL RIGHT TO HOLD . . . ANY OFFICE

Section 10. A governor who asks, receives, or agrees to receive any bribe upon any understanding that the governor's official opinion, judgment, or action shall be influenced thereby, or who gives or offers, or promises the governor's official influence in consideration that any member of the legislative assembly shall give the member's official vote or influence on any particular side of any question or matter upon which the member may be required to act in the member's official capacity, or who menaces any member by the threatened use of the governor's veto power, or who offers or promises any member that the governor will appoint any particular person or persons to any office created or thereafter to be created, in consideration that any member shall give the member's official vote or influence on any matter pending or thereafter to be introduced into either house of the legislative assembly, or who

[372] State v. Dewing, 131 N.W.2d 434, 439 (1964).

[373] State v. Olson, 260 N.W. 586 (1935).

[374] Id., p. 589.

[375] State v. Olson, 286 N.W.2d 262, 270–271 (1979).

threatens any member that the governor will remove any person or persons from office or position with intent in any manner to influence the action of that member, must be punished in the manner now, or that may hereafter be, provided by law, and upon conviction thereof forfeits all right to hold or exercise any office of trust or honor in this state.

The Supreme Court has not decided any cases involving this section.

THE LIEUTENANT GOVERNOR SHALL SUCCEED TO THE OFFICE OF GOVERNOR WHEN A VACANCY OCCURS

Section 11. The lieutenant governor shall succeed to the office of governor when a vacancy occurs in the office of governor. If, during a vacancy in the office of governor, the lieutenant governor is unable to serve because of death, impeachment, resignation, failure to qualify, removal from office, or disability, the secretary of state shall act as governor until the vacancy is filled or the disability removed.

When Thomas H. Moodie was elected governor in November 1934, Attorney General P. O. Sathre commenced legal action asserting that Moodie had not been a resident of the state for the five years preceding the election, and therefore was not qualified to serve as governor. The Supreme Court agreed and declared the office of governor vacant. In so doing, the Court discussed this section, and pointed out:

> The general function of the Lieutenant Governor is to act in event the Governor cannot or does not exercise the powers and perform the duties of his office. He must possess the same qualifications as the Governor. These qualifications are not affected by the particular type or nature of the disability which prevents the Governor from acting. . . . The Lieutenant Governor, elected at the same election, does possess the required qualifications. He has been chosen by the people to act as Governor in event the Governor fails to qualify, or is unable to act because of disability.[376]

LIEUTENANT GOVERNOR SHALL SERVE AS PRESIDENT OF THE SENATE

Section 12. The lieutenant governor shall serve as president of the senate. If the senate is equally divided on a question, the lieutenant governor may vote on procedural matters and on substantive matters if the lieutenant governor's vote would be decisive.

---

[376] State v. Moodie, 258 N.W. 558, 567 (1935).

At one time in the state's history, it was assumed that the lieutenant governor, acting as president of the Senate, could not cast a tie-breaking vote on pending bills. The lieutenant governor's authority to break ties was limited to procedural matters and the Supreme Court approved that procedure.[377] This section was changed to its present form by an amendment to the constitution which became effective July 1, 1997.

---

377 State v. Freed, 251 N.W. 2d 898, 906 (1977).

Article VI

Judicial Branch

JUDICIAL POWER OF THE STATE IS VESTED IN A UNIFIED JUDICIAL SYSTEM

Section 1. The judicial power of the state is vested in a unified judicial system consisting of a supreme court, a district court, and such other courts as may be provided by law.

The Legislature, exercising the power granted to it in this section, has created a Court of Appeals'[378] Small Claims Courts,[379] Juvenile Courts,[380] and Municipal Courts.[381]

In writing the North Dakota Constitution, the framers followed the format of the U.S. Constitution and created three branches of government—a legislative branch, an executive branch, and a judicial branch. In commenting upon this arrangement the North Dakota Supreme Court has stated: "In this state, as in all other states of the Union, the essential functions of government are divided among three departments, the legislative, executive, and judicial. This court has

[378] NDCC Section 27-02.1-01.

[379] NDCC Chapter 27-08.1. See also: NDCC Section 29-01-15.

[380] NDCC Chapter 27-20.

[381] NDCC Chapter 40-18; NDCC Section 29-01-01; NDCC Section 29-01-15.

early held that these grants were in their nature exclusive and that neither department could exercise any of the functions of the other."[382]

Throughout the state's history, the North Dakota Supreme Court has jealously guarded the independence of the judiciary. For example, when the Legislature gave the secretary of state authority to determine whether a corporation authorized to do business in the state was guilty of unfair business practices, the Supreme Court held the law to be unconstitutional. Commenting upon the distribution of powers among the three branches of government, Justice B. F. Spalding wrote: "The question of the distribution of the powers of government to the legislative, executive, and judicial departments under the Constitution has been passed upon many times and by nearly every court of this country, and there can no longer be any doubt that each department is supreme within its own sphere or that the judicial power of this state has been exclusively vested, under... [the Constitution] in the courts."[383]

In addressing the duties assigned to the secretary of state by the Legislature, the Court declared: "We are of the opinion that the Legislature by this act attempted to confer upon the Secretary of State powers which are clearly judicial in their nature, and that the act is to that extent invalid."[384]

The Court reached the same result when the Legislature established a State Bonding Department in the Office of the Commissioner of Insurance and assigned to the commissioner duties which the Court concluded were judicial. In this case, the Court explained: "Judicial power determines what the law is, and what the rights of the parties are with reference to transactions already had, and, wherever an act undertakes to determine a question of right or obligation of property, as the foundation upon which it proceeds, such act is to that extent a judicial one."[385]

The Supreme Court has been more willing to allow the Legislature to assign nonjudicial powers to the courts. For example, the Court upheld a law requiring district court judges to issue druggists' permits because it was of the opinion that such a duty was quasi-judicial.[386] The Court also upheld legislation requiring the

---

[382] State v. Baker, 288 N.W. 202, 204 (1939). See also: Riverview Place, Inc. v. Cass County, 448 N.W.2d 635, 638 Note 3 (1989).

[383] State v. Blaisdell, 132 N.W. 769, 772 (1911).

[384] Id., p. 776.

[385] State v. Taylor, 145 N.W. 425, 429 (1913). See also: Becker County Sand & Gravel Co. v. Wosick, 245 N.W. 454 (1932) where the Supreme Court held unconstitutional a law permitting a Board of County Commissioners to assess damages in condemnation cases. And see: Paluck v. Bd. of Cty. Commissioners, Stark County, 307 N.W.2d 852 (1981) where the Court held unconstitutional a legislative created Tax Appeals Board. In both of these cases, the Court concluded that the tasks assigned to the Boards were judicial and therefore could be exercised only by courts.

[386] Kermott v. Bagley, 124 N.W. 397, 399 (1910).

Supreme Court to employ a Code Revision Commission to annotate the constitution, the rules of practice and procedure, and the laws of the state.[387]

But when the Legislature gave District Courts the power to hear and rule on annexation petitions prepared by municipal authorities, the Supreme Court held the law to be unconstitutional as "an impermissible delegation of legislative power."[388]

THE SUPREME COURT SHALL . . . HAVE APPELLATE JURISDICTION

> **Section 2.** The supreme court shall be the highest court of the state. It shall have appellate jurisdiction, and shall also have original jurisdiction with authority to issue, hear, and determine such original and remedial writs as may be necessary to properly exercise its jurisdiction. The supreme court shall consist of five justices, one of whom shall be designated chief justice in the manner provided by law.

Early in our history the Legislature provided that the Supreme Court should "try the cause anew"[389] on appeal in cases originally tried to the court below without a jury. The Court held this legislation to be constitutional.

In discussing the phrase "try the cause anew," the Court declared: "This language, it is apparent, was not used with exact accuracy. The case is not tried anew. There is no new evidence or any evidence adduced in this court. . . . This Court simply reviews the record, and the practical and necessary result of such review is to correct the errors, if any, either of the law or fact, into which the court below may have fallen."[390]

In cases originally tried before a jury, however, the rule is different. In such cases, "[t]he right to jury trial means that the ultimate determination of issues of fact is to be by the jury under proper guidance and direction of the court."[391]

Sometimes the question before the Court relates to the constitutionality of a statute and no facts are at issue in the case. Of such situations, the Supreme Court has said: "Whether a statute violates the United States or North Dakota constitutions is a question of law and is, therefore, fully reviewable by this court."[392]

---

387 State v. Baker, 288 N.W. 202 (1939).

388 City of Carrington v. Foster County, 166 N.W.2d 377, 385 (1969). See also: Glaspell v. City of Jamestown, 88 N.W. 1023 (1902).

389 Christianson v. Farmers' Warehouse Ass'n., 67 N.W. 300, 301 (1896). The Legislature has provided that the Supreme Court justices and District Court judges shall elect a chief justice, who shall serve for a term of five years. (NDCC Section 27-02-01.)

390 Id., p. 301. See also: State v. City of Williston, 8 N.W.2d 564, 567 (1943).

391 Jury, 47 Am. Jur. 2d, Section 15, p. 723.

392 Best Products Co., Inc. v. Spaeth, 461 N.W.2d 91, 96 (1990).

The Supreme Court Shall Have . . . Original Jurisdiction

A court has original jurisdiction if a case can be started in that court. The North Dakota Supreme Court has pointed out, however, that the original jurisdiction given to it under this section "extends only to those cases in which the question presented is *publici juris,* wherein the sovereignty of the state, the franchises or prerogatives of the state, or the liberties of its people are affected. . . . The interest of the state must be primary, not incidental, and the public, the community at large, must have an interest or right which may be affected."[393]

As a general rule, the attorney general of the state is the person to request the Supreme Court to exercise its original jurisdiction. "It is true," the Court has written, "that ordinarily the consent or refusal of the Attorney General should be secured in initiating the exercise of the original jurisdiction of this court for the reason that ordinarily the Attorney General is the legal representative of the interests of the state, its sovereignty, franchises, and liberties of the people."[394]

In the exercise of its original jurisdiction, the Supreme Court has the authority to issue writs of prohibition, mandamus, quo warranto, injunction, and habeas corpus.

"The writ of prohibition," the Court has said, "is not a writ of right, but is available only when an inferior court, body, or tribunal is about to act without or in excess of jurisdiction."[395] Furthermore: "'A writ of prohibition is to be used sparingly and only in cases where there is an inadequate remedy by appeal, or in those cases where other equitable principles justify its use.'"[396]

The Supreme Court granted a writ of prohibition against Thomas D. Ewing, judge of the Stark County Court upon the application of Sheriff Harold Schneider. Judge Ewing had instituted contempt proceedings against Sheriff Schneider because the sheriff had refused to obey Judge Ewing's order regarding the over-crowded conditions of the county jail. In granting the writ, the Court held that Judge Ewing had "no jurisdiction over the subject matter nor the person of the petitioner [Sheriff Schneider]."[397]

The writ of mandamus derives its meaning from the word mandate. It is, therefore, an order from a superior court to a lower court or government official to compel the court or official to perform some duty.

---

[393] State ex rel. Link v. Olson, 286 N.W.2d 262, 266 (1979).

[394] State v. Langer, 177 N.W. 408, 413 (1919).

[395] Schneider v. Ewing, 310 N.W.2d 581, 585–586 (1981).

[396] Id., p. 586.

[397] Schneider v. Ewing, 310 N.W.2d 581, 584 (1981).

The Supreme Court has issued such a writ "to compel one who has no color of title to an office to surrender it to one who holds the prima facie title to it."[398]

The Court also issued a writ of mandamus to the county auditor of Ward County requiring him to give notice of an election concerning the division of Ward County and the formation of Renville County. The Court wrote: "The auditor was without authority to refuse to give notice of the election upon the proposition of the creation of Renville County."[399]

When County Judge Lawrence O'Connell refused to allow reporters from the *Williston Herald* to inspect criminal records, the *Herald* sought a writ of mandamus seeking the right to inspect the court's records. In granting the writ, Chief Justice Alvin C. Strutz wrote for the Supreme Court: "We believe that it is the right of the public to inspect the records of judicial proceedings after such proceedings are completed and in the docket of the court."[400]

The writ of quo warranto is defined as: "A common law writ designed to test whether a person exercising power is legally entitled to do so."[401]

The North Dakota Supreme Court used this writ to determine whether A. G. Burr was legally acting as a judge after being appointed to that position by the governor. After examining the legislation creating the new judgeship, the Court concluded that the Legislature intended the position to be filled by election and not by appointment by the governor. Burr, therefore, was not qualified to act as judge.[402]

After Governor William Langer was convicted of conspiracy to defraud the U.S. Government, Lieutenant Governor Ole H. Olson sought a writ of quo warranto questioning the right of Governor Langer to remain in office. The Court concluded that because of Langer's conviction he was no longer a "qualified elector" and thus disqualified to hold the office of governor. The Court declared: "We . . . conclude from a review of the authorities that, when a defendant is convicted of a felony in this state, his disqualification as an elector attaches immediately, and that this disqualification is not suspended by his appeal and the furnishing of a supersedeas bond."[403]

In a quo warranto proceeding to determine whether Thomas H. Moodie had been a resident of the state for the five years necessary to make him eligible to be governor, the Court held that it would be necessary for it to consider the disputed facts surrounding Moodie's residence. The Court declared: "This is the

---

[398] State v. Archibald, 66 N.W. 234, 235 (1896).

[399] State v. Fabrick, 117 N.W. 860, 864 (1908).

[400] State v. O'Connell, 151 N.W. 2d 758, 763 (1967).

[401] Henry Campbell Black, *Black's Law Dictionary* (St. Paul, MN: West Publishing Co. 1990), p. 1256.

[402] State v. Burr, 113 N.W. 705, 711 (1907).

[403] State v. Langer, 256 N.W. 377, 391 (1934).

first time in the history of this court that it has been confronted with the trial and determination of disputed questions of fact in a quo warranto proceeding instituted in this court."[404] After examining the facts, the Court concluded that Moodie had not been a resident for five years preceding the election and therefore was not qualified to be governor.

After an election to create a new county out of existing McLean County, several voters commenced legal action seeking to challenge the election results. While this action was pending, the McLean County auditor proceeded to organize the new county. Attorney General Andrew Miller, acting on behalf of several voters in McLean County, then sought an injunction from the Supreme Court to prevent the formation of the new county while the voters' lawsuit was pending. The Supreme Court granted this writ and explained its decision: "By this proceeding, . . . we are not asked to determine the validity of the alleged organization of Stevenson county. That question is directly involved and will be adjudicated in the pending . . . case. In the interest of the public and all concerned such proceeding should be speedily tried and determined by the district court."[405]

When a petition was presented to the Supreme Court to test the right of Fred McLean to hold the office of chairman of the Central Committee of the Democratic Party, the Court refused to get involved. "These matters," the Court declared, "are for political or party discipline, and not for the intervention of the courts. We cannot oust the said McLean from his chairmanship, for there is no other claimant, and the franchises and prerogatives of the state are not involved, as he is in no sense a public officer."[406]

In describing a writ of habeas corpus, the U.S. Supreme Court said: "A writ of *habeas corpus* is not like an action to recover damages for an unlawful arrest or commitment, but its objective is to ascertain whether the prisoner can lawfully be detained in custody; and if sufficient ground for his detention by the government is shown, he is not to be discharged for defects in the original arrest or commitment."[407]

When it was argued that Section 2 does not give the Supreme Court jurisdiction to issue writs of habeas corpus, the Court responded: "Although . . . [the Constitution does not contain] specific reference to habeas corpus, we believe that the provision in Article VI, Section 2, that this Court has original jurisdiction to issue, hear, and determine such original and remedial writs as may be necessary to exercise its jurisdiction, includes the authority to issue original writs of habeas corpus."[408]

---

[404] State v. Moodie, 258 N.W. 558, 561 (1935).

[405] State v. Miller, 131 N.W. 282, 287 (1911).

[406] State v. McLean, 159 N.W. 847, 853 (1916).

[407] Nishimura Ekiu v. United States, 142 U.S. 651, 662 (1892).

[408] Jensen v. State, 373 N.W.2d 894, 897 (1985).

In addition to the writs discussed above, the Supreme Court has interpreted this section to give it superintending control over lower courts. The Court, in discussing this supervisory control, has written:

> The power of general superintending control over inferior courts allows the Supreme Court, in a proper case, to control the course of litigation in district courts and "to prevent injustice in cases when there is no appeal, or when the remedy by appeal is inadequate." . . . Superintending jurisdiction enables this court to control a lower court, "which though within its jurisdiction, is by mistake of law, or willful disregard of it, doing a gross injustice and there is no adequate remedy by appeal."[409]

One rather unusual case in which the Court granted a supervisory writ involved the question of whether the attorney general had authority to hire outside counsel to prosecute an action against a company for allegedly installing asbestos in the state's public buildings. District Judge Gail Hagerty had issued an order prohibiting the attorney general from using retained counsel on a contingent fee basis.

Referring to its grant of a supervisory writ, the Court declared: "Here, the case is extraordinary, the injustice if the trial court erred is significant and the Attorney General has no adequate alternative remedy. We conclude this is an appropriate case in which to exercise our supervisory jurisdiction."[410] The Court then held that the attorney general did have authority to hire outside counsel in this case and pay them on a contingent fee basis.

SUPREME COURT SHALL . . . PROMULGATE RULES OF PROCEDURE

> **Section 3.** The supreme court shall have authority to promulgate rules of procedure, including appellate procedure, to be followed by all the courts of this state; and, unless otherwise provided by law, to promulgate rules and regulations for the admission to practice, conduct, disciplining, and disbarment of attorneys at law.
>
> The chief justice shall be the administrative head of the unified judicial system. He may assign judges, including retired judges, for temporary duty in any court or district under such rules and regulations as may be promulgated by the supreme court. The chief justice shall appoint a court administrator for the unified court system. Unless otherwise provided by law, the powers, duties, qualifications, and terms of the office of court administrator, and other court officials, shall be as provided by rules of the court.

---

[409] Spence v. North Dakota Dist. Court, 292 N.W.2d 53, 57 (1980).

[410] State v. Hagerty, 580 N.W.2d 139, 142 (1998).

In commenting upon its rule-making power, the Supreme Court has pointed out:

> Our state constitution's creation of three branches of government apportions the different classes of power, implicitly excluding each branch of state government from overriding the functions of the other branches. . . . However, "[w]e have recognized that there is an interplay between statutory procedures and rules promulgated by this court." . . . While this court has "final authority over procedural rules," . . . "statutorily enacted rules of procedure are in effect until superseded or amended by our court." . . . Under N.D. Const., Art VI, Sec. 3, "a procedural rule adopted by this court must prevail in a conflict with a statutory procedure rule."[411]

The Court found such a conflict when it compared a statutory rule requiring a defendant to supply a prosecutor with certain information whenever the defendant requests information from the prosecutor. This statutory rule conflicted with a Supreme Court rule that restricted the amount of information the defendant was required to disclose.

In concluding that the Court's rule covering this question prevailed, Justice William Neumann, writing for the Court, declared: "The statute directly conflicts with Rule 16, which requires only limited pretrial disclosure of information, while allowing additional disclosure by order or agreement. Under Article VI, Sec. 3, N.D. Const., a procedural rule adopted by this court must prevail in a conflict with a statutory procedural rule."[412]

When a conflict does exist between a statutory procedural rule and a Supreme Court rule, the Court will try to reconcile the conflict. The Court did just that when it upheld a statutory rule providing visitation rights to grandparents if a district court made findings of fact "'that visitation would be in the best interests of the minor and would not interfere with the parent–child relationship.'"[413] The Court concluded that even though the Court's Procedural Rule provided that "'[f]indings of fact'" were unnecessary, such findings would be important in this case to determine if visitation by the grandparents was in the best interests of the child and did not interfere with the child–parent relationship.

The Supreme Court Shall . . . Promulgate Rules . . . for Admission to Practice . . . Law

Acting under the authority given by this section, the Supreme Court has promulgated detailed rules relating to the admission to practice law;[414] relating to the

[411] Traynor v. Leclerc, 561 N.W. 2d 644, 647 (1997).

[412] State v. Hanson, 558 N.W.2d 611, 615 (1996).

[413] Schempp-Cook v. Cook, 455 N.W.2d 216, 217 (1990).

[414] Admission to Practice Rules, North Dakota Rules of Court, pp. 793–805.

professional conduct of lawyers;[415] and rules for lawyer discipline.[416] The Court has also adopted rules for continuing education of lawyers.[417]

Those rules require that the applicant be "of good moral character," have a "juris doctor or equivalent degree from a law school approved . . . for accreditation by the American Bar Association," and pass a bar examination.[418]

The Supreme Court considers the qualification of an applicant to the bar being of "good moral character" absolutely essential. In describing what constitutes good moral character, the Court, quoting from a California Supreme Court case, declared: "Good moral character has also been defined to include qualities of honesty, fairness, candor, trustworthiness, observance of fiduciary responsibility, [observance] of the laws of the state and the nation and respect for the rights of others and for the judicial process."[419]

In denying the application of R. Frank Layon to be admitted to the North Dakota Bar, the State Bar Board found that Layon had failed to disclose eight criminal charges against him, and 25 separate motor vehicle violations. That he also had "a past history of conversion and the misappropriation of monies in his possession which were held under a trust relationship."[420]

In denying Layon's application, the Court declared: "We conclude that the letters of support and testimony on behalf of Layon do not overcome the evidence in this case disclosing present lack of good moral character."[421]

Applicants for admission to the bar have often complained "that the tests were arbitrary and capricious and were not valid tests of the applicant's legal education and qualifications."[422] The courts, including the North Dakota Supreme Court, however, have disagreed. In response to this claim, the Supreme Court has written: "No expert witness in the field of testing was presented nor was any evidence introduced regarding the reliability of essay-type tests. They are probably more accurate and real than some other types. A mere assertion or allegation is not sufficient to place the examination in jeopardy."[423]

Rarely does a court admit an applicant to the practice of law who has failed any part of the bar examination. The Court did that, however, in the case of David C. Thompson, whose grade on part of the exam was three points below passing. Thompson's scores on the other parts of the examination were well

---

[415] North Dakota Rules of Professional Conduct, North Dakota Rules of Court, pp. 807–873.

[416] North Dakota Rules for Lawyer Discipline, North Dakota Rules of Court, pp. 875–904.

[417] North Dakota Rules for Continuing Legal Education, North Dakota Rules of Court, pp. 961–965.

[418] See Admission to Practice Rules 1, 2, 5, and 6.

[419] Layon v. North Dakota State Bar Bd., 458 N.W.2d 501, 503 (1990).

[420] Id., p. 504.

[421] Id., p. 512.

[422] Dinger v. State Bar Bd., 312 N.W.2d 15, 17 (1981).

[423] Id., p. 20.

above passing grade. The evidence indicated that except for the failing grade in one part of the exam, Thompson was well qualified to practice law. On that basis, four of the justices voted to admit him. In voting to admit Thompson, Justice Vernon R. Pederson wrote: "The testing process is certainly entitled to prima facie validity but not when the evidence indicates that, in a specific case, it fails to fairly measure qualifications. Thompson has demonstrated that he is qualified. A certificate of admission should be issued."[424]

The Supreme Court Shall . . . Promulgate Rules . . . for . . . Disciplining, and Disbarment of Attorneys

Justice Harvey B. Knudson enunciated the responsibility of a lawyer to the community in which he or she practices as follows: "No member of the community is charged with the exercise of a higher degree of good faith, fairness, and honesty in his dealings with others, and in his treatment of clients, than an attorney at law. He is an officer of the court, and should be possessed of a high appreciation of ethical and moral duties."[425]

In what may have been the first case in which the Supreme Court was called upon to disbar an attorney, Justice N. C. Young wrote: "The power to discipline attorneys, who are officers of the court, is an inherent and incidental power in courts of record, and one which is essential to an orderly discharge of judicial functions. To deny its existence is equivalent to a declaration that the conduct of attorneys towards courts and clients is not subject to restraint."[426]

The Court, relying on that power, disbarred Leslie A. Simpson. The Court summed up its conclusion: "His general attitude towards the administration of justice and his conduct as an attorney have come under our immediate observation during the progress of these proceedings, and both confirm the conclusion that he lacks that high sense of personal and professional integrity which is a paramount qualification in an attorney and counselor at law."[427]

In commenting upon lawyers' conduct generally, the Supreme Court has pointed out: "We have repeatedly said a lawyer's conversion of clients funds is impossible to condone and is one of the least excusable acts of misconduct for which a lawyer can be disciplined."[428]

---

[424] Petition of Thompson, 342 N.W.2d 393, 403 (1983).

[425] In re Christianson, 175 N.W.2d 8, 11 (1970).

[426] In re Simpson, 83 N.W. 541, 553 (1900).

[427] Id., p. 552.

[428] In re Reinstatement of Montgomery, 612 N.W.2d 278, 282 (2000).

The Supreme Court's power to discipline attorneys includes the power to place an offender on probation for a while,[429] or to suspend a lawyer for a period of time.[430]

Because only those persons licensed in North Dakota can practice law in this state, a lawyer who is not licensed in North Dakota is not entitled to collect fees for legal services rendered here.[431] Furthermore, it is a crime to practice law without a license in North Dakota.[432]

SUPREME COURT SHALL NOT DECLARE . . . [A LAW] UNCONSTITUTIONAL UNLESS . . . FOUR MEMBERS . . . SO DECIDE

Section 4. A majority of the supreme court shall be necessary to constitute a quorum or to pronounce a decision, provided that the supreme court shall not declare a legislative enactment unconstitutional unless at least four members of the court so decide.

Although this section prevents the Supreme Court from holding a state law unconstitutional unless four justices agree to the opinion, the Court nevertheless does issue an opinion in which three members of the court join.[433]

When four justices do not agree on whether a state law is unconstitutional, the Court may look for other grounds to reach its result. Such was the case of Cora Kroeplin, who was sentenced to 18 months' imprisonment with the requirement that she be imprisoned "at no other place"[434] than Bismarck. Because a state law permitted the director of institutions to arrange for prisoners to be incarcerated in a prison in another state, Attorney General Allen Olson sought an order of the Court permitting transfer of Kroeplin to a prison in Minnesota.

Although only three justices were of the opinion that the statute permitting incarceration in another state was unconstitutional, the Court did agree that before such a transfer could be made, due process required that an inmate be given notice and an opportunity to be heard with regard to whether such transfer should be made.

---

[429] Matter of Maragos, 285 N.W.2d 541 (1979).

[430] Matter of Disciplinary Action Against Larson, 512 N.W.2d 454 (1994).

[431] Ranta v. McCarney, 391 N.W.2d 161 (1986).

[432] State v. Niska, 380 N.W.2d 646 (1986).

[433] Benson v. N. D. Workmen's Comp. Bureau, 283 N.W.2d 96 (1979). See also: Bismarck Public School Dist. 1 v. State, 511 N.W.2d 247 (1994).

[434] State ex rel. Olson v. Maxwell, 259 N.W.2d 621, 624 (1977).

WHEN A JUDGMENT . . . IS REVERSED, MODIFIED, OR CONFIRMED . . . THE REASONS SHALL BE CONCISELY STATED IN WRITING

Section 5. When a judgment or order is reversed, modified, or confirmed by the supreme court, the reasons shall be concisely stated in writing, signed by the justices concurring, filed in the office of the clerk of the supreme court, and preserved with a record of the case. Any justice dissenting may give the reason for his dissent in writing over his signature.

Requiring the Supreme Court to state in writing the reasons for its decision allows the cases to be cited as authority in subsequent similar cases. It also identifies the specific issues decided by the Court and makes those issues final in any future action in the same case. The Supreme Court has written: "If an appellate court has passed on a legal question and remanded the case for further proceedings, that decided legal question becomes the law of the case."[435]

APPEALS SHALL BE ALLOWED FROM DECISIONS OF LOWER COURTS

Section 6. Appeals shall be allowed from decisions of lower courts to the supreme court as may be provided by law.

In commenting on this section, Chief Justice James Morris declared: "Thus it will be seen that no right of appeal from the district courts is conferred by the Constitution. That right is left to statutory provisions and must be exercised in accordance therewith. An appeal, therefore, embraces only that which is contemplated by the law enacted by the legislature and must be taken within the time that the legislature has seen fit to provide."[436]

The Legislature has provided for appeals in both civil[437] and criminal cases.[438]

THE JUSTICES . . . SHALL BE CHOSEN BY THE ELECTORS OF THE STATE FOR TEN-YEAR TERMS

Section 7. The justices of the supreme court shall be chosen by the electors of the state for ten-year terms, so arranged that one justice is elected every two years. They shall hold office until their successors are duly qualified, and shall receive compensation as provided by law, but the compensation of any justice shall not be diminished during his term in office.

---

[435] Poyzer v. Amenia Seed and Grain Co., 409 N.W.2d 107, 108–109 (1987).

[436] State v. McClelland, 10 N.W.2d 798, 801 (1943).

[437] NDCC Chapter 28-27.

[438] NDCC Chapter 29-28.

Early in the state's history a conflict arose as to when justices were to take office. The controversy occurred because the constitution originally set the term of the first three justices to commence on the first Monday in December 1889. Justices who were elected in November 1916 claimed that they too were entitled to take office on the first Monday in December. The Supreme Court disagreed being of the opinion that the December date related only to the first justices elected to the Court, and that thereafter justices took office on the first Monday in January the same as other state officers.[439]

North Dakota Century Code, Section 27-02-01 provides that the chief justice of the Supreme Court shall be elected to a term of five years by "the judges of the supreme court and district courts."

THE DISTRICT COURT SHALL HAVE ORIGINAL JURISDICTION

Section 8. The district court shall have original jurisdiction of all causes, except as otherwise provided by law, and such appellate jurisdiction as may be provided by law or by rule of the supreme court. The district court shall have authority to issue such writs as are necessary to the proper exercise of its jurisdiction.

District courts have general jurisdiction in civil cases.[440] Generally, a civil action in the District Court is commenced by the issuance and service of a summons. "Once a summons is served in the manner prescribed by law," Justice Beryl J. Levine has written, "the court acquires personal jurisdiction and subject matter jurisdiction if the case is within the court's subject matter jurisdiction provided by law."[441]

District courts also have jurisdiction in cases involving government condemnation of property,[442] divorces,[443] guardianships,[444] and custody of minor children.[445] The administration of trusts,[446] and the supervision of probate are also matters within the jurisdiction of the District Court.[447]

---

[439] State v. Robinson, 160 N.W. 514 (1916).

[440] Nodak Mut. Farm Bureau v. Kosmatka, 619 N.W.2d 852 (2000). See also: NDCC Section 27-05-06.

[441] United Accounts, Inc. v. Teladvantage, Inc., 499 N.W.2d 115, 117 (1993).

[442] Becker County Sand & Gravel Co. v. Wosick, 245 N.W. 454 (1932).

[443] Schillerstrom v. Schillerstrom, 32 N.W.2d 106, 123 (1948).

[444] In re Thoreson's Guardianship, 4 N.W.2d 822 (1942). See also: NDCC Chapter 30.1-28. GUARDIANSHIP OF INCAPACITATED PERSONS.

[445] Jordana v. Corley, 220 N.W.2d 515 (1974).

[446] ADMINISTRATION OF TRUSTS, NDCC Chapter 59-04.

[447] UNIFORM PROBATE CODE, NDCC Title 30.1-01.

The District Court is the Juvenile Court in North Dakota.[448] As a Juvenile Court, it has the power over delinquent children[449] and to terminate parental rights.[450] In discussing delinquent children, the Supreme Court has pointed out: "Proceedings under the so-called juvenile law are not prosecutions for crime. . . . The court inquires into the actions of the juvenile and those in charge of him. The main purpose is to determine what is the best to do for him. This may require an investigation of his habits, language and actions."[451]

With regard to terminating parental rights, Justice Dale V. Sandstrom has written for the Court: "To terminate parental rights, the State must prove by clear and convincing evidence (1) the child is deprived, (2) the conditions and causes of the deprivation are likely to continue, and (3) the child is suffering, or will in the future suffer serious physical, mental, moral, or emotional harm."[452]

Two other examples of the District Court's jurisdiction are its power to declare laws unconstitutional and to certify to the Supreme Court questions the answers to which are doubtful.

In commenting on the District Court's power to declare laws unconstitutional, the Court pointed out: "The district court is one of the primary bulwarks in our judicial system. The framers of our Constitution contemplated and designated the district court as a court of general jurisdiction."[453]

When certifying questions to the Supreme Court, "[t]he trial court must first exercise its discretion in determining that the questions to be certified are doubtful and it must be made to appear that the case in which they arise will depend wholly or principally upon the construction of law applicable to the questions certified."[454]

One area of the law which occupies much of the docket of District Courts is its jurisdiction over felony criminal cases. Writing for the Supreme Court in 1926, Justice John Burke pointed out: "The district court has jurisdiction over all criminal offenses and exclusive original jurisdiction over all felonies, and of all persons brought therein, charged with the commission of crime."[455]

NDCC Section 27-05-06, 4 provides that District Courts shall have: "Jurisdiction of appeals from all final judgments of municipal judges and from the determinations of inferior officers, boards, or tribunals, in such cases and pursuant to such regulations as may be prescribed by law."

---

[448] UNIFORM JUVENILE COURT ACT, NDCC Chapter 27-20.

[449] NDCC Section 27-20-03, 1.a

[450] NDCC Section 27-20-03, 1.c.

[451] State v. Smith, 25 N.W.2d 270, 271 (1946).

[452] In re W. E., 619 N.W.2d 494, 496 (2000).

[453] State ex rel. DeKrey v. Peterson, 174 N.W.2d 95, 100 (1970).

[454] City of Grand Forks v. Grand Forks County, 139 N.W.2d 242, 248 (1965).

[455] State v. Overby, 209 N.W. 552, 554 (1926).

Inferior officers, boards, and tribunals include the following: State Tax Commissioner,[456] Commissioner of Insurance,[457] Board of Barber Examiners,[458] Public Service Commission,[459] and the Workers Compensation Bureau.[460] The decisions of many other administrative agencies can also be appealed to the District Court.[461]

Although the constitution does not specifically prohibit the Legislature from giving courts the power to legislate, that prohibition is inherent in the state's constitutional system. The Supreme Court addressed that question in a case wherein the Legislature gave District Courts the power to exclude land from the corporate limits of cities.

In holding the law to be unconstitutional, the Court pointed out that

> it is undisputed that the delegation of legislative functions to the district courts is not contemplated by the constitution, and that the three departments of government provided for in the constitution are distinct from each other; the powers of each being therein separately defined. It is therein provided that the executive department shall enforce the laws, the legislative department shall enact, repeal, or amend the laws, and the judicial department shall construe them.[462]

THE STATE SHALL BE DIVIDED INTO JUDICIAL DISTRICTS

> **Section 9.** The state shall be divided into judicial districts by order of the supreme court. In each district, one or more judges, as provided by law, shall be chosen by the electors of the district. The term of office shall be six years, and a district judge shall hold office until his successor is duly qualified. The compensation of district judges shall be fixed by law, but the compensation of any district judge shall not be diminished during his term of office.

Acting pursuant to the authority given by this section, the Supreme Court has established seven (7) judicial districts, with forty-two district judges.[463]

---

[456] Langer v. State, 28 N.W.2d 523 (1947).

[457] Evanson v. Wigen, 221 N.W.2d 648 (1974).

[458] Wagner v. N. D. Board of Barber Examiners, 186 N.W.2d 570 (1971).

[459] Petition of Village Board of Wheatland, 42 N.W.2d 321 (1950).

[460] Ehli v. N.D. Workers' Compensation Bureau, 447 N.W.2d 313 (1989).

[461] NDCC Section 28-32-15, 3.a.

[462] Glaspell v. City of Jamestown, 88 N.W. 1023, 1024 (1902).

[463] N.D. Supreme Court Administrative Rule 6, Judicial Districts, and Rule 7 Designation of judgeships and chambers with assignments. See also: NDCC Section 27-05-01, Judicial districts number of judges.

A District Judge Shall Hold Office until His Successor Is Duly Qualified

The Supreme Court discussed the question of a judge holding "office until his successor is duly qualified," in the case of *State v. Friederich*.[464] In this case, the person elected to be a district judge died 10 days before he was to take office on January 2. The then incumbent judge resigned and Governor John E. Davis immediately appointed Ray E. Friederich to fill the vacancy.

Governor William L. Guy, who took office in January, immediately declared the office vacant because of the death of the person previously elected. He then appointed Frank E. Foughty to fill the vacancy.

When the question of which of the two individuals was entitled to hold the office reached the Supreme Court, it held that the person appointed immediately after the death of the incumbent was entitled, under this section, to hold the office until his successor had been duly qualified. Referring to the constitution, the Court pointed out: "The only method it prescribes is by election when the office is occupied by an incumbent holding under a lawful tenure."[465] In this case, the person appointed after the death of the sitting judge was the incumbent and entitled to hold office until an election was held to fill that vacancy.

SUPREME COURT JUSTICES AND DISTRICT JUDGES SHALL BE . . . LEARNED IN THE LAW

> **Section 10.** Supreme court justices and district judges shall be citizens of the United States and residents of this state, shall be learned in the law, and shall possess any additional qualifications prescribed by law. Judges of other courts shall be selected for such terms and shall have such qualifications as may be prescribed by law.
>
> No justice of the supreme court or judge of the district court of this state shall engage in the practice of law, or hold any public office, elective or appointive, nor judicial in nature. No duties shall be imposed by law upon the supreme court or any of the justices thereof, except such as are judicial, nor shall any of the justices exercise any power of appointment except as herein provided. No judge of any court of this state shall be paid from the fees of his office, nor shall the amount of his compensation be measured by fees, other moneys received, or the amount of judicial activity of his office.

The Supreme Court dealt with the meaning of "learned in the law" when Torfin A. Teigen sought to have his name placed on the ballot for election as a Supreme Court justice. Although Teigen had not been admitted to the bar, he had graduated from the Minneapolis College of Law.

---

464 108 N.W.2d 681 (1961).

465 Id., p. 691.

Writing for a majority, Chief Justice Ralph Erickstad declared, "if we are to continue our practice of examining through the auspices of the State Bar Board those who have received Law Degrees from the finest law schools in this country to determine their qualifications to practice law before the highest court of this State, it would seem to follow that we must require that those who seek to sit on the highest court of the State demonstrate first that they are qualified."[466]

No Duties Shall Be Imposed . . . upon the Supreme Court . . . Except Such as Are Judicial

In 1939, the Legislature directed the Supreme Court to create a Code Revision Commission "to annotate the Constitution, to prepare, annotate and index a set of rules of practice and procedure for all courts of the state and to revise, annotate and index the laws of the state."[467] The validity of this law was challenged on the grounds that "it imposes upon the Supreme Court duties other than judicial and confers upon the judges thereof powers of appointment in violation of . . . [this section] of the State Constitution."[468]

The Supreme Court disagreed and said: "Our Constitution is not to be construed as rigidly classifying all the functions of government as being either legislative, executive or judicial."[469] Furthermore, the Court pointed out that for many years it had been regulating and controlling the admission to the bar under laws previously enacted by the Legislature.

Judge Harvey J. Miller, in commenting upon the Court's involvement in admission to the bar pointed out: "If the strict construction contended for by the Realtor is placed upon the limitations of power contained in . . . [this section] then it would appear that the foregoing statutes relating to the State Bar Board are unconstitutional."[470]

Another facet of the doctrine of separation of powers is the limitation on the scope of the Court's review of administrative decisions. For example, the Supreme Court has written: "It is not the function of the judiciary to act as a super board, substituting its judgment for that of the administrator whose decision is being reviewed."[471] The Court's function is to determine whether the administrative agency had jurisdiction of the case; whether the agency had applied the law correctly, and finally, whether or not the agency had acted "arbitrarily, oppressively, or unreasonably."[472]

---

[466] Petition of Teigen, 221 N.W.2d 94, 99 (1974).

[467] State v. Baker, 288 N.W. 202 (1939).

[468] Id., p. 203.

[469] Id., p. 205.

[470] Id., pp. 205-206.

[471] Barnes County v. Garrison Diversion, etc., 312 N.W.2d 20, 25 (1981).

[472] Id., p. 26.

WHEN ANY JUSTICE OR JUDGE HAS A CONFLICT OF INTEREST . . . THE CHIEF JUSTICE . . . SHALL ASSIGN A JUDGE

Section 11. When any justice or judge has a conflict of interest in a pending cause or is unable to sit in court because he is physically or mentally incapacitated, the chief justice, or a justice acting in his stead, shall assign a judge, or retired justice, or judge, to hear the cause.

This section leaves the decision to disqualify himself or herself to the justice or judge. In discussing such a decision, the Supreme Court has written: "When a district judge concludes that his impartiality might reasonably be questioned, and he accordingly disqualifies himself, the Supreme Court has the authority pursuant to . . . [this section] of the North Dakota Constitution . . . to assign an alternate judge. The assignment cannot be challenged at this time."[473]

Although this section does not deal with the extent to which litigants can demand a change of judge, the Legislature has provided for such situations.[474] In commenting upon this legislation, the Supreme Court has pointed out: "That legislation, . . . eliminated the former requirement of an affidavit of prejudice to get a change of judge, and adopted the present procedure that allows a party to get a change of judge by filing a written demand for change of judge, which must state that it is filed in good faith and not for the purpose of delay."[475]

ASSEMBLY MAY PROVIDE FOR THE RETIREMENT, DISCIPLINE AND REMOVAL OF JUDGES

Section 12.1. The legislative assembly may provide for the retirement, discipline and removal of judges of the supreme court and district court. The removal procedure provided for herein may be used in addition to the impeachment proceedings provided for in article XI, sections 8, 9, and 10.

The Legislature has provided for the retirement of judges in NDCC Chapter 27–17 Retirement of Judges.

A JUDICIAL NOMINATING COMMITTEE MUST BE ESTABLISHED

Section 13.

1. A judicial nominating committee must be established by law. The governor shall fill any vacancy in the office of supreme court justice or district court

---

473 Dangerfield v. Markel, 278 N.W.2d 364, 371 (1979).

474 NDCC Section 29-15-21. Demand for change of judge.

475 Traynor v. Leclerc, 561 N.W.2d 644, 647–648 (1997).

judge by appointment from a list of candidates nominated by the committee, unless the governor calls a special election to fill the vacancy for the remainder of the term. Except as provided in subsection 2, an appointment must continue until the next general election, when the office must be filled by election for the remainder of the term.
2. An appointment must continue for at least two years. If the term of the appointed judgeship expires before the judge has served at least two years, the judge shall continue in the position until the next general election immediately following the service of at least two years.
3. Notwithstanding sections 7 and 9 of this article, the term of the judge elected at the subsequent general election provided for in subsection 2 is reduced to the number of years remaining in the subsequent term after the appointee has served at least two years.

The Legislature has established a Judicial Nominating Committee as required by this section.[476]

[476] NDCC Chapter 27-25. JUDICIAL NOMINATING COMMISSION.

Article VII

Political Subdivisions

THIS ARTICLE IS TO PROVIDE FOR MAXIMUM LOCAL SELF-GOVERNMENT BY ALL POLITICAL SUBDIVISIONS

Section 1. The purpose of this article is to provide for maximum local self-government by all political subdivisions with a minimum of duplication of functions.

Although this section has undergone some changes since first adopted in 1889, its basic meaning is still the same. For example, in 1923 the Legislature gave cities the power to regulate the height and size of buildings. When that statute was attacked as being unconstitutional, the Supreme Court responded: "This section is the only provision in the Constitution relating to municipal corporations, and it leaves the Legislature entirely free to make regulations for the organization, government, and orderly building of cities by general law."[477]

The Supreme Court has also pointed out: "Since the Constitution directs the Legislative Assembly to provide, by general law, for the organization of municipal corporations, these municipal corporations, . . . become agencies of the State and have only the powers expressly conferred upon them by the Legislature, or such as may be necessarily implied from the powers expressly granted."[478]

---

[477] City of Bismarck v. Hughes, 208 N.W. 711, 713 (1926).

[478] Parker Hotel Company v. City of Grand Forks, 177 N.W.2d 764, 768 (1970).

ASSEMBLY SHALL PROVIDE . . . FOR THE ESTABLISHMENT AND THE GOVERNMENT OF ALL POLITICAL SUBDIVISIONS

Section 2. The legislative assembly shall provide by law for the establishment and the government of all political subdivisions. Each political subdivision shall have and exercise such powers as provided by law.

Some of the powers the Legislature has conferred upon cities include authority to construct parking lots,[479] establish parking meter zones,[480] to pave and improve streets,[481] to create zoning within the city,[482] and to annex land to the city.[483] Cities have also been given the authority to adopt a home rule charter.[484]

The Legislature has provided that meetings of the governing body of a city must be "open to the public."[485]

When the City Council of Westhope held a private meeting at which it authorized a paving project, the Supreme Court held that the actions of the Council taken at the meeting were void. The Court said: "Thus the cases hold that the public is entitled to have the City Council meet at the times specified by the statute or legal ordinance so as to prevent the council from doing business in any secret meeting. Any proceedings had at a meeting held at other times than so specified are void and illegal."[486]

COUNTIES . . . ARE HEREBY DECLARED TO BE COUNTIES OF THE STATE OF NORTH DAKOTA

Section 3. The several counties of the state of North Dakota as they now exist are hereby declared to be counties of the state of North Dakota.

Being "counties of the state of North Dakota" does not give counties any autonomy. The Supreme Court, for example, has pointed out: "This political subdivision of the state could speak and act only in the manner and on the matters prescribed by the Legislature in statutes enacted pursuant to constitutional authority."[487]

---

[479] Fisher v. City of Minot, 188 N.W.2d 745 (1971).

[480] State v. Brekke, 28 N.W.2d 598 (1947).

[481] Green v. Beste, 76 N.W.2d 165 (1956). See also: Parker Hotel Company v. City of Grand Forks, 177 N.W.2d 764 (1970).

[482] Eck v. City of Bismarck, 302 N.W.2d 739 (1981).

[483] City of Fargo v. Annexation Review Commission, 148 N.W.2d 338 (1967).

[484] NDCC Chapter 40-05.1. See also: Litten v. City of Fargo, 294 N.W.2d 628 (1980).

[485] NDCC Section 40-06-02. Meetings to be public—Journal of proceedings to be kept.

[486] Green v. Beste, 76 N.W.2d 165, 170 (1956). This section also applies to other political subdivisions, such as Water Resource Districts. See: BN. v. Benson County Water Resource Dist., 618 N.W.2d 155, 157 (2000).

[487] McHenry County v. Northern Trust Co., 200 N.W. 888, 893 (1924).

An example of a county acting in excess of its authority is the case of *Murphy v. Swanson*,[488] wherein the county commissioners of Burleigh County employed F. O. Hellstrom as an assistant state's attorney, to investigate property which might have escaped taxation. Hellstrom was to be paid $200 plus 10 percent of the taxes subsequently collected.

In an action brought by several county taxpayers, who argued that the county did not have authority to employ Hellstrom, the Supreme Court noted that the Board of County Commissioners had no authority to assess taxes nor to collect them. "The law," the Court declared, "expressly reposes in the various local officers the duties pertaining to the assessment of property, and places in the county treasurer the power and duty to collect such taxes as may be assessed and levied."[489]

ASSEMBLY SHALL PROVIDE BY LAW FOR RELOCATING COUNTY SEATS WITHIN COUNTIES

> **Section 4.** The legislative assembly shall provide by law for relocating county seats within counties, but it shall have no power to remove the county seat of any county.

The Legislature has enacted laws providing for the relocating of county seats.[490] These laws require the Board of County Commissioners to call an election when they receive a petition signed by electors "equal to thirty-three percent of the votes cast in the county for the office of governor at the preceding gubernatorial election."[491] A petition to remove a county seat must receive an affirmative vote of two-thirds of "all the legal votes cast" on the question.[492]

In discussing the purpose of the statutes relating to removal of a county seat, Justice James E. Robinson wrote, in a concurring opinion: "The purpose of the statute is to give the people of a county a fair opportunity to go to the polls and vote for the location or relocation of their county seat when it is not on a river or railroad, because it is a well-known fact that a county seat should be on some line of traffic and commerce, and readily accessible to the public."[493]

---

[488] 198 N.W. 116 (1924).

[489] Id., p. 119.

[490] NDCC Chapter 11.4. COUNTY SEATS—PERMANENTLY LOCATING AND REMOVING.

[491] NDCC Section 11-04-04. County seats—Removal—Petition—Election.

[492] NDCC Section 11-04-08. Affirmative vote necessary to remove county seat—Notice of result.

[493] Bugbee v. Steele County, 170 N.W. 321, 324 (1918).

NO PORTION OF ANY COUNTY . . . SHALL BE ANNEXED . . . OR DISSOLVED UNLESS A MAJORITY OF THE ELECTORS . . . APPROVE

Section 5. Methods and standards by which all or any portion of a county or counties may be annexed, merged, consolidated, reclassified, or dissolved shall be as provided by law. No portion of any county or counties shall be annexed, merged, consolidated, or dissolved unless a majority of the electors of each affected county voting on the question so approve.

The requirement that actions affecting the boundaries of counties be approved by a majority of the voters was before the Supreme Court in the case of *State v. Thompson*.[494] Although the votes of six precincts were not counted, the canvassing board concluded that the voters had approved the creation of a new county out of an existing county. In commenting upon the action of the canvassing board, Justice E. B. Goss wrote: "If the constitutional provision can be circumvented and virtually set aside by any such presumptions as here urged from a canvass of a portion of the vote, it is the equivalent of saying that the Constitution does not mean what it says when it requires the adoption of the proposition 'by a majority of all the legal votes cast in each county at such election.'"[495]

The Legislature has provided statutes by which counties can be "annexed, merged, consolidated, reclassified, or dissolved."[496]

ASSEMBLY SHALL PROVIDE . . . FOR THE ESTABLISHMENT . . . OF HOME RULE IN COUNTIES AND CITIES

Section 6. The legislative assembly shall provide by law for the establishment and exercise of home rule in counties and cities. No home rule charter shall become operative in any county or city until submitted to the electors thereof and approved by a majority of those voting thereon. In granting home rule powers to cities, the legislative assembly shall not be restricted by city debt limitations contained in this constitution.

The Legislature has adopted comprehensive legislation to create and govern home rule cities.[497]

Becoming a home rule city, however, does not give the city unlimited authority as to how it will govern itself. For example, after Fargo became a home rule city, it attempted to change its form of government from a commission form to a council form. Several residents brought an action seeking to prevent that change,

---

[494] 139 N.W. 960 (1913).

[495] Id., p. 967.

[496] NDCC Chapter 11-01. NAMES AND BOUNDARIES OF COUNTIES.

[497] NDCC Chapter 40-05.1. HOME RULE IN CITIES.

arguing that the city had no authority to do so. Judge John O. Garaas agreed with the petitioners and the Supreme Court affirmed. The Court said: "(W)e conclude that the legislature did not intend, and the statutory provisions do not give, home rule cities the authority to select any form of government it may desire."[498]

Counties may also adopt home rule by a vote of the people.[499]

ASSEMBLY SHALL . . . PROVIDE BY LAW FOR OPTIONAL FORMS OF GOVERNMENT FOR COUNTIES

Section 7. The legislative assembly shall also provide by law for optional forms of government for counties, but no optional form of government shall become operative in any county until submitted to the electors thereof at a special or general election, and approved by a majority of those voting thereon.

Until one of the optional forms of county government is adopted by any county, the fiscal and administrative affairs of the county shall be governed by a board of county commissioners as provided by law.

The Legislature has enacted legislation permitting counties to adopt a County Consolidated Office Form of County Government. This form of government gives the Board of County Commissioners the authority to appoint county officers.[500]

Counties are also permitted to adopt a County Managership form of government, which requires the election of a county manager who is given certain powers with regard to the operation of the county.[501]

EACH COUNTY SHALL PROVIDE FOR LAW ENFORCEMENT, ADMINISTRATIVE AND FISCAL SERVICES

Section 8. Each county shall provide for law enforcement, administrative and fiscal services, recording and registration services, educational services, and any other governmental services or functions as may be provided by law. Any elective office provided for by the counties shall be for a term of four years. Elective officers shall be elected by the electors in the jurisdiction in which the elected officer is to serve. A candidate for election must be a resident in the jurisdiction in which they are to serve at the time of the election. The office of sheriff shall be elected.

---

498 Litten v. City of Fargo, 294 N.W.2d 628, 634 (1980).

499 NDCC Chapter 11-09.1. HOME RULE COUNTIES.

500 NDCC Section 11-08-06. Officers in county adopting consolidated office form of government.

501 NDCC Section 11-09-12. Powers and duties of county manager.

The Legislature has provided for the election of a county auditor, registrar of deeds, clerk of the District Court, county treasurer, county coroner, state's attorney, and sheriff. After December 31, 2002, some of the clerks of the District Court will be state officials and will no longer be elected.[502]

QUESTIONS OF THE FORM OF GOVERNMENT . . . MAY BE PLACED UPON THE BALLOT

Section 9. Questions of the form of government to be adopted by any county or on the elimination or reinstatement of elective county offices may be placed upon the ballot by petition of electors of the county equal in number to twenty-five percent of the votes cast in the county for the office of governor at the preceding gubernatorial election.

The Supreme Court has not decided any cases involving this section.

AGREEMENTS.. . . FOR COOPERATIVE OR JOINT ADMINISTRATION . . . MAY BE MADE BY ANY POLITICAL SUBDIVISION

Section 10. Agreements, including those for cooperative or joint administration of any powers or functions, may be made by any political subdivision with any other political subdivision, with the state, or with the United States, unless otherwise provided by law or home rule charter. A political subdivision may by mutual agreement transfer to the county in which it is located any of its powers or functions as provided by law or home rule charter, and may in like manner revoke the transfer.

Section 11. The power of the governing board of a city to franchise the construction and operation of any public utility or similar service within the city shall not be abridged by the legislative assembly.

The Supreme Court has not decided any cases involving the above two sections.

[502] NDCC Section 11-10-02, and NDCC Chapter 27-05.2 CLERK OF DISTRICT COURT FUNDING AND FEES.

Article VIII

Education

ASSEMBLY SHALL MAKE PROVISION FOR THE ESTABLISHMENT AND MAINTENANCE OF A SYSTEM OF PUBLIC SCHOOLS

Section 1. A high degree of intelligence, patriotism, integrity and morality on the part of every voter in a government by the people being necessary in order to insure the continuance of that government and the prosperity and happiness of the people, the legislative assembly shall make provision for the establishment and maintenance of a system of public schools which shall be open to all children of the state of North Dakota and free from sectarian control. The legislative requirement shall be irrevocable without the consent of the United States and the people of North Dakota.

Section 2. The legislative assembly shall provide for a uniform system of free public schools throughout the state, beginning with the primary and extending through all grades up to and including schools of higher education, except that the legislative assembly may authorize tuition, fees and service charges to assist in the financing of public schools of higher education.

Section 3. In all schools instruction shall be given as far as practicable in those branches of knowledge that tend to impress upon the mind the vital importance of truthfulness, temperance, purity, public spirit, and respect for honest labor of every kind.

Section 4. The legislative assembly shall take such other steps as may be necessary to prevent illiteracy, secure a reasonable degree of uniformity in course of study, and to promote industrial, scientific and agricultural improvements.

In discussing the power of the Legislature over education, the Supreme Court has declared: "The legislature is given the power under Article VIII of the North Dakota Constitution to establish a complete and efficient system for the education of the youth of the state. The inhabitants of a school district have no property rights in the boundaries thereof."[503]

The Court has also said the Legislature "can provide for the boundaries and changes of boundaries of school districts, for the levy of taxes for school purposes and for such other matters as to it seems necessary in order to carry out the provisions of the constitution."[504]

In a dispute over whether the superintendent of Public Instruction or the Legislature has the authority to prescribe courses for the schools, the Supreme Court held that authority rests with the Legislature. Writing for the Court, Justice H. A. Bronson declared: "We have no hesitancy in stating that the Legislature of this state possesses the power to regulate or supervise the course of study in the common schools of this state."[505]

When Paula Kadrmas and Marsha Hall brought suit against the Dickinson Public Schools, asserting that the district was obligated to provide free bus transportation to school for their children, Judge Donald L. Jorgensen disagreed and the Supreme Court affirmed his decision. The Court said that Section 2 "does not require the state or school districts to provide free transportation for students to and from school."[506]

When Eldred N. Dornacker brought legal action against Mildred Olson, Trail County Auditor, he argued that the constitution's limitation on the power of the state to levy taxes to defray "the expenses of the state," prevented the levy of taxes by counties for schools in excess of the constitutional limitation.[507] The Supreme Court disagreed and pointed out that the constitutional limitation on state taxation "does not become involved unless a property tax levy is made by the State directly."[508]

The Supreme Court was required to interpret the words "free from sectarian control" when it had before it a case involving four teachers who wore religious habits in the classroom because they were nuns. The Court found "no evidence and no claim that any of the teachers departed in any manner from their line of

---

503 In re Township 143 North, Range 55 West, Cass County, 183 N.W.2d 520, 533 (1971).

504 Anderson v. Peterson, 54 N.W.2d 542, 551 (1952).

505 State v. Totten, 175 N.W. 563, 566 (1919).

506 Kadrmas v. Dickinson Public Schools, 402 N.W.2d 897, 902 (1987). This decision was affirmed in Kadrmas v. Dickinson Public Schools, 487 U.S. 450 (1988).

507 Dornacker v. Olson, 248 N.W.2d 844, 849 (1976).

508 Id., p. 851.

duty and gave or sought to give instruction in religious or sectarian subjects or that they conducted . . . any religious exercises, or that they sought to impress their own religious beliefs while acting as teachers."[509]

On the basis of this evidence, the Court declared: "We are all agreed that the wearing of the religious habit described in the evidence here does not convert the school into a sectarian school, or create sectarian control within the purview of the Constitution."[510]

The Legislature has enacted comprehensive legislation making school attendance mandatory. The Supreme Court upheld that legislation when it affirmed the convictions of Paul Shaver and Dennis Steinwand, members of the Bible Baptist Church, who were sending their children to the Bible Baptist School which was not approved by the Superintendent of Public Instruction. The Court pointed out: "The Constitution of North Dakota recognizes that 'a high degree of intelligence, patriotism, integrity and morality on the part of every voter in a government by the people' is necessary 'in order to insure the continuance of that government and the prosperity and happiness of the people.'"[511]

The Supreme Court was called upon to address this issue again when Kathy Rivinius and Ronald Weikum were arrested and convicted for sending their children to a religious school not approved by the Superintendent of Public Instruction. In response to the defendants' arguments that Article I, Section 3 of the North Dakota Constitution guaranteed them the "free exercise and enjoyment" of religion, Justice Paul M. Sand, in referring to Article VIII, Sections 1–4, wrote: "These constitutional provisions all disclose that the state has a compelling interest in requiring minimum standards of education to insure adequate education of the children of the state to enable them to be viable citizens in the community."[512]

In 1988, the Supreme Court upheld the convictions of Deborah and Lawrence Anderson, who were not sending their children to school, but instead were teaching them at home. The Andersons believed "that God had given them responsibility for their children, including their education, and that their religious convictions require them to teach their children at home."[513]

In 1989, the Legislature enacted comprehensive legislation permitting and regulating home-based education.[514]

The courts have had the opportunity to deal with the question of whether school districts must provide education to handicapped students. In each case,

---

[509] Gerhardt v. Heid, 267 N.W. 127, 135 (1936).

[510] Id.

[511] State v. Shaver, 294 N.W.2d 883, 895-896 (1980). See also: NDCC Chapter 15-34.1. COMPULSORY SCHOOL ATTENDANCE.

[512] State v. Rivinius, 328 N.W.2d 220, 228 (1982).

[513] State v. Anderson, 427 N.W.2d 316, 317 (1988).

[514] NDCC Sections 15-34.1-06 thru 13.

the Supreme Court has responded in the affirmative. For the Court, the answer was clear. "Under our state constitution," the Court declared, "all children in North Dakota have the right to a public school education."[515]

In *Cardiff v. Bismarck Public School Dist.*,[516] the Supreme Court considered the question of whether free public education included free textbooks. The Court responded that it did and therefore held that the Bismarck Public School District could not charge a rental fee for the use of its books.

ALL COLLEGES . . . FOR . . . WHICH LANDS HAVE BEEN GRANTED . . . SHALL REMAIN UNDER THE . . . CONTROL OF THE STATE

Section 5. All colleges, universities, and other educational institutions, for the support of which lands have been granted to this state, or which are supported by a public tax, shall remain under the absolute and exclusive control of the state. No money raised for the support of the public schools of this state shall be appropriated to or used for the support of any sectarian school.

When the Agricultural College Dormitory Association of Fargo, North Dakota, received permission from the State Board of Administration to erect a dormitory on the campus of the agricultural college now known as North Dakota State University, Maurice Kaufman brought an action seeking to prevent the dormitory from being built. Kaufman argued that the arrangement with the Dormitory Association violated this section. The District Court disagreed and the Supreme Court affirmed. "The statute under consideration here," Justice A. M. Christianson noted, "does not purport to authorize the board of administration to make law. The Legislature has made the law. It has assumed the responsibility and discharged the duty placed upon it by the Constitution. It has declared the policy. It has prescribed the rule of action."[517]

A BOARD OF HIGHER EDUCATION . . . IS HEREBY CREATED

Section 6.

1. A board of higher education, to be officially known as the state board of higher education, is hereby created for the control and administration of the following state educational institutions, to wit:

   a. The state university and school of mines, at Grand Forks, with their substations.

[515] Lapp v. Reeder Public School Dist. No. 3, 491 N.W.2d 65, 67 (1992). See also: In Interest of G. H., 218 N.W.2d 441 (1974).

[516] 263 N.W.2d 105 (1978).

[517] State v. Davis, 229 N.W. 105, 109 (1930).

b. The state agricultural college and experiment station, at Fargo, with their substations.
c. The school of science, at Wahpeton.
d. The state normal schools and teachers colleges, at Valley City, Mayville, Minot and Dickinson.
e. The school of forestry, at Bottineau.
f. And such other state institutions of higher education as may hereinafter be established.[518]

2. a. The state board of higher education consists of eight members. The governor shall appoint seven members who are qualified electors and taxpayers of the state, and who have resided in this state for not less than five years immediately preceding their appointments. These seven appointments are subject to confirmation by the senate.

   The governor shall appoint as the eighth member of the board a full-time resident student in good academic standing at an institution under the jurisdiction of the state board.

In addition to the institutions named above, the Legislature has placed the following institutions under the control of the State Board of Higher Education: Bismarck State College, Lake Region State College (Devils Lake), and Williston State College.[519]

In discussing the creation of the State Board of Higher Education, one writer has written:

> The particular form given to the [State] Board [of Higher Education] as a constitutionally autonomous body grew out of the highly charged political atmosphere brought about in the state during its fourth and fifth decades by the activities of William "Wild Bill" Langer and the Nonpartisan League. . . . In 1937, "Wild Bill" Langer was the Governor and three of the five Board of Administration members were his appointees. That year the Board instituted what was to be called "The Purge" by firing seven faculty and staff members of the North Dakota Agricultural College, including the state county agent leader. The Board also relieved the Director of the Experiment Station and Extension Service from his duties and accepted the resignation of the College president. The stated reasons for the actions were "economy and efficiency," but many people believed they were intended to give Langer control of Experiment Station and Extension Service funds and appointments, including the ability to allocate about $20,000,000 per year in benefit payments to farmers under

[518] The section contains detailed information concerning the creation and operation of the State Board of Education.

[519] NDCC Section 15-10-01. State board of education—Institutions administered by board.

the Agricultural Adjustment Act and to use farm and home demonstration agents for political purposes.[520]

Although Section 6 gives the governor the authority to appoint members of the State Board of Higher Education, his appointive power is limited to selections from three candidates selected by five officials designated in this section.

Although the Board is given substantial authority, its power is administrative and not legislative. The Supreme Court made this clear when it considered the validity of legislation giving the Board authority to build facilities without specifying where those facilities were to be built. In striking down this legislation, the Court declared: "It is clear that . . . [the] powers vested in the State Board of Higher Education are administrative. The constitutional provision does not create a 'miniature legislature.' The Board of Higher Education became a part of the executive branch of government."[521]

The powers of the Board of Higher Education include the power to discharge faculty members of the institutions of higher education. The Board exercised that power in the case of *Posin v. State Board of Higher Education*.[522] Although the Board was not required to give faculty members a formal hearing, the Supreme Court pointed out: "It is clear from the record before us that not only were the appellants allowed all of the rights to which they were entitled under the College constitution, but in addition thereto a formal hearing was had in which they participated and were represented by counsel."[523]

---

[520] Richard B. Crockett, *Constitutional Autonomy and the North Dakota State Board of Higher Education*, 54 North Dakota Law Review 530, 530–532 (1977–1978). See also: NDCC Chapter 15-10. THE STATE BOARD OF HIGHER EDUCATION.

[521] Nord v. Guy, 141 N.W.2d 395, 402 (1966).

[522] 86 N.W.2d 31 (1957).

[523] Id., p. 36.

Article IX

Trust Lands

ALL PROCEEDS OF THE PUBLIC LANDS . . . SHALL BE AND REMAIN A PERPETUAL TRUST FUND

Section 1. All proceeds of the public lands that have heretofore been, or may hereafter be granted by the United States for the support of the common schools in this state; all such per centum as may be granted by the United States on the sale of public lands; the proceeds of property that shall fall to the state by escheat; all gifts, donations, or the proceeds thereof that come to the state for support of the common schools, or not otherwise appropriated by the terms of the gift, and all other property otherwise acquired for common schools, shall be and remain a perpetual trust fund for the maintenance of the common schools of the state. Only the interest and income of the fund may be expended and the principal shall be retained and devoted to the trust purpose. All property, real or personal, received by the state from whatever source, for any specific educational or charitable institution, unless otherwise designated by the donor, shall be and remain a perpetual trust fund for the creation and maintenance of such institution, and may be commingled only with similar funds for the same institution. Should a gift be made to an institution for a specific purpose, without designating a trustee, such gift may be placed in the institution's fund; provided that such a donation may be expended as the terms of the gift provide.

> The interest and income of each institutional trust fund held by the state shall, unless otherwise specified by the donor, be appropriated by the legislative assembly to the exclusive use of the institution for which the funds were given.
>
> The proceeds of all bonuses, or similar payments, made upon the leasing of coal, gas, oil, or any other mineral interests under, or reserved after sale of, grant lands for the common schools or institutional lands shall be deposited in the appropriate trust fund as created by this section.

At the time North Dakota was admitted to the Union, the United States granted to it 3,191,770.28 acres of land "for the support and maintenance of the common schools, buildings at the state capitol, and for various educational and charitable institutions."[524]

In commenting upon this grant in 1903, Chief Justice N. C. Young of the North Dakota Supreme Court said: "Perhaps it is not necessary to state that by acceptance of the grant for educational purposes . . . a trust was created, the character of which was fixed by the terms of the grant. By the mere acceptance of the grant the honor of the state was pledged to the observance of the obligation of the trust; that is, to maintain the permanency of the trust fund and to use the interest thereof only for the support of the several schools to which it was dedicated."[525]

An example of where the Court intervened to protect school lands is the case of *State v. Murphy*.[526] This case involved land which had been given to the state and used for an agricultural experiment station. In 1925, the Legislature directed that the land be conveyed to Williams County to be used as a county poor farm.

Those seeking to uphold the transfer argued that using the land for an experiment station was not an "educational purpose" and therefore such transfer did not violate this section of the constitution. The Supreme Court disagreed. "The maintenance of experimental farms or stations," Justice Sveinbjorn Johnson declared,

> under express legislative sanction, in different parts of the state, and under the supervision of the Agricultural College, is simply another aspect of the policy spreading scientific or other knowledge through extension departments and extension work. We are constrained to the conclusion that the donation of the land to the state in the case at bar was distinctly for an "educational purpose," within the meaning of . . . [this section] of the Constitution.[527]

---

[524] Thomas O. Smith, *State Lands! What Are We Doing*. 51 North Dakota Law Review 477 (1975). The Legislature has enacted legislation providing for the investment of trust lands. See NDCC Chapter 15-03. INVESTMENT OF FUNDS.

[525] State v. McMillan, 96 N.W. 310, 315 (1903).

[526] 210 N.W. 53 (1926).

[527] Id., p. 54.

INCOME OF THIS FUND . . . SHALL BE . . . USED . . . FOR THE BENEFIT OF THE COMMON SCHOOLS

Section 2. The interest and income of this fund together with the net proceeds of all fines for violation of state laws and all other sums which may be added thereto by law, shall be faithfully used and applied each year for the benefit of the common schools of the state and no part of the fund shall ever be diverted, even temporarily, from this purpose or used for any other purpose whatever than the maintenance of common schools as provided by law.

Because the farming industry had suffered from economic turndown, in 1935 the Legislature gave the Board of University and School Lands permission "'to reduce, scale down, or throw off the interest that may be due upon any land contract or real estate mortgage, or rentals, to the end that justice may be done in dealing with our farmers and to enable the farmers indebted to the Board of University and School Lands to pay their debts and retain their property.'"[528]

Attorney General P. O. Sathre brought an action asserting that such action by the Board would violate this section of the constitution. Because only three justices were of the opinion that the law was unconstitutional, the statute was upheld.[529] Justice A. M. Christianson, writing for himself and Judge H. L. Berry, declared:

> It must be presumed that the statute was enacted to enable the Board of University and School Lands better to perform its duties. . . . The Board of University and School Lands has no power to utilize the funds or interest income for any purpose except those specified in the Constitution. Its great and primary duty is to safeguard the fund and properly direct the investment thereof, and if a case arises where the proper safeguarding of the fund requires that interest be remitted in whole or in part, the board may do so.[530]

In 1992, the Supreme Court had before it the question of whether the phrase "the net proceeds of all fines for violation of state laws," as used in this section, included fees charged for violation of weight limitations on highways. The Court held that such fees were not fines.

"The overload charges in the case at hand," the Court wrote, "are for the extraordinary use of the highway and are assessed on a pro rata basis for exceeding the legal weight restriction. . . . The primary purpose of assessing the charges is to compensate the state for possible damage to its highways and the proceedings are civil in nature."[531]

---

[528] State v. Board of University and School Lands, 262 N.W. 60, 62 (1935).

[529] Article VI, Section 4 provides that in order for the Court to declare a law unconstitutional, four members of the Court must agree.

[530] Supra note 5, p. 69.

[531] State ex. rel. Backes v. A Motor Vehicle, 492 N.W.2d 595, 598 (1992).

"THE BOARD OF UNIVERSITY AND SCHOOL LANDS"

Section 3. The superintendent of public instruction, governor, attorney general, secretary of state and state treasurer comprise a board of commissioners, to be denominated the "board of university and school lands." Subject to the provisions of this article and any law that may be passed by the legislative assembly, the board has control of the appraisement, sale, rental, and disposal of all school and university lands, and the proceeds from the sale of such lands shall be invested as provided by law.

The Board Has Control of the Appraisement, Sale, Rental, and Disposal of All School and University Lands

The Board's authority under this section was questioned in *Fuller v. Board of University and School Lands*.[532] In this case, E. H. Fuller sought to force the Board to convey certain property to him which he claimed he purchased at an auction sale. The Board refused to do so, being of the opinion that there had been fraud and collusion between Fuller and other bidders at the sale.

In finding in favor of the Board, the Court pointed out: "It suffices that it [the Board] had evidence and information, and, acting thereon in the exercise of discretion, disapproved the sale; presumably the board did its duty. This court will not weigh in this mandamus case the evidence that was before the board, but, instead, recognizes that this board was charged by law with a duty—that of approving or disapproving this contract of sale—and that it has performed its duty, inasmuch as it has acted in this matter."[533]

The Legislature has enacted legislation governing the investment of the permanent funds of common schools and other public institutions.[534]

The Board's power with regard to investments, however, is not unlimited. For example, when the Board sought to satisfy a real estate mortgage it held, without requiring the payment of past due interest, the Court said it could not do so. The Court pointed out that "the board has no power to comprise a claim for past due interest unless authorized by the Legislature."[535]

Once the Board sells school land without reserving to the state an interest in coal deposits, the Board may not thereafter rescind the sale even though the land does contain coal. Writing for the Court, Justice Thomas J. Burke declared:

> A consideration of the foregoing constitutional and statutory provisions, makes it clear that, while the sales of state lands are surrounded with multiple safeguards to insure against illegal sales, inadequate price and fraud and collusion and to procure an

---

[532] 129 N.W. 1029 (1911).

[533] Id., p. 1032.

[534] NDCC Chapter 15-03. INVESTMENT OF FUNDS.

[535] State v. Hanson, 256 N.W. 201, 204 (1934).

avoidance of contracts of sale for such reasons prior to the issuance of a patent; it was nevertheless the constitutional and legislative intent that after a good faith determination by the board that the sales were not subject to such infirmities, and the issuance of patents to the lands sold, that all questions of legality should be concluded and the sales should be final and irrevocable.[536]

THE PUBLIC OFFICERS DESIGNATED BY LAW SHALL CONSTITUTE BOARDS OF APPRAISAL

Section 4. The public officers designated by law shall constitute boards of appraisal and under the authority of the state board of university and school lands shall appraise all school lands within their respective counties which they may from time to time recommend for sale at their actual value under the prescribed terms and shall first select and designate for sale the most valuable lands.

The Legislature has designated the county superintendent of schools, the chairman of the Board of County Commissioners, and the county auditor of each county as the County Board of Appraisers.[537]

ASSEMBLY SHALL PROVIDE FOR THE SALE OF ALL SCHOOL LANDS

Section 5. After one year from the assembling of the first legislative assembly the lands granted to the state from the United States for the support of common schools, may be sold upon the following conditions and no other; No more than one-fourth of all such lands shall be sold within the first five years after the same become salable by virtue of this section. No more than one-half of the remainder within ten years after the same become salable as aforesaid. The residue may be sold at any time after the expiration of said ten years. The legislative assembly shall provide for the sale of all school lands subject to the provisions of this article. In all sales of lands subject to the provisions of this article all minerals therein, including but not limited to oil, gas, coal, cement materials, sodium sulfate, sand and gravel, road material, building stone, chemical substances, metallic ores, uranium ores, or colloidal or other clays, shall be reserved and excepted to the state of North Dakota, except that leases may be executed for the extraction and sale of such materials in such manner and upon such terms as the legislative assembly may provide.

---

[536] State v. Oster, 61 N.W.2d 276, 278–279 (1953). See also: Haag v. State Board of University and School Lands, 219 N.W.2d 121 (1974).

[537] NDCC Section 15-06-02. County board of appaisers—How composed.

The Legislature has defined the lands granted to the state by the United States as "original grant lands."[538]

The Supreme Court has held that when the Board of University and School Lands sells original grant lands, it has the burden of determining if there are minerals on the land. If the Board sells original grant land believing that the land does not contain minerals, the Board cannot later claim ownership of all the minerals found on the land. However, where a statute specifically provides for a reservation to the state of 50 percent of any minerals on the land, the state is entitled to that 50 percent even though the grant does not reserve them. In explaining this, Justice Robert Vogel wrote that "once it is admitted that future discoveries and future technology may make coal subject to development at a later time even though it was not subject to profitable development at the time of contract, there is no logical reason for holding that the State cannot reserve coal in lands which contain coal but are not 'coal lands' . . . at the time of the contract."[539]

As pointed out above, at the time North Dakota was admitted to the Union, it received land from the United States "'*for public buildings at the capital of*'"[540] the state. Such land, however, is not considered original grant land, and therefore the disposition thereof is governed by statute rather than by this section of the constitution. That was the conclusion of the Court in *Abbey v. State*,[541] where the Court upheld a reservation of 50 percent of all oil, natural gas, and minerals transferred as required by law.

ALL SALES . . . SHALL BE AT PUBLIC AUCTION AND TO THE HIGHEST BIDDER

> **Section 6.** No original grant school or institutional land shall be sold for less than the fair market value thereof, and in no case for less than ten dollars ($10.00) per acre, provided that when lands have been sold on contract and the contract has been canceled, such lands may be resold without reappraisement by the board of appraisal. The purchaser shall pay twenty (20) percent of the purchase price at the time the contract is executed; thereafter annual payments shall be made of not less than six (6) percent of the original purchase price. An amount equal to not less than three (3) percent per annum of the unpaid principal shall be credited to interest and the balance shall be applied as payment on principal as credit on purchase price. The purchaser may pay all or any installment or installments not yet due to any interest paying date. If the purchaser so desires, he may pay the entire balance due on his contract

[538] NDCC Section 15-06-01. Original grant lands defined.

[539] Haag v. State Board of University and Schools Lands, 219 N.W.2d 121, 130 (1974).

[540] Abbey v. State, 202 N.W.2d 844, 849 (1972).

[541] 202 N.W.2d 844 (1972).

with interest to date of payment at any time and he will be entitled to proper conveyance.

All sales shall be held at the county seat of the county in which the land to be sold is situated, and shall be at public auction and to the highest bidder, and notice of such sale shall be published once each week for a period of three weeks prior to the day of sale in a legal newspaper published nearest the land and in the newspaper designated for the publication of the official proceedings and legal notices within the county in which said land is situated.

No grant or patent for such lands shall issue until payment is made for the same; provided that the land contracted to be sold by the state shall be subject to taxation from the date of the contract. In case the taxes assessed against any of said lands for any year remain unpaid until the first Monday in October of the following year, the contract of sale for such land shall, if the board of university and school lands so determine, by it, be declared null and void. No contract of sale heretofore made under the provisions of this section of the constitution as then providing shall be affected by this amendment, except prepayment of principal may be made as herein provided.

Any of said lands that may be required for townsite purposes, school-house sites, church sites, cemetery sites, sites for other educational or charitable institutions, public parks, airplane landing fields, fairgrounds, public highways, railroad right of way, or other railroad uses and purposes, reservoirs for the storage of water for irrigation, irrigation canals, and ditches, drainage ditches, or for any of the purposes for which private lands may be taken under the right of eminent domain under the constitution and laws of this state, may be sold under the provisions of this article, and shall be paid in full at the time of the sale, or at any time thereafter as herein provided. Any of said lands and any other lands controlled by the board of university and school lands, including state coal mineral interests, may, with the approval of said board, be exchanged for lands and coal mineral interests of the United States, the state of North Dakota or any county or municipality thereof as the legislature may provide, and the lands so acquired shall be subject to the trust to which the lands exchanged therefor were subject, and the state shall reserve all mineral and water power rights in land so transferred, except coal mineral interests approved for exchange by the board of university and school lands under this section.

When any of said lands have been heretofore or may be hereafter sold on contract, and the purchaser or his heirs or assigns is unable to pay in full for the land purchased within twenty years after the date of purchase and such contract is in default and subject to being declared null and void as by law provided, the board of university and school lands may, after declaring such contract null and void, resell the land described in such contract to such purchaser, his heirs or assigns, for the amount of the unpaid principal, together with interest thereon reckoned to the date of such resale at the rate of not less than three (3%) percent, but in no case shall the resale price be more than the original sale price; such contract of resale shall be upon the terms herein provided, provided this section shall be deemed self-executing insofar as the provisions for resale herein made are concerned.

The Legislature has enacted comprehensive legislation to implement this section.[542]

When the State Highway Commission attempted to secure a right of way over school land, the Supreme Court held that the land could not be condemned and that the Highway Commission must follow the requirements of ths section and purchase the land.

"(T)he . . . [Highway Commission] concede[s]," Justice William L. Nuessle wrote, "that title to school lands may not be acquired through condemnation proceedings, and that where title in fee to such lands is taken the requirements of the Constitution as to sale, price, manner, etc., must be complied with."[543]

Because state lands are not subject to taxation, this section provides that when such land is sold, it "shall be subject to taxation from the date of the contract." This section, however, also provides that when taxes on the land remain unpaid, the Board of University and School Lands may declare the contract "null and void." These parts of this section came into play when Towner County attempted to levy taxes on school land previously sold under a contract which the state had cancelled when the purchaser had defaulted in making payments.

The Court pointed out that the Legislature had provided that at the time of the sale of school land, the purchaser's contractual interest was subject to taxation. In explaining this the Court declared: "The State does not tax its own property, and had the legislative assembly failed to provide a means for taxing the interest of the purchaser, . . . the land would have been free from taxation until title passed."[544]

ALL LANDS RECEIVED BY THE STATE . . . SHALL BE . . . SOLD IN THE SAME MANNER AND UNDER THE SAME LIMITATIONS

Section 7. All lands received by the state for any specific educational or charitable institution shall be appraised and sold in the same manner and under the same limitations and subject to all the conditions as to price and sale as provided in this constitution for the appraisal and sale of lands for the benefit of common schools. However, a distinct and separate account shall be kept by the proper officers of each of said funds and the limitations as to the time in which school land may be sold shall apply only to lands granted for the support of common schools.

---

[542] NDCC Chapter 15-08. PROVISIONS RELATING TO ORIGINAL GRANT AND TO NONGRANT LANDS.

[543] State Highway Commission v. State, 297 N.W. 194, 196 (1941).

[544] State v. Towner County, 283 N.W. 63, 68 (1938).

Although this section has been referred to in several Supreme Court cases, it has not been a deciding factor in these cases.[545] The Legislature has, however, provided procedures for the sale and lease of nongrant lands.[546]

ASSEMBLY SHALL . . . PROVIDE . . . FOR THE LEASING OF LANDS GRANTED TO THE STATE

Section 8. The legislative assembly shall have authority to provide by law for the leasing of lands granted to the state for educational and charitable purposes; but no such law shall authorize the leasing of said lands for a longer period than five years. Said lands shall only be leased for pasturage and meadow purposes and at a public auction after notice as heretofore provided in case of sale; provided, that all of said school lands now under cultivation may be leased, at the discretion and under the control of the board of university and school lands, for other than pasturage and meadow purposes until sold. All rents shall be paid in advance.

Provided further, that coal lands may also be leased for agricultural cultivation upon such terms and conditions and for such a period, not exceeding five years, as the legislature may provide.

This section makes a distinction between school lands generally, which can be leased "for pasturage and meadow purposes," and "lands now under cultivation," which may be leased "for other than pasturage and meadow purposes." When called upon to explain the authority of the Board with regard to lands under cultivation, the Court wrote: "We do not think that . . . [this section] of the Constitution in any way circumscribes or limits the power of the board to lease lands which were sold, put in cultivation, and have reverted to the state to any greater extent or in any different manner than it circumscribes and limits the board's power with respect to school lands under cultivation at the time the Constitution was adopted."[547]

The extent to which the Board of University and School Lands may lease school lands for the exploration of oil and gas was considered by the Court in the case of *State v. Amerada Petroleum Corp.*[548] Richard P. Rausch had brought an action seeking to have a lease made by the state to Amerada Petroleum Corp. for the exploration of oil and gas declared invalid.

Rausch argued that the lease violated this section, but the Court disagreed. "The constitution providing as it does through [this] Section . . . for certain restrictions upon the leasing of lands granted to the state for educational and charitable purpose deals exclusively with leases for pasturage, meadow purposes,

[545] See: State v. Amerada Petroleum Corporation, 71 N.W.2d 675, 683 (1955).

[546] NDCC Chapter 15-07. SALE AND LEASE OF NONGRANT LANDS.

[547] Wittmayer v. Security State Bank, 211 N.W. 436, 440 (1926).

[548] 49 N.W.2d 14 (1951).

and purposes of cultivation. References to leasing in that section do not embrace or include leases for the purpose of exploring for or exploiting subsurface minerals."[549]

NO LAW SHALL . . . BE PASSED . . . GRANTING . . . ANY PRIVILEGES BY REASON OF THE OCCUPATION . . . OF . . . LANDS

Section 9. No law shall ever be passed by the legislative assembly granting to any person, corporation or association any privileges by reason of the occupation, cultivation or improvement of any public lands by said person, corporation or association subsequent to the survey thereof by the general government. No claim for the occupation, cultivation or improvement of any public lands shall ever be recognized, nor shall such occupation, cultivation or improvement of any public lands ever be used to diminish either directly or indirectly, the purchase of said lands.

When Cass County levied certain assessments upon land for the construction of a drain, the Court held that school land served by the drain could not be assessed for its construction. "This tract," Justice N. C. Young declared, "is a portion of the lands granted by the United States to this state in trust for school purposes. The provisions of the grant and its acceptance forbid the imposition of assessments."[550]

ASSEMBLY MAY PROVIDE FOR THE SALE . . . OF ALL PUBLIC LANDS . . . GRANTED BY THE UNITED STATES TO THE STATE

Section 10. The legislative assembly may provide by law for the sale or disposal of all public lands that have been, or may hereafter be granted by the United States to the state for purposes other than set forth in article IX, section 1. The legislative assembly in providing for the appraisal, sale, rental, and disposal of the same shall not be subject to the provisions and limitations of article IX, sections 1 through 11.

The Supreme Court cited this section in a case involving an agreement between the Board of Administration and the Agricultural College Dormitory Association of Fargo under which the Dormitory Association agreed to build and operate a dormitory on land set aside for the building of the Agricultural College.

When Maurice Kaufman sought to prevent the erection of the dormitory at the Agricultural College, Fargo, in addition to arguing that the project violated

---

549 Id., p. 23. See: NDCC Chapter 38-11. LEASE OF MINERALS ON PUBLIC LAND; and NDCC Chapter 15-05. LEASING COAL, OIL, GAS, AND OTHER RIGHTS.

550 Erickson v. Cass County, 92 N.W. 841, 848 (1902).

Article VIII, Section 5, he also asserted that the dormitory project violated this section. The Supreme Court disagreed and pointed out that the U.S. Congress had specifically "granted its consent that the tract of land in question be released from the operations of the grant, and that the state of North Dakota might appropriate the same for the Agricultural College."[551] "The site acquired in this manner," the Court declared, "is obviously no more subject to the provisions of the Constitution relating to school and institutional lands than would be a site which had been acquired by purchase from a private owner."[552] This section, therefore, supported the Board's lease of this land for dormitory purposes.

ASSEMBLY SHALL PASS . . . LAWS FOR THE SAFEKEEPING, TRANSFER, AND DISBURSEMENT OF THE STATE SCHOOL FUNDS

Section 11. The legislative assembly shall pass suitable laws for the safekeeping, transfer and disbursement of the state school funds; and shall require all officers charged with the same or the safekeeping thereof to give ample bonds for all moneys and funds received by them, and if any of said officers shall convert to his own use in any manner or form, or shall loan with or without interest or shall deposit in his own name, or otherwise than in the name of the state of North Dakota, or shall deposit in any banks or with any person or persons, or exchange for other funds or property any portion of the school lands aforesaid or purposely allow any portion of the same to remain in his own hands uninvested, except in the manner prescribed by law, every such act shall constitute an embezzlement of so much of the aforesaid school funds as shall be thus taken or loaned or deposited, or exchanged or withheld and shall be a felony; and any failure to pay over, produce or account for, the state school funds or any part of the same entrusted to any such officer, as by law required or demanded, shall be held and be taken to be prima facie evidence of such embezzlement.

The Supreme Court has not decided any cases involving this section.

THE FOLLOWING PUBLIC INSTITUTIONS OF THE STATE ARE PERMANENTLY LOCATED AT THE PLACES . . . NAMED

Section 12. The following public institutions of the state are permanently located at the places hereinafter named, each to have the lands specifically granted to it by the United States in the Act of Congress approved February 22, 1889, to be disposed of and used in such manner as the legislative assembly may prescribe subject to the limitations provided in the article on school and public lands contained in this constitution.

1. The seat of government at the city of Bismarck in the county of Burleigh.

---

[551] State v. Davis, 229 N.W. 105, 111 (1930).

[552] Id.

2. The state university and the school of mines at the city of Grand Forks, in the county of Grand Forks.
3. The North Dakota state university of agriculture and applied science at the city of Fargo, in the county of Cass.
4. A state normal school at the city of Valley City, in the county of Barnes, and the legislative assembly, in apportioning the grant of eighty thousand acres of land for normal schools made in the Act of Congress referred to shall grant to the said normal school at Valley City, as aforementioned, fifty thousand (50,000) acres, and said lands are hereby appropriated to said institution for that purpose.
5. The school for the deaf and dumb of North Dakota at the city of Devils Lake, in the county of Ramsey.
6. A state training school at the city of Mandan, in the county of Morton.
7. A state normal school at the city of Mayville, in the county of Traill, and the legislative assembly in apportioning the grant of lands made by Congress in the Act aforesaid for state normal schools shall assign thirty thousand (30,000) acres to the institution located at Mayville, and said lands are hereby appropriated for said purpose.
8. A state hospital for the insane at the city of Jamestown, in the county of Stutsman. And the legislative assembly shall appropriate twenty thousand acres of the grant lands made by the Act of Congress aforesaid for other educational and charitable institutions to the benefit and for the endowment of said institution, and there shall be located at or near the city of Grafton, in the county of Walsh, an institution for the feebleminded, on the grounds purchased by the secretary of the interior for a penitentiary building.

In 1916, a petition was filed with Secretary of State Thomas Hall to amend this section to move the seat of government from Bismarck to New Rockford, North Dakota. Attorney General Henry J. Linde, acting on behalf of taxpayer Otto Bauer, sought a writ from the Supreme Court preventing Secretary Hall from putting the issue on the ballot. The Supreme Court, in granting the writ, held that at that time the constitution could not be amended by the initiative process.[553] Article III, Section 9 of the constitution now permits amendment by the initiative process.

In discussing the status of the State Normal School at Valley City, and the other institutions created by this section, the Supreme Court has written: "This institution and the other state educational and charitable institutions are not legal and independent entities, but are mere agencies or instrumentalities through which the state promotes its educational and charitable interests, and for the support of which all of the taxable property of the state is chargeable;

[553] State v. Hall, 159 N.W. 281 (1916).

and the power of their trustees to contract debts is limited by legislative appropriations."[554]

The authority of the Board of Administration over the institutions listed in this section was at issue when a dispute arose over whether the city of Grafton or Otter Tail Power Company should provide electricity to the Grafton State School.

Otter Tail Power had been given a contract by the Board to supply the electricity, but the Public Service Commission challenged that decision, being of the opinion that it had the final say about who the electricity supplier should be. District Judge Albert Lundberg disagreed and held that the PUC had no authority to interfere with the decision of the Board of Administration and the Supreme Court agreed.

> The Grafton State School is a state institution whose foundation rests upon . . . [this section] of the North Dakota Constitution. . . . The Board of Administration is an agency of the state created for the purpose of administering and managing the School and other specified institutions. It has the power vested in it by statute either expressly or by reasonable implication. When exercising those powers it is acting as an instrumentality of the state.[555]

THE FOLLOWING PUBIC INSTITUTIONS ARE PERMANENTLY LOCATED AS PROVIDED

Section 13. The following public institutions are located as provided, each to have so much of the remaining grant of one hundred seventy thousand acres of land made by the United States for "other educational and charitable institutions" as is allotted by law:

1. A soldiers' home, when located, or such other charitable institution as the legislative assembly may determine, at the city of Lisbon in the county of Ransom, with a grant of forty thousand acres of land.
2. The school for the blind at the city of Grand Forks in the county of Grand Forks or at such other location as may be determined by the legislative assembly to be in the best interests of the students of such institution and the state of North Dakota.
3. A school of forestry, or such other institution as the legislative assembly may determine, at such place in one of the counties of McHenry, Ward, Bottineau, or Rolette, as the electors of said counties may determine by an election for that purpose, to be held as provided by the legislative assembly.

---

[554] State v. McMillan, 96 N.W. 310, 317 (1903).

[555] City of Grafton v. Otter Tail Power Company, 86 N.W.2d 197, 201 (1957).

4. A school of science or such other educational or charitable institution as the legislative assembly may prescribe, at the city of Wahpeton in the county of Richland, with a grant of forty thousand acres.
5. A state college at the city of Minot in the county of Ward.
6. A state college at the city of Dickinson in the county of Stark.
7. A state hospital for the mentally ill at such place within this state as shall be selected by the legislative assembly.

No other institution of a character similar to any one of those located by article IX, section 12, or this section shall be established or maintained without an amendment of this constitution.

When this section was originally adopted it did not contain a reference to the creation of a "state college at the city of Minot." In November 1910, however, the voters amended the section to add a provision creating a "state normal school at the city of Minot."

Shortly thereafter, Attorney General Andrew Miller brought an action seeking to permanently enjoin the State Board from creating the normal school at Minot. At that time, the last paragraph of this section prohibited the establishment of any similar institution "without a revision of this Constitution." Miller, argued "that the word . . . revision . . . was associated only with the calling and holding of a constitutional convention, with the power to make or submit complete or partial changes in the Constitution as it might deem expedient."[556] The Supreme Court agreed that "the language employed in this proviso is ambiguous and its meaning not free from doubt."[557] After examining the debates at the Constitutional Convention, Chief Justice Burleigh F. Spalding wrote for the Court: "In other words, we are satisfied that the convention and voters all believed it [revision] was used in its popular sense and meant precisely the same as though *amendment* [emphasis added] had been used."[558]

When the Legislature established a soldier's home at Lisbon, as required by this section, it provided:

> **Object of veterans' home.** The object of the veterans' home is to provide basic care as defined under chapter 23-09.3 and long-term care as defined under chapter 23–16 for:
>
> 1. All veterans as defined in section 37-01-40 and all honorably discharged soldiers of the North Dakota national guard who heretofore or hereafter may become permanently disabled from any cause while in the line and discharge of duty.

[556] State v. Taylor, 133 N.W. 1046, 1048 (1911).

[557] Id., p. 1050.

[558] Id., p. 1051.

2. The spouses and surviving spouses of those mentioned in subsection 1 if they meet the requirements for admission under section 37-15-10.[559]

Although Peter W. Skeffington, a veteran, was "suffering with paralysis and confined to his bed and unable to take care of himself,"[560] he was denied admission to the home because he was not indigent. Skeffington argued, however, that the home was for "all honorably discharged" veterans. Judge Frank P. Allen disagreed and so did four justices of the Supreme Court. Judge Allen and the four justices were of the opinion that "when facilities were not at hand to accommodate all, to so manage the institution that those really in need should first be benefited"[561] was acceptable.

Justice R. H. Grace dissented because he was of the opinion that the word "all" in the statute meant exactly that. "It is my opinion," Justice Grace wrote, "that any old soldier, sailor, or marine who has served in the United States army or navy, and who has been honorably discharged, if he is disabled . . . as a matter of strict legal right is entitled to be admitted to the Soldiers' Home if he wishes to be."[562]

The Legislature has established the School of Forestry at Bottineau, North Dakota,[563] and the state hospital for the mentally ill at Jamestown, North Dakota.[564]

---

[559] NDCC Section 37-15-02. Object of veterans' home.

[560] State v. Seigfried, 168 N.W. 62, 63 (1918).

[561] Id.

[562] Id., p. 65. Originally this section did not restrict eligibility to members of the "North Dakota national guard."

[563] NDCC Section 15-16-01.

[564] NDCC Section 25-02-01.

Article X

Finance and Public Debt

ASSEMBLY SHALL BE PROHIBITED FROM . . . LEVYING OF A TAX ON THE ASSESSED VALUE OF REAL OR PERSONAL PROPERTY

Section 1. The legislative assembly shall be prohibited from raising revenue to defray the expenses of the state through the levying of a tax on the assessed value of real or personal property.

When called upon to do so, the Supreme Court defined taxation as "the inherent power in the government to raise funds with which to promote the general welfare and protection of its citizens."[565] Furthermore, the Court wrote: "A tax is an enforced contribution for public purposes and is in no way dependent upon the will or the express consent of the person taxed."[566] Originally, this section permitted the state to levy a tax "not to exceed in any one year four (4) mills on the dollar of the assessed valuation of all taxable property in the state."

In construing the section in its original form, the Supreme Court held that the limitation did not apply to local levies for public schools. "We conclude that . . . [this section] of the Constitution," Justice Vernon Pederson wrote, "was adopted with the understanding that its provisions did not limit local levies for

[565] State v. Kromarek, 52 N.W.2d 713, 715 (1952).

[566] Id.

public schools. Neither does . . . [this section] limit the State in expending revenues not raised by a property tax levy, for the maintenance of the public school system."[567]

The section was amended to its present form in 1980.

THE POWER OF TAXATION SHALL NEVER BE SURRENDERED

> **Section 2.** The power of taxation shall never be surrendered or suspended by any grant or contract to which the state or any county or other municipal corporation shall be a party.

After extensive negotiations between the office of the State Tax Commissioner and a taxpayer, an agreement was reached as to the amount of sales and use taxes the taxpayer was obligated to pay. Subsequently, however, the tax commissioner reassessed the tax due and imposed penalties and interest on the taxpayer. The taxpayer's response was to commence legal action seeking to prevent the reassessment, claiming that during its previous negotiations with the tax department it had been assured that the taxes due were those as originally assessed. The tax commissioner responded that to prevent the tax department from levying the additional taxes would, in effect, be a violation of this section. The Supreme Court disagreed. The Court declared: "The public's interest in revenue collection in this case is outweighed by the taxpaying public's interest in being entitled to rely on statements made by the Department official authorized to make decisions. It would belittle the office and title which . . . [the representative of the tax department] holds to otherwise."[568]

EVERY LAW IMPOSING A TAX SHALL STATE DISTINCTLY THE OBJECT OF THE SAME

> **Section 3.** No tax shall be levied except in pursuance of law, and every law imposing a tax shall state distinctly the object of the same, to which only it shall be applied. Notwithstanding the foregoing or any other provisions of this constitution, the legislative assembly, in any law imposing a tax or taxes on, in respect to or measured by income, may define the income on, in respect to or by which such tax or taxes are imposed or measured or may define the tax itself by reference to any provision of the laws of the United States as the same may be or become effective at any time or from time to time, and may prescribe the exceptions or modifications to any such provision.

When Gene A. Benson appealed his conviction for not filing state income tax returns for the years 1982 and 1983, he argued that his wages were not subject to

---

[567] Dornacker v. Olson, 248 N.W.2d 844, 850–851 (1976).

[568] Blocker Drilling Canada, Ltd. v. Conrad, 354 N.W.2d 912, 922 (1984).

the North Dakota income tax laws. In affirming Benson's conviction, the Supreme Court pointed out that the state income tax laws refer to federal income tax laws for the definition of taxable income. "For federal income tax purposes," the Court pointed out, "[federal law] defines gross income as all income from whatever source including compensation for services."[569]

In upholding a statute which transferred excess funds in the hail insurance revolving fund to the state equalization fund to be expended for schools, Justice A. M. Christianson, for the Court, declared:

> The very idea that an excess or surplus which is not needed for the purpose for which it has been raised must lie idle and unused and that the Legislature must impose additional tax burdens upon the taxpayers to meet necessary governmental expenses when such burdens can be obviated by an appropriation of the surplus or excess is in conflict with the object that . . . [this section] of the Constitution is intended to accomplish.[570]

Justice A. G. Burr disagreed and dissented. He argued that the decision was "based on the fallacy that the purpose for which the money is raised has been accomplished."[571] "The hail insurance department," he pointed out, "has not been wound up. It does not cease to exist. The state is not going out of the business of insuring crops against hail. The purpose for which the fund was raised is still in existence."[572]

But the Court struck down a legislative attempt to transfer funds from the Permanent Hail Surplus Fund to the Real Estate Bond Interest Payment Fund. In referring to the Permanent Hail Surplus Fund, the Court declared: "This fund is raised by a tax, a constitutional tax. It is a constitutional fund appropriated for a specific purpose, and can be used in no other way. The appropriation, or the loaning, of the fund for any other purpose would violate . . . [this section] of the Constitution, which provides that every law imposing a tax shall state distinctly the object of the same to which only it shall be applied."[573]

The courts have been confronted with the question of whether license fees for certain occupations are taxes and therefore must comply with the provisions of this section. In *Ex parte Bryan*[574] the Supreme Court considered whether the licensing of taxicabs was a tax and therefore a violation of Section 3. Justice

---

569 State v. Benson, 376 N.W.2d 36, 40 (1985).

570 State v. Hopton, 265 N.W. 395, 402 (1936).

571 Id., p. 408.

572 Id. The Supreme Court upheld diversion of funds in Stinson v. Thorson, 158 N.W. 351 (1916) transfer of funds from teachers' fund to the general school fund; State v. Hauge, 164 N.W. 289 (1917) transfer of funds from the county tuition fund to the STATE TEACHERS' INSURANCE AND RETIREMENT FUND.

573 Brye v. Dale, 250 N.W. 99, 104 (1933).

574 264 N.W. 539 (1936).

James Morris responded for the Court: "The petitioners contend that the fees required are excessive and unreasonable for the purposes of regulation and must therefore be considered to constitute a tax. The record here submitted discloses nothing which supports this contention. The fees are not so large as to be per se excessive. The presumption is that such regulatory fees are reasonable until the contrary appears."[575]

When the Legislature increased court filing fees, several individuals brought legal action contesting the legality of such fees. The complainants argued that the fees were taxes and therefore must comply with Section 3. The Supreme Court agreed, but concluded that the Legislature had specifically provided what the increase in fees was to be used for. Justice Alvin C. Strutz wrote for the Court: "The law specifically states the object of the tax. It provides that all funds received under its provisions 'shall be used for legal research and education, and supervision and improvement of the judicial system of the state of North Dakota.'"[576]

The Court reached the same conclusion when it upheld a $50 fee for filing an action for divorce, the proceeds from which were specifically designated for a "'displaced homemaker program.'"[577] Although the Legislature specifically stated that at "'least ninety-five percent of the funds appropriated . . . must be used . . . for the direct provision of displaced homemaker services,'"[578] that did not make the tax unconstitutional.

ALL TAXABLE PROPERTY . . . SHALL BE ASSESSED . . . [WHERE] IT IS SITUATED

Section 4. All taxable property except as hereinafter in this section provided, shall be assessed in the county, city, township, village or district in which it is situated, in the manner prescribed by law. The property, including franchises of all railroads operated in this state, and of all express companies, freight line companies, dining car companies, sleeping car companies, car equipment companies, or private car line companies, telegraph or telephone companies, the property of any person, firm or corporation used for the purpose of furnishing electric light, heat or power, or in distributing the same for public use, and the property of any other corporation, firm or individual now or hereafter operating in this state, and used directly or indirectly in the carrying of persons, property or messages, shall be assessed by the state board of equalization in a manner prescribed by such state board or commission as may be provided by law. But should any railroad allow any portion of its railway to be used for any purpose other than the operation of a railroad thereon, such portion of its railway, while so used shall be assessed in a manner provided for the assessment of other real property.

---

575 Id., p. 541.

576 Menz v. Coyle, 117 N.W.2d 290, 298 (1962).

577 Gange v. Clerk of Burleigh Cty. D. Court, 429 N.W.2d 429, 431 (1988).

578 Id., p. 435.

In *State v. Taylor*,[579] the Court was confronted with the argument that it was unconstitutional for the government to spend tax receipts in a municipality other than the one in which the taxes were levied. To this argument, the Court responded:

> But we are aware of no constitutional requirement that taxes levied for a general purpose must be expended and disbursed in the taxing district in which they were collected. If this were true, every department, not only of the state, but also of county, government, would soon cease to operate.[580]

In reaching this decision, the Court upheld a state bonding fund to cover county, city, village, school district, and township officers with the premiums to be paid by each of these government entities.

Although this section speaks in terms of assessing property for taxation purposes, the Supreme Court has upheld a license tax on automobiles in lieu of other taxes,[581] and an income tax.[582] "The income tax," Justice A. M. Christianson wrote, "is a charge against the taxpayer and is not a charge upon any specific property. [This section] of the Constitution applies only to taxes levied upon real property as such and has no application to taxes that are levied upon income resulting in whole or in part upon real property."[583]

Railroads have had mixed results in their attempts to have their taxes declared unconstitutional under this section. When the Board of Equalization assessed the taxes of the Northern Pacific Ry. Co. for 1939, the railroad sought to have the assessment set aside, but the Supreme Court refused to do so. "The Constitution," the Court declared,

> makes no provision for an appeal from, or review of, the determinations made by the State Board of Equalization in making assessments under . . . [this section] of the Constitution. Hence, all honest determinations of the Board, within the scope of its authority are final. . . . Courts may . . . inquire whether a determination is fraudulent, and set it aside for fraud; but a determination of the Board is binding upon the courts unless it is shown clearly that the determination was made fraudulently, or in such wrongful arbitrary or capricious manner as to constitute in effect fraud in law or an act in excess of jurisdiction.[584]

When the Board of Equalization used a 7 percent capitalization rate in determining the value of the Soo Line Railroad Company's property for tax purposes, the railroad appealed, arguing that the rate was unrealistic and improper.

---

[579] 156 N.W. 561 (1916).

[580] Id., p. 576.

[581] State v. Wetz, 168 N.W. 835 (1918).

[582] State v. Nichols, 265 N.W. 859 (1935).

[583] Id., p. 876.

[584] Northern Pac. Ry. Co v. State, 299 N.W. 696, 699–700 (1941).

The Supreme Court agreed and wrote: "The use of a higher percentage of assessed value for centrally assessed property than that which is used for locally assessed property is impermissible."[585] The Court, however, let stand the assessment already made, but required the Board of Equalization to make its rates uniform beginning with the 1981 taxable year.

Whether a pipeline was part of the real estate and therefore subject to local assessment, or whether it was separated from the land and therefore taxable by the Board of Equalization was the question before the Court in *Phillips Nat. Gas. Co. v. State Board of Equalization.*[586] District Judge Donald L. Jorgensen had held that the pipelines were real property and therefore subject to local taxation. The Supreme Court disagreed, and reversed.

Writing for the Court, Justice Herbert L. Meschke declared: "We therefore conclude that the pipeline systems operated by the plaintiffs fall within the phrase, 'and the property of any other corporation, firm or individual now or hereafter operating in this state, and used directly or indirectly in the carrying of persons, property or messages.'"[587]

The case of *Northern Pacific Ry. Co. v. Morton County,*[588] presented the Court with the question to what extent can railroad property that is being "used for any purpose other than the operation of a railroad thereon" be taxed by local taxing authorities. At issue was the taxation of elevators, lumberyards, and oil tank stations located on railroad property. The railroad argued that because its right of way was assessed and taxed by the State Board of Equalization, counties could not tax these sites. The Supreme Court, however, disagreed and pointed out that this section specifically requires that railway property not used for railway purposes be "assessed in a manner provided for the assessment of other real property."

In referring to this section and Section 5, Justice E. B. Goss pointed out:

> These constitutional provisions recognize that a roadbed of a railroad may be applied to two uses: First, the railroad use in the strict sense of the term for which the railroad must hold its right of way intact as a public carrier to fulfill its duty under its charter and grant of roadway, and which may be assessed in its entirety as railroad property devoted to railroad use. . . . And these sections of the Constitution contemplate a second and subordinate right of user under permission and by others; a temporary use, as compared with the permanent railroad use, other than for railroad purposes. Otherwise . . . [the last part of Section 4] was wholly unnecessary.[589]

---

585 Soo Line Railroad Company v. State, 286 N.W.2d 459, 465 (1979).

586 402 N.W.2d 906 (1987).

587 Id., p. 909.

588 156 N.W. 226 (1915).

589 Id., p. 231.

The Court also held that requiring those leasing the railroad's property for an elevator, lumberyard, or oil tank station to pay taxes to the county, even though the railroad right of way was being taxed by the state, was not double taxation.

> While the property as right of way is taxed to the railroad upon a basis of railroad user by the power authorized to assess for such purposes, it is as against the railroad strictly a railroad tax. But the tax levied for the use made and against the lessee upon the site as for property "not taxed in the same manner as other property" is a tax against the property possessed by the tenant. It is not the same class of tax. Nor is the same property taxed.[590]

TAXES SHALL BE UNIFORM UPON THE SAME CLASS OF PROPERTY

> **Section 5.** Taxes shall be uniform upon the same class of property including franchises within the territorial limits of the authority levying the tax. The legislative assembly may by law exempt any or all classes of personal property from taxation and within the meaning of this section, fixtures, buildings and improvements of every character, whatsoever, upon land shall be deemed personal property. The property of the United States, to the extent immunity from taxation has not been waived by an act of Congress, property of the state, county, and municipal corporations, to the extent immunity from taxation has not been waived by an act of the legislative assembly, and property used exclusively for schools, religious, cemetery, charitable or other public purposes shall be exempt from taxation. Except as restricted by this article, the legislative assembly may provide for raising revenue and fixing the situs of all property for the purpose of taxation. Provided that all taxes and exemptions in force when this amendment is adopted shall remain in force until otherwise provided by statute.

The first case in which the Supreme Court interpreted this section involved a state law permitting a county to enter on its tax list the amount of unpaid seed liens made by the county to farmers. The law made the lien a tax upon the farmer's land and became a first lien upon the grain raised.[591] In commenting upon the application of this section, Chief Justice Guy C. H. Corliss declared: "Practically every state constitution embodies a provision for uniformity in taxation. The great purpose of such articles is to prevent unjust discrimination in taxation. Whenever there is a tax violative of the terms of such a provision, we must expect to find the tax an unjust one."[592] Furthermore, the Chief Justice wrote:

> And yet no one can pretend that there is any uniformity in a system of taxation that imposes upon one or a few citizens, and upon his or her property, in addition to the

[590] Id., p. 232.

[591] Yeatman v. King, 51 N.W. 721, 722 (1892).

[592] Id., p. 723.

> burden resting upon all alike, an additional sum as a tax. We must therefore conclude that which creates a plain violation of the terms of such a fundamental provision, if regarded as a tax, and yet bears no semblance to unjust discrimination, cannot possibly be a tax at all.[593]

In discussing this section's requirement that taxes be uniform, the Court has written:

> Uniformity of taxation is demanded by . . . our constitution. . . . It has ever been the aim of the legislature to realize this universal demand of constitutional law. Nevertheless, absolute uniformity and equality in taxation has ever remained a Utopian project—accessible in theory, but never reached in practice. Inequalities and injustice in taxation, more or less pronounced, always have existed, and, from the necessities of the cause, it would seem that they must exist. But this has not generally been supposed sufficient to invalidate a tax. If it were, the collection of revenue would instantly and permanently cease.[594]

An example of the "inequalities and injustice" in taxation is the case of *Minneapolis & Northern Elevator Co. v. Trail County*,[595] wherein the Court upheld a tax levied against an elevator for the grain held therein even though the elevator did not own the grain. In response to the argument that the Legislature had no authority to levy this tax, the Court declared: "There is no constitutional provision which makes it imperative that it [the tax] be assessed against the owner."[596]

When the Legislature established a tax of 3 cents on each acre of land containing lignite coal and other minerals, the Supreme Court declared the law unconstitutional as a violation of this section. What concerned the justices was the fact that the tax rate of 3 cents an acre had no relation to the value of the minerals on the land. Writing for the Court, Justice John Burke pointed out: "Each tract sold, upon which the mineral rights are reserved, is taxed the same as every other tract, regardless of the value or kind or amount of mineral, or whether there is any mineral at all. Mineral reserves of gold, if any, or oil, would pay 3 cents an acre the same as mineral reserves of lignite coal or mineral of even less or of no value."[597] Furthermore, the Justice declared: "To be uniform property taxes must be laid with regard to the value, or some other characteristic of the property which justifies a classification. The tax in question is not uniform upon the

---

[593] Id. See also: Strand v. Marin, 152 N.W. 280 (1915); Davis v. McLean County, 204 N.W. 459 (1925); Federal Farm Mortgage Corp. v. Falk, 270 N.W. 885 (1936).

[594] Shattuck v. Smith, 69 N.W. 5, 6 (1896).

[595] 82 N.W. 727 (1900).

[596] Id., p. 728.

[597] Northwestern Improvement Co. v. State, 220 N.W. 436, 439 (1928).

same class of property in the taxing territory as required . . . [by this section] of the Constitution and is therefore void."[598]

Not all classifications of property which may result in different taxation are a violation of this section. For example, the Supreme Court upheld the taxation of "real property" which included machinery and equipment used for refining oil and gas and sugar beets. District Judge Eugene A. Burdick had held the law to be a violation of this section because the tax law did not include "the machinery and equipment of other processors of raw materials such as lignite coal or potatoes."[599]

The Supreme Court characterized this section as having the same meaning as the Equal Protection Clause of the Fourteenth Amendment to the U.S. Constitution. "This restriction," the Court declared, "does not require the adoption of an iron rule of equal taxation or prevent differences in taxation or discretion in the selection of subjects or reasonable classifications of subjects for taxation."[600]

Acting pursuant to the second clause of this section, the Legislature has adopted legislation exempting 39 different interests from taxation.[601]

Because this section exempts property of federal, state, and local governments from taxation, the requirement of uniformity in taxation does not apply. In explaining this exemption, the Supreme Court has written: "State land is not in the same class as privately owned land. The constitutional provision [of uniformity] is not violated by the withdrawal of State land from taxation. As State land it may lie dormant for decades, and yet the privately owned land situated within the taxing district be subjected to tax burden for the purpose of carrying on governmental purposes in school and township government. As soon as sold the land goes on the tax list."[602]

Questions have been raised as to the point in time when property becomes state property and is therefore exempt from taxation. The Court gave this answer to the question: "Taxes levied and not due are not liens upon the real estate, and after the State acquires title to the land, no tax lien can attach so long as the State holds it. It is not subject to taxation, and the taxes that ordinarily thereafter would have become due can not exist. Therefore such taxes must be cancelled and abated of record."[603]

The Legislature has enacted legislation to implement this section's exemption for "property used exclusively for . . . religious, . . . charitable or other public

---

[598] Id., p. 440. See also: Northwestern Imp. Co. v. Morton County, 47 N.W.2d 543 (1951).

[599] Signal Oil and Gas Company v. Williams County, 206 N.W.2d 75, 81 (1973).

[600] Id., pp. 81–82.

[601] NDCC Section 57-02-08. Property exempt from taxation.

[602] State v. Towner County, 283 N.W. 63, 68 (1938).

[603] State v. Divide County, 283 N.W. 184, 190 (1938).

purposes."[604] In *Lutheran Campus Council v. Board of County Commissioners, Ward County*,[605] the question before the Court was whether property owned by the Lutheran Campus Council and occupied by a minister who worked full time counseling students and faculty at a state college was exempt from taxation as being used for religious purpose. The Court held that the property was tax exempt, under two subsections of the statute. "It is exempt under subsection 7," the Court noted, "as a dwelling belonging to a religious organization intended or ordinarily used for the residence of a minister in charge of the services of the church.... It is exempt under subsection 9 as a dwelling intended and ordinarily used for the residence of a minister in charge of religious services of the religious corporation."[606]

The mere fact that property may be owned by a charitable institution does not automatically entitle it to a tax exemption. That was the Court's decision in *Y.M.C.A. of N.D. State Univ. v. Board of County Com'rs.*[607] In this case, the YMCA owned and operated two apartment buildings for students on the campus of North Dakota State University, Fargo. In upholding the denial of a tax exemption, the Court pointed out: "From the facts disclosed by the record, the apartments are not devoted to charitable purposes and are not used in carrying out the charitable purposes of the University YMCA."[608]

This section applies to property taxation but does not apply to other kinds of taxation. For example, it does not apply to special assessments,[609] occupations tax,[610] income tax,[611] or the tax on operating receipts of telephone companies.[612]

Two other kinds of taxes for which this section does not apply are automobile license fees,[613] and fees for filing actions in the courts, even though the fees were given to the State Bar Association for "legal research and education, and for supervision and improvement of the judicial system of the State of North Dakota."[614]

ASSEMBLY MAY PROVIDE FOR . . . AN ANNUAL POLL TAX

Section 6. The legislative assembly may provide for the levy, collection and disposition of an annual poll tax of not more than one dollar and fifty cents on every male

[604] NDCC Section 57-02-08.

[605] 174 N.W.2d 362 (1970).

[606] Id., p. 366.

[607] 198 N.W.2d 241 (1972).

[608] Id., p. 247.

[609] Rolph v. City of Fargo, 76 N.W. 242, 245 (1898). See also: Gallaher v. City of Fargo, 64 N.W.2d 444 (1954); Chernick v. City of Grand Forks, 210 N.W.2d 73 (1973).

[610] In re Lipschitz, 95 N.W. 157 (1903).

[611] State v. Nichols, 265 N.W. 859 (1935).

[612] Souris River Telephone Mutual Aid Corp. v. State, 162 N.W.2d 685 (1968).

[613] State v. Kromarek, 52 N.W.2d 713 (1952).

[614] Menz v. Coyle, 117 N.W.2d 290, 294 (1962).

inhabitant of this state over twenty-one and under fifty years of age, except paupers, idiots, insane persons and Indians not taxed.

There is no poll tax in North Dakota. If the state were to adopt a poll tax, the Twenty-Fourth Amendment to the U. S. Constitution would prohibit such a tax in elections involving the president, vice president, senators, or representatives in Congress.

LEGISLATURE MAY BY LAW PROVIDE FOR . . . AN ACREAGE TAX ON LANDS WITHIN THE STATE

Section 7. The legislature may by law provide for the levy and collection of an acreage tax on lands within the state in addition to the limitations specified in article X, section 1, of the constitution. The proceeds of such tax shall be used to indemnify the owners of growing crops against damages by hail, provided that lands used exclusively for public roads, rights of way of common carriers, mining, manufacturing or pasturage may be exempt from such tax.

Section 8. The legislative assembly shall pass all laws necessary to carry out the provisions of this article.

Section 9. The legislative assembly may provide for the levy of a tax upon lands within the state for the purpose of creating a fund to insure the owners of growing crops against losses by hail. The legislative assembly may classify lands within the state, and divide the state into districts on such basis as shall seem just and necessary, and may vary the tax rates in such districts in accordance with the risk, in order to secure an equitable distribution of the burden of the tax among the owners of such lands.

In 1919, the Legislature implemented these sections by adopting the State Hail Insurance Act and creating the State Hail Insurance Department.[615] In 1967, the Legislature repealed the Act and the State Hail Insurance Department was abolished.[616]

THERE SHALL BE . . . LEVIED . . . ONE MILL . . . UPON . . . TAXABLE PROPERTY [FOR] THE . . . STATE MEDICAL CENTER

Section 10.

1. Upon the adoption of this amendment to the Constitution of the State of North Dakota there shall be annually levied by the state of North Dakota one mill upon all of the taxable property located within the state of North Dakota which, when

[615] State v. Nestos, 187 N.W. 233 (1922).

[616] See: Chapter 232 Session Laws 1967 and Chapter 244 Session Laws 1977.

collected, shall be covered into the state treasury of the state of North Dakota and placed to the credit of the North Dakota state medical center at the university of North Dakota; said fund shall be expended as the legislature shall direct for the development and maintenance necessary to the efficient operation of the said North Dakota state medical center.

2. This amendment shall be self-executing, but legislation may be enacted to facilitate its operation.

Acting pursuant to Section 10, the Legislature has created the North Dakota State Medical Center at the University of North Dakota, Grand Forks.[617]

MOTOR FUEL EXCISE AND LICENSE TAXATION . . . SHALL BE . . . USED SOLELY FOR CONSTRUCTION OF . . . PUBLIC HIGHWAYS

Section 11. Revenue from gasoline and other motor fuel excise and license taxation, motor vehicle registration and license taxes, except revenue from aviation gasoline and unclaimed aviation motor fuel refunds and other aviation motor fuel excise and license taxation used by aircraft, after deduction of cost of administration and collection authorized by legislative appropriation only, and statutory refunds, shall be appropriated and used solely for construction, reconstruction, repair and maintenance of public highways, and the payment of obligations incurred in the construction, reconstruction, repair and maintenance of public highways.

In order to have funds available for highway construction, the people approved an initiated measure authorizing the State Highway Department to issue and sell highway revenue anticipation certificates redeemable out of taxes on motor fuels. Being of the opinion that this procedure for financing highway construction violated this section of the constitution, H. E. Syvertson brought an action against Highway Commissioner N. Owen Jones seeking to prevent him from issuing the certificates. Judge Fred Jansonius upheld the initiative and the Supreme Court affirmed.

"Clearly the people intended by . . . [this section]" the Court declared, "to make the scope broad enough to include such device as the one adopted here—the issuance and sale of certificates of indebtedness. The initiative measure specifically limits expenditures to the construction, and reconstruction and the payment of any obligation arising from such construction, and reconstruction."[618]

This section's requirement that highway funds be "used solely for construction, reconstruction, repair and maintenance of public highways," has spawned

---

[617] NDCC Chapter 15-52. STATE MEDICAL CENTER.

[618] State v. Jones, 23 N.W.2d 54, 62 (1946).

some litigation. For example, the Court has upheld the expenditure of funds for constructing a new highway approach to a bridge over the Yellowstone River in McKenzie County, even though the approach was not part of the state highway system. The Court was of the opinion that the expenditure of these funds was consistent with the section's requirement that funds be used for "maintenance of public highways."[619]

The Court has also upheld the use of highway funds to reimburse a telephone company for the cost of relocating telephone facilities in connection with highway improvement projects;[620] the purchase of sign control rights outside of the access right of way to a highway;[621] and for the payment for a bridge or culvert over a drainage ditch which crossed a highway.[622]

ALL PUBLIC MONEYS . . . SHALL BE PAID OVER . . . TO THE STATE TREASURER

Section 12.

1. All public moneys, from whatever source derived, shall be paid over monthly by the public official, employee, agent, director, manager, board, bureau, or institution of the state receiving the same, to the state treasurer, and deposited by him to the credit of the state, and shall be paid out and disbursed only pursuant to appropriation first made by the legislature; provided, however, that there is hereby appropriated the necessary funds required in the financial transactions of the Bank of North Dakota, and required for the payment of losses, duly approved, payable from the state hail insurance fund, state bonding fund, and state fire and tornado fund, and required for the payment of compensation to injured employees or death claims, duly approved, payable from the workmen's compensation fund, and required for authorized investments made by the board of university and school lands, and required for the financial operations of the state mill and elevator association, and required for the payment of interest and principal of bonds and other fixed obligations of the state, and required for payments required by law to be paid to beneficiaries of the teachers' insurance and retirement fund, and required for refunds made under the provisions of the Retail Sales Tax Act, and the State Income Tax Law, and the State Gasoline Tax Law, and the Estate and Succession Tax Law, and the income of any state institution derived from permanent trust funds, and the funds allocated under the law to the state highway department and the various counties for the construction, reconstruction, and maintenance of public roads.

---

[619] McKenzie County v. Lamb, 298 N.W. 241 (1941).

[620] Northwestern Bell Telephone Co. v. Wentz, 103 N.W.2d 245 (1960).

[621] Newman v. Hjelle, 133 N.W.2d 549 (1965).

[622] Brenna v. Hjelle, 161 N.W.2d 356 (1968).

This constitutional amendment shall not be construed to apply to fees and moneys received in connection with the licensing and organization of physicians and surgeons, pharmacists, dentists, osteopaths, optometrists, embalmers, barbers, lawyers, veterinarians, nurses, chiropractors, accountants, architects, hairdressers, chiropodists, and other similarly organized, licensed trades and professions; and this constitutional amendment shall not be construed to amend or repeal existing laws or Acts amendatory thereof concerning such fees and moneys.

2. No bills, claims, accounts, or demands against the state or any county or other political subdivision shall be audited, allowed, or paid until a full itemized statement in writing shall be filed with the officer or officers whose duty it may be to audit the same, and then only upon warrant drawn upon the treasurer of such funds by the proper officer or officers.

3. This amendment shall become effective on July 1, 1939.

Early in the state's history, the Supreme Court considered this section's requirement that public moneys be paid out "only pursuant to appropriation first made by the legislature." At the time, the Court was considering the validity of a statute providing for a reward of fifty dollars "to any person . . . for the arrest and conviction of each and every person who violates" certain provisions of the law. In concluding that the statute was not an appropriation of funds, the Court wrote: "The purpose of limiting by law the amount which may be expended for a definite purpose, and requiring that it be stated in the act relating to the particular subject, is to enable the Legislature and state officials to approximate in advance the total amount of appropriations made so they be kept within the power of the state to pay."[623]

"[W]e think an appropriation," the Court declared, "in the sense that word is used in our Constitution, is the setting apart from the public revenue of a definite sum of money for the specified object in such a manner that the officials of the government are authorized to use the amount so set apart, and no more, for that object."[624]

The Court has examined a number of different kinds of expenditures made by the state to determine whether such expenditures were required to be appropriated by the Legislature. Some of those which the Court held did not require a specific appropriation include payments from hail insurance fund,[625] state bonding fund,[626] workers' compensation fund,[627] and the allocation of gas tax

---

623 State v. Holmes, 123 N.W. 884, 886 (1909).

624 Id., pp. 886–887.

625 State v. Jorgenson, 150 N.W. 565 (1915).

626 State v. Taylor, 156 N.W. 561 (1916).

627 State v. Olson, 175 N.W. 714 (1919).

receipts.[628] In *Menz v. Coyle,*[629] the Court held that court filing fees could be paid to the State Bar Association for use in legal research and education, but the Bar Association was required to get approval of the Legislature before the funds could be disbursed.

The Court reached a different conclusion when it held that fees for brand inspection and registration were public funds and therefore were required to be deposited in the state treasury. The Legislature had given the Stockman's Association the responsibility of monitoring brands and provided that the fees therefrom were to be paid to the Association for their services.

Writing for the Supreme Court, Justice Dale V. Sandstrom, quoting from a previous case involving the duties of the Stockman's Association, pointed out:

> "In this instance, the State of North Dakota, through the North Dakota Stockman's Association, is selling neither a commodity nor a service in trade or business. It is in competition with no one. It is exercising purely a governmental function in policing the sale of livestock in the state through having inspectors inspect livestock for brand markings. No one other than the State of North Dakota, through the North Dakota Stockman's Association, has been authorized to do such inspecting and make charge therefor."[630]

The Court also held that special assessments for street improvements levied against property of North Dakota State University required an appropriation by the Legislature before they could be paid. "Very few state agencies or departments," Justice Paul M. Sand wrote, "are legally capable of generating funds to pay for special assessments. The great majority are dependent upon appropriations by the Legislature for all expenditures. We must assume that the Legislature was aware that NDSU does not have any funds, other than those appropriated, for the payment of special assessments."[631]

This section specifically provides for payment of refunds under the Retail Sales Act, the State Income Tax Law, the State Gasoline Tax Law, and the Estate and Succession Tax Law. In *Ford Motor Co. v. Baker,*[632] the Court held that the

---

[628] Department of State Highways v. Baker, 290 N.W. 257 (1940). See also: King v. Baker, 299 N.W. 247 (1941).

[629] Menz v. Coyle, 117 N.W.2d 290 (1962). See also: Gange v. Clerk of Burleigh Cty. D. Court, 429 N.W.2d 429 (1988). The Court also upheld a contingent fee arrangement which the attorney general made with attorneys who participated in a lawsuit in which the state brought an action for damages for asbestos installed in public buildings. (State v. Hagerty, 580 N.W.2d 139 (1988).

[630] Billey v. North Dakota Stockman's Ass'n., 579 N.W.2d 171, 175 (1998).

[631] City of Fargo, Cass County v. State, 260 N.W.2d 333, 338 (1977).

[632] 300 N.W. 435 (1941). See also: Boe v. Steele County, 19 N.W.2d 921 (1945) overpayment of estate taxes.

Ford Motor Co. was entitled to a refund of income taxes without a legislative appropriation covering such refund.

NO FURTHER INDEBTEDNESS SHALL BE INCURRED BY THE STATE UNLESS EVIDENCED BY A BOND ISSUE

> **Section 13.** The state may issue or guarantee payment of bonds, provided that all bonds in excess of two million dollars shall be secured by first mortgage upon real estate in amounts not to exceed sixty-five percent of its value; or upon real or personal property of state-owned utilities, enterprises, or industries, in amounts not exceeding its value, and provided further, that the state shall not issue or guarantee bonds upon property of state-owned utilities, enterprises, or industries in excess of ten million dollars.
>
> No further indebtedness shall be incurred by the state unless evidenced by a bond issue, which shall be authorized by law for certain purposes, to be clearly defined. Every law authorizing a bond issue shall provide for levying an annual tax, or make other provision, sufficient to pay the interest semiannually, and the principal within thirty years from the date of the issue of such bonds and shall specially appropriate the proceeds of such tax, or of such other provisions to the payment of said principal and interest, and such appropriation shall not be repealed nor the tax or other provisions discontinued until such debt, both principal and interest, shall have been paid. No debt in excess of the limit named herein shall be incurred except for the purpose of repelling invasion, suppressing insurrection, defending the state in time of war or to provide for the public defense in case of threatened hostilities.

This section was amended in 1918 to permit the Legislature to issue up to $2 million in bonds which need not be "secured by a first mortgage upon real estate." In 1919, the Legislature authorized the issuance of $2 million in bonds to establish the Bank of North Dakota. Secretary of State Thomas Hall, however, refused to issue more than $1,588,000 of said bonds because he was of the opinion that amount plus the state's present debt of $412,000, making a total of $2 million, was all the indebtedness permitted by this section. The Supreme Court disagreed and approved the issuance of the full $2 million in bonds.

Writing for the Court, Justice Richard H. Grace pointed out:

> As we view the matter, the existing indebtedness was not intended to be included in . . . [this section] there being no expressed statement to that effect included therein. In order to include existing indebtedness . . . [this section] should have expressly so stated. It not having expressly so stated, we are of the opinion and so hold that the $2,000,000 of bonds which the state may issue or guarantee the payment of are in addition to the existing indebtedness.[633]

[633] State v. Hall, 173 N.W. 763, 765 (1919).

In 1944, by the initiative process, the people approved a highway construction law that permitted the state to issue "'highway revenue anticipation certificates in a total aggregate amount not exceeding twelve million three hundred sixty thousand dollars ($12,360,000.00).'"[634]

The state, acting on behalf of H. E. Syvertson, brought an action seeking to have the law declared unconstitutional. One of the arguments made against the law was that it violated that part of this section providing that "further indebtedness shall be incurred by the state . . . [only if] evidenced by a bond issue."

The Supreme Court, in upholding the law, declared: "Where a law provides for public utilities or improvements, for a revenue therefrom and that all indebtedness created is payable solely from that revenue and not from state taxation this indebtedness is not taken into consideration in determining the debt limit of the state or municipality."[635] This theory is called the "'special fund doctrine'"[636]

The Court did not apply this doctrine in *State ex rel. Lesmeister v. Olson*[637] when it struck down legislation authorizing the issuance of bonds to finance a pipeline to bring water from the Missouri River to the water-short southwestern part of the state. These pipeline bonds were to be paid from the money produced by the oil extraction tax rather than from any revenue generated by the project.

The Court wrote:

> We believe that allowing a special fund exemption for bonds funded from excise taxes would, in effect, nullify the debt limitation and remove the protections which the people of the State of North Dakota reserved unto themselves in Article X, Section 13, of the Constitution. We hold that bonds funded by any general State tax, excise or ad valorem, constitute a "debt" of the State within the meaning of the constitutional debt limitation.[638]

STATE MAY ISSUE BONDS . . . TO MAKE LOANS TO . . . CONSTRUCT . . . POWER AND GENERATING . . . FACILITIES

Section 14.

1. Notwithstanding any other provision in the constitution, and for the purpose of promoting the economic growth of the state, the development of its natural resources, and the prosperity and welfare of its people, the state may issue bonds and use the proceeds thereof to make loans to privately or cooperatively owned

---

[634] State v. Jones, 23 N.W.2d 54, 57 (1946).

[635] Id., p. 60.

[636] Id.

[637] 354 N.W.2d 690 (1984).

[638] Id., p. 698.

enterprises to plan, construct, acquire, equip, improve, and extend facilities for converting natural resources into power and generating and transmitting such power, and to acquire real and personal property and water and mineral rights needed for such facilities.

2. The state may issue general obligation bonds for this purpose to an amount which, with all outstanding general obligation bonds, less the amount of all money on hand and taxes in process of collection which are appropriated for their payment, will not exceed five percent of the full and true value of all the taxable property in the state, to be ascertained by the last assessment made for state and county purposes; but nothing herein shall increase or diminish the limitations established by other provisions of the constitution on the amount of bonds therein authorized to be issued.

3. The state may also issue revenue bonds for the purpose of providing part or all of the funds required for any project undertaken under subsection 1, payable solely from sums realized from payments of principal and interest on money loaned for such project, and from other similar projects if so determined by the legislature, and from the liquidation of security given for such payments. Revenue bonds issued for any project shall not exceed the cost thereof, including all expenses reasonably incurred to complete and finance the project, but shall not be subject to any other limitation of amount.

4. The full faith and credit of the state shall be pledged for the prompt and full payment of all bonds issued under subsection 2. Its obligation with respect to bonds issued under subsection 3 shall be limited to prompt and full performance of such covenants as the legislature may authorize to be made respecting the enforcing of the provisions of underlying loan agreements and the segregation, accounting, and application of bond proceeds and of loan payments and other security pledged for the payment of the bonds. All bonds authorized by subsections 1 and 3, inclusive, shall mature within forty years from their respective dates of issue, but may be refunded at or before maturity in such manner and for such term and upon such conditions as the legislature may direct. Any such bonds may, but need not be, secured by mortgage upon real or personal property acquired with the proceeds of the same or any other issue of general obligation or revenue bonds, or upon other property mortgaged by the debtor. Pledges of revenues and mortgages of property securing bonds of any issue may be prior or subordinate to or on a parity with pledges and mortgages securing any other issue of general obligation or revenue bonds, as determined by the legislature from time to time in conformity with any provisions made for the security of outstanding bonds.

5. The legislature shall pass such laws as are appropriate to implement this amendment.

6. If any subsection of this amendment, or any part of a subsection, or any application thereof to particular circumstances should be held invalid for any reason, such invalidity shall not affect the validity of all remaining provisions of this amendment

which may be given effect without that which is declared invalid, as applied to any circumstances and for this purpose all subsections and parts of subsections and applications thereof are declared to be severable.

When the Economic Development Commission approved a $7,000 loan to Minnekota Power Co-operatives, Inc., of Grand Forks to extend the transmission of power generated from the use of lignite coal, Harold J. Kelly sought to prevent the loan from being made. Kelly argued that the loan was not for a public purpose and therefore violated this section. The Court responded:

> The court . . . takes judicial notice of the fact that the vast lignite coal resources underlying the western half of this state have attracted relatively meager amounts of private capital during the first seventy-five years of statehood. Current enterprise in the development of lignite coal as a major natural resource in the generation of electrical energy is largely dependent on loans made to cooperative electric companies by the federal government. The development of a major natural resource of the state for the common good where adequate amounts of private capital are lacking would seem to be the highest order of public purpose.[639]

DEBT . . . SHALL NEVER EXCEED FIVE PER CENTUM UPON THE ASSESSED VALUATION OF THE TAXABLE PROPERTY

Section 15. The debt of any county, township, city, town, school district or any other political subdivision, shall never exceed five per centum upon the assessed value of the taxable property therein; provided that any incorporated city may, by a two-thirds vote, increase such indebtedness three per centum on such assessed value beyond said five per centum limit, and a school district, by a majority vote may increase such indebtedness five percent on such assessed value beyond said five per centum limit; provided also that any county or city by a majority vote may issue bonds upon any revenue-producing utility owned by such county or city, or for the purchasing or acquiring the same or building or establishment thereof, in amounts not exceeding the physical value of such utility, industry or enterprise.

In estimating the indebtedness which a city, county, township, school district or any other political subdivision may incur, the entire amount, exclusive of the bonds upon said revenue-producing utilities, whether contracted prior or subsequent to the adoption of this constitution, shall be included; provided further that any incorporated city may become indebted in any amount not exceeding four per centum of such assessed value without regard to the existing indebtedness of such city for the purpose of constructing or purchasing waterworks for furnishing a supply of water to the inhabitants of such city, or for the purpose of constructing sewers, and

---

639 Kelly v. Guy, 133 N.W.2d 853, 857 (1965).

> for no other purposes whatever. All bonds and obligations in excess of the amount of indebtedness permitted by this constitution, given by any city, county, township, town, school district, or any other political subdivision shall be void.

Much of the litigation relating to this section has dealt with the question whether the issuance of bonds exceeded the limitations contained therein. For example, when the city of Grand Forks sought to issue new bonds to provide funds to redeem existing bonds, the Court concluded that would violate the constitutional debt limit. The Court did not accept the argument that the debt limit would be exceeded only until the prior bonds were paid. Writing for the Court, Chief Justice Guy C. H. Corliss pointed out:

> But it is urged that, inasmuch as their issue will result in only a temporary, and not in a permanent, increase of the city indebtedness, the prohibition of the constitution does not apply. We do not so construe the fundamental law. The language is that the debt shall never exceed the specified percentage of the assessed valuation. One day's continuation of such excess is as much within the condemnation both of the letter and of the spirit of the constitution as a year's continuation thereof.[640]

The Court has been confronted with governmental financing arrangements which are not as clear-cut as in the Grand Forks case above. For example, the Court held that when a school district entered into contracts for the construction of a new school, the debt limit was exceeded even though the payments under the contract were to be made in installments. "After a careful consideration of the question," the Court declared, "we deem the sound rule relating to contracts of the nature of those before us to be that an indebtedness within the meaning of . . . [Section 15] of our Constitution was created against the district at the time these contracts were entered into."[641]

When the contractor in this case brought an action asserting that not being paid for work already done on the school was inequitable, the Court disagreed.

Justice James E. Robinson, however, dissented. He wrote: "No opinion of the court should ever be written with the appearance of cynical indifference to the cause of right and justice. If we must sustain plunder and theft, it should be done with tears and regret."[642]

The Supreme Court has consistently held that indebtedness which is paid out of a special assessment or other specific funds is not to be considered in determining whether a municipality's debt limit has been exceeded.[643]

---

[640] Birkholz v. Dinnie, 72 N.W. 931 (1897).

[641] Anderson v. International School Dist. No. 5, 156 N.W. 54, 57 (1916).

[642] Bartelson v. International School Dist. No. 5, 174 N.W. 78, 80 (1919).

[643] Vallelly v. Board of Park Com'rs., 111 N.W. 615 (1907) special assessments; Lang v. City of Cavalier, 228 N.W. 819, 823 (1930) installation of electrict light plant; Thomas v. McHugh, 256 N.W. 763, 772 (1934) electric light plant; Schrieber v. City of Mohall, 268 N.W. 445, 450 (1936) sewer and waterworks; Marks v. City of Mandan, 296 N.W. 39, 47 (1941) sewer system; Ferch v. Housing Authority of

Some other decisions the Court has made regarding governmental debt limits are: (1) concluding that even if the assessed valuation of the property within a school district shrinks so that the outstanding indebtedness exceeds the debt limit, the indebtedness is still valid;[644] (2) holding that a judgment against a city does not affect the city's indebtedness and therefore does not violate this section;[645] and even though a school district and a municipality have identical boundaries, each has its own debt limit.[646]

POLITICAL SUBDIVISION . . . [MUST] PROVIDE FOR . . . AN ANNUAL TAX . . . TO PAY THE INTEREST AND . . . PRINCIPAL

> **Section 16.** Any city, county, township, town, school district or any other political subdivision incurring indebtedness shall, at or before the time of so doing, provide for the collection of an annual tax sufficient to pay the interest and also the principal thereof when due, and all laws or ordinances providing for the payment of the interest or principal of any debt shall be irreparable until such debt be paid.

In *Marks v. City of Mandan,*[647] the plaintiffs brought an action seeking to require the city of Mandan to levy a tax upon all taxable property in order to pay special assessment warrants which the city could not pay because of a deficiency in the special assessments from which the warrants were supposed to be paid. The city argued that under this section it was required to levy the tax before the warrants were issued and to do so now would be a violation of this section. The Court disagreed, and pointed out that because the warrants were funded with special assessments, there was no city debt until there was a default in these assessments. "If the obligations are to be paid only from special funds," Justice James Morris wrote, "it would be wholly superfluous to also require the levy of an annual tax under the provision of this section of the constitution."[648]

While this section requires the municipality to levy a tax "sufficient to pay the interest and also the principal" of an indebtedness, the Supreme Court has held that the section "does not require that an equal amount be collected each year for the payment of a specific debt."[649] The Court reached this conclusion when several taxpayers in Stutsman County brought an action seeking to secure a reduction in the assessed valuation of their land. In defending against the

---

Cass County, 59 N.W.2d 849, 867 (1953) slum clearance low cost housing; State v. Jones, 23 N.W.2d 54, 60 (1946) highway construction.

[644] Jones v. Brightwood Ind. School Dist. No. 1, 247 N.W. 884, 887 (1933).

[645] G. W. Jones Lumber Co. v. City of Marmath. 272 N.W. 190, 195 (1937).

[646] Baldwin v. Board of Education, 33 N.W.2d 473 (1948).

[647] 296 N.W. 39 (1941).

[648] Id., p. 47.

[649] Werner v. Riebe, 296 N.W. 422, 430 (1941).

reduction, the county argued that such reduction would create a deficiency in the sinking fund established to pay its indebtedness in violation of this section.

"This section," the Court declared, "does not require that an equal amount be collected each year for the payment of a specific debt. . . . It is the constitutional duty of the taxing officials to levy annually such sums as will be reasonably adequate for debt service. If by reason of errors in assessment or other mistakes, too small a sum is collected, the deficit thus occurring does not necessarily render the laws under which it occurs unconstitutional."[650]

In *Pelkey v. City of Fargo*,[651] the Court had before it this question: May a city be required to submit to a vote of the people a repeal of a charter for the issuance of bonds for the construction of a multi-purpose dome facility where the bonds have already been issued and the city has received the funds? The Court's answer: "The City of Fargo incurred a debt when it issued the bonds. Consequently, we agree with the City of Fargo that because the bonds for construction of the dome have been issued the charter provision and implementing ordinance imposing the sales and use tax are irreparable until the bonds have been paid."[652]

Justice Gerald W. VandeWalle dissented. He expressed concern that "[t]he majority opinion would encourage a municipality which may have committed errors in its proceedings to issue bonds with unseeming haste in order to avoid any challenge to the validity of the proceedings although it intends to hold the proceeds in a special fund for some time because it is not yet prepared to proceed with the improvement for which the bonds were issued."[653]

NO BOND . . . IS VALID UNLESS . . . ISSUED PURSUANT TO LAW AND IS WITHIN THE DEBT LIMIT

> **Section 17.** No bond or evidence of indebtedness of the state is valid unless it has endorsed thereon a certificate, signed by the auditor and secretary of state showing that the bond or evidence of debt is issued pursuant to law and is within the debt limit. No bond or evidence of debt of any county, or bond of any township or other political subdivision is valid unless it has endorsed thereon a certificate signed by the officer authorized by law to sign such certificate, stating that said bond or evidence of debt is issued pursuant to law and is within the debt limit.

Kidder County Auditor John C. Taylor refused to issue a warrant for payment of certain fees and expenses of Sheriff Hiram S. Darling because, he argued, the warrant would have caused the debt limit of the county to be exceeded. District Judge W. H. Winchester, however, ordered Taylor to issue the warrant

---

650 Id., p. 430. See also: State v. Rasmusson, 300 N.W. 25, 27 (1941).

651 453 N.W.2d 801 (1990).

652 Id., p. 803.

653 Id., p. 805.

because the county had previously levied taxes sufficient to pay the warrant. The Supreme Court affirmed. "Under the rule of construction which we have concluded to adopt as controlling this case," the Court said, "the indebtedness of Kidder County will not be augmented by issuing the warrant in question, and thereby anticipating the collection of existing tax levies to the amount of such warrant."[654]

THE STATE, ANY COUNTY OR CITY MAY MAKE INTERNAL IMPROVEMENTS AND MAY ENGAGE IN ANY INDUSTRY

> **Section 18.** The state, any county or city may make internal improvements and may engage in any industry, enterprise or business, not prohibited by article XX of the constitution, but neither the state nor any political subdivision thereof shall otherwise loan or give its credit or make donations to or in aid of any individual, association or corporation except for reasonable support of the poor, nor subscribe to or become the owner of capital stock in any association or corporation.

The extent to which a city may engage in business was before the Court in *Gripentrog v. City of Wahpeton.*[655] Justice Alvin C. Strutz gives these facts about the case:

> The City of Wahpeton, in order to secure additional employment for its people and in order to encourage industrial activity and development and to generally improve the welfare of the Wahpeton community, proposes to issue not to exceed $2,000,000 worth of revenue bonds for the acquisition of a site and for construction of a sugar beet processing plant near the city. It then proposes to lease such plant to the defendant Southern Red River Valley Sugarbeet Corporation under authority which it claims is granted to it by . . . the North Dakota Century Code.[656]

Donald M. Gripentrog, believing that the proposed lease to the Sugarbeet Corporation violated this section of the constitution, brought suit against the city. District Judge Clifford Schneller disagreed and the Supreme Court, being of the opinion that the city's proposal was for a "public purpose," upheld Judge Schneller's decision.

This section, Justice Strutz wrote, "does not prohibit the making of loans or giving credit or making donations in connection with a city's engaging in any industry, enterprise, or business. . . . What it does prohibit is for a city 'otherwise' to make loans or give its credit or make donations."[657]

---

654 Darling v. Taylor, 75 N.W. 766, 767 (1898).

655 126 N.W.2d 230 (1964).

656 Id., p. 232.

657 Id., p. 237. For a similar result see: Patterson v. City of Bismarck, 212 N.W.2d 374 (1973).

The state became directly involved in industry when the Legislature created the Bank of North Dakota and the State Mill and Elevator Association in 1919. Referring to the Bank of North Dakota, the Supreme Court has written: "Keeping in mind that it is the purpose of the state of North Dakota to engage in the banking business, and in pursuance of said purpose, has established a system of banking, under the name of the 'Bank of North Dakota,' . . . and that such bank is a state industry or institution."[658]

In approving the establishment of a state mill and elevator, the Court declared: "We are thoroughly convinced that the establishment and maintaining of state-owned elevators and state-owned mills for the marketing and manufacturing of wheat and other small grains produced in the state of North Dakota is a public purpose."[659]

The Court also upheld the action of the Economic Development Commission of North Dakota making a loan of $7,000 to Minnekota Power Co-operatives, Inc., to assist the company in extending its power transmission lines. The Court, finding the same public purpose as in *Gripentrog*, pointed out: "It seems clear that if the state were to engage directly in the business of transmitting power generated by the lignite generation plant as a means of making electric power available to the consuming public, the public purpose test would be met."[660]

The question of whether the government's action is a loan or a grant of its credit or a donation has been before the courts in other types of situations. For example, the Court was forced to consider the legality of the State Teachers' Insurance and Retirement Fund.

In order to provide a retirement system for teachers, the Legislature created a fund to which the teachers and school boards both contributed. In response to the assertion that the school board's participation in this fund violated this section, the Court declared: "As to the teachers' pensions the decisions of the courts are more uniform and favorable to the theory that the payments are not donations but in the nature of added compensation for long and faithful service in the public interest."[661]

In 1929, the Legislature authorized the organization of nonprofit associations to build and maintain dormitories on several of the campuses of state educational institutions.

The state, acting on behalf of Maurice Kaufman, brought an action seeking to have this legislation declared unconstitutional. One of the arguments made against the legislation was that allowing the dormitories to be constructed on

---

[658] Green v. Fraizer, 176 N.W. 11, 15 (1920), affirmed 253 U.S. 233 (1920).

[659] Id., p. 20. See NDCC Chapter 6-09. BANK OF NORTH DAKOTA; and NDCC Section 54-18. North Dakota Mill and Elevator Association.

[660] Kelly v. Guy, 133 N.W.2d 853, 856 (1965).

[661] Payne v. Board of Trustees, 35 N.W.2d 553, 556 (1948). See also: Walker v. Omdahl, 242 N.W.2d 649 (1976) where the Court upheld "inflationary increases in living expenses of state officials."

the campus was a violation of this section. The Supreme Court disagreed. "It is true," Justice A. M. Christianson pointed out,

> the statute permits a portion of the campus to be occupied by a dormitory erected by the institutional holding association; but the dormitory may be operated only for the benefit and use of the educational institution. In short, it may be used only to facilitate the work of that institution. The Legislature has determined that there is such an existent need for a dormitory as to justify the construction thereof upon the terms and conditions prescribed in the act.[662]

Sometimes a close relationship with the government is sufficient to justify the expenditure of public funds and thus not violate this section. Such was the case of *Menz v. Coyle*.[663] At issue in this case was a state law requiring courts to collect a fee when actions are filed in District Courts. The fees collected were then paid to the State Bar Association, which uses the funds for legal research, education, and supervision and improvement of the legal system.

In holding that this section was not violated, Justice Alvin C. Strutz pointed out that while the Bar Association was not a state organization, it was so closely aligned with the government that it really wasn't a private organization either. Justice Strutz wrote:

> Surely an association whose existence is regulated and controlled by law, whose members are made public officers by the Constitution itself, and whose activities are regulated and controlled for the benefit of the public, who can be compelled to represent indigent citizens without pay, and whose members are subject to disbarment for violation of rules and regulations established pursuant to law, cannot be held to be a private association existing only for the benefit of its members.[664]

Sometimes the Legislature has enacted laws which the Court has found to violate this section. For example, in 1943 the Legislature provided that land which the state had acquired through a foreclosure could be sold to the previous owner, his widow, or lineal descendants at a price lower than the actual value. Emmanuel Herr, a prospective purchaser of land, brought an action to prevent the sale to a descendant of the former owner. Among the legal arguments made by Herr was that such a sale would violate this section because he was willing to pay more than the amount which the family members were required to pay under the statute.

The Supreme Court agreed. Herr "insists," the Court said, "that the statute violates . . . [this section] of the Constitution of North Dakota in that it makes a

---

[662] State v. Davis, 229 N.W. 105, 112 (1930).

[663] 117 N.W.2d 290 (1982).

[664] Id., p. 300.

donation to a privileged buyer by enabling him to buy at the appraised value, though others are ready and willing to pay a greater price. We think the contention is well grounded."[665]

The extent to which the state may provide "reasonable support of the poor" was before the Court early in the state's history when in 1890 the Legislature authorized "counties to issue bonds to procure seed grain for needy farmers resident therein."[666]

Attorney General George F. Goodwin brought an action on behalf of the state to prevent Nelson County from issuing bonds to help the county's farmers secure seed grain. After an extensive examination of the law relating to the power of the Legislature to meet the general needs of the poor, the Supreme Court concluded:

> In our opinion, this power [to aid the poor] is conferred in the organic law expressly to meet the exigencies of the situation then existing, and that it is our duty to give it that effect. We believe, and so hold, that the class referred to in the exception contained in . . . [this section] of the state constitution is the poor and destitute farmers of the state, and that the first legislature which met after the state was admitted has, by the seed-grain statute, put a proper construction upon the language in question. We therefore refuse to grant the writ applied for, and hold that the seed-grain statute is a valid enactment.[667]

When considering whether the North Dakota Old Age Assistance Fund violated this section, the Court held: "Need was one of the basic qualifications of an applicant and it was the element of need that brought the Act within the exception of Section . . . [18] of the Constitution which prohibits donations except for the reasonable support of the poor."[668]

ASSEMBLY . . . [MAY] PROVIDE . . . FOR THE . . . OPERATION OF . . . GRAIN ELEVATORS . . . IN MINNESOTA OR WISCONSIN

> **Section 19.** The legislative assembly is hereby authorized and empowered to provide by law for the erection, purchasing or leasing and operation of one or more terminal grain elevators in the states of Minnesota or Wisconsin, or both, to be maintained and operated in such manner as the legislative assembly shall prescribe, and provide for inspection, weighing and grading of all grain received in such elevator or elevators.

---

[665] Herr v. Rudolph, 25 N.W.2d 916, 922 (1947). For a similar case see: Solberg v. State Treasurer, 53 N.W.2d 49 (1952). But see: State v. Amerada Petroleum Corporation, 71 N.W.2d 675 (1955) for a different result.

[666] State v. Nelson County, 45 N.W. 33 (1890).

[667] Id., p. 37.

[668] State v. Borge, 283 N.W. 521, 525–526 (1939).

The Supreme Court has not decided any cases involving this section.

ASSEMBLY IS AUTHORIZED . . . TO PROVIDE . . . FOR THE . . . OPERATION OF ONE OR MORE TERMINAL GRAIN ELEVATORS

> **Section 20.** The legislative assembly is hereby authorized and empowered to provide by law for the erection, purchasing or leasing and operation of one or more terminal grain elevators in the state of North Dakota, to be maintained and operated in such manner as the legislative assembly shall prescribe, and provide for inspection, weighing and grading of all grain received by such elevator or elevators.

This section was discussed by Federal District Judge Charles F. Amidon in 1919 in a case brought by 42 taxpayers to prevent the state from issuing bonds and spending money for, among other things, the erection of grain elevators.[669]

Judge Amidon, in discussing the plight of North Dakota farmers in having to market their products through grain terminals in Minnesota, points out: "There these products pass into the hands of large commission houses, elevator and milling companies and live stock concerns. These interests are combined, not only in corporations, chambers of commerce, boards of trade, and interlocking directorates, but in millions of understandings which arise among men having common interests and living through long terms of years in the daily intercourse of great cities."[670]

This system, Judge Amidon wrote, had an effect upon the people in North Dakota.

> The people have thus come to believe that the evils of the existing system consist, not merely in the grading of grain, its weighing, its dockage, the price paid and the disparity between the price of different grades and the flour-producing capacity of the grain. They believe that the evil goes deeper; that the whole system of shipping the raw materials of North Dakota to these foreign terminals is wasteful and hostile to the best interests of the state.[671]

Judge Amidon then discusses the effect the system had upon the people: "Year by year the conviction deepened, in steadily increasing majorities, that the public ownership of terminal elevators, mills, and packing houses is the only effective remedy to correct the evils from which they believe themselves to be suffering. Their decision is not a popular whim, but a deliberate conviction,

---

[669] Scott v. Frasier, 258 F. 669 (1919), reversed on other grounds, 253 U.S. 243 (1920).

[670] Id., p. 678.

[671] Id., p. 679

arrived at as a result of full discussion and repeated presentations of the subject at polls."[672]

In upholding the constitutionality of this section, Judge Amidon concluded: "It is hopeless to expect a population consisting of farmers scattered over a vast territory as the people of this state are to create any private business system that will change the system now existing. The only means through which the people of the state have had experience in joint action is their state government."[673]

NOT LESS THAN FIFTEEN PERCENT OF THE TAX . . . FOR SEVERING COAL SHALL BE PLACED INTO A PERMANENT TRUST

Section 21. Not less than fifteen percent of the tax imposed for severing coal shall be placed into a permanent trust fund in the state treasury to be held in trust and administered by the board of university and school lands, which shall have full authority to invest said trust funds as provided by law, and may loan moneys from the fund to political subdivisions as provided by law. The interest earned on the moneys in said trust fund shall be used first to replace uncollectible loans made from the fund, and the balance shall be credited to the general fund of the state. Up to fifty percent of the taxes collected and deposited in the permanent trust fund during a biennium may be appropriated by the legislative assembly for lignite research development, and marketing as provided by law. An additional twenty percent of the taxes collected and deposited in the permanent fund during the biennium may be appropriated by the legislative assembly for clean coal demonstration projects approved by the industrial commission.

The Legislature has implemented this section by creating a Coal Severance Tax.[674]

ASSEMBLY MAY PROVIDE . . . FOR A PERCENTAGE . . . FROM TAXES . . . BE . . . CREDITED TO A SPECIAL TRUST FUND

Section 22. The legislative assembly may provide by law for a percentage of revenue from taxes imposed on the extraction or production of oil to be allocated and credited to a special trust fund, to be known as the resources trust fund. The principal and income of the resources trust fund may be expended only pursuant to legislative appropriation for:

1. Constructing water-related projects, including rural water systems, and
2. Funding of programs for energy conservation.

---

[672] Id., pp. 679–680.

[673] Id., p. 680.

[674] NDCC Chapter 57-61. COAL SEVERANCE TAX.

The Legislature has implemented this section by allocating 20 percent of the Oil Extraction Tax Development Fund to water projects and energy conservation.[675]

ASSEMBLY MAY PROVIDE FOR . . . COMPENSATION TO . . . MEMBERS OF THE REGULAR ACTIVE DUTY ARMED FORCES

Section 23. The legislative assembly may provide for the payment of adjusted compensation to North Dakota residents who were members of the regular active duty armed forces and who served in the Persian Gulf theatre or in the Grenada, Lebanon, or Panama areas of armed conflict as designated by the President of the United States or to heirs of North Dakota residents who were members of the regular active duty armed forces and who died while on orders to or from the Persian Gulf theatre or in the Grenada, Lebanon, or Panama areas of armed conflict as designated by the President of the United States. The legislative assembly may provide a direct appropriation or provide for the issuance, sale, and delivery of bonds of the state of North Dakota in such principal amounts as determined by the legislative assembly to be necessary for the payment of adjusted compensation under this section. Adjusted compensation under this section may be paid at such rates, terms of service, and conditions as the legislative assembly provides.

Pursuant to the authority granted under this section, the Legislature has provided that veterans shall be paid $50 for each month of domestic service and $100 for each month of foreign service during Operation Desert Storm. Veterans who had received a Purple Heart were to be paid $2,500 in lieu of the monthly payments. Heirs of deceased veterans were entitled to the payments which the veteran would have received.[676]

TWENTY PERCENT OF THE REVENUE FROM OIL EXTRACTION TAXES . . . MUST BE ALLOCATED AS FOLLOWS

Section 24. Twenty percent of the revenue from oil extraction taxes from taxable oil produced in this state must be allocated as follows:

1. Fifty percent must be deposited in the common schools trust fund.
2. Fifty percent must be deposited in the foundation and stabilization fund in the state treasury, the interest income of which must be transferred to the state general fund on July first of each year. The principal of the foundation and stabilization fund may be expended only upon order of the governor, who may direct such a transfer only to offset foundation aid

[675] NDCC Section 57-51.1-07. Allocation of moneys in oil extraction tax development fund.

[676] NDCC Section 37-26-02. Payment of adjusted compensation for domestic and foreign service.

reductions that were made by executive action pursuant to law due in a revenue shortage.

The Supreme Court has not decided any cases involving this section.

THE VETERANS' POSTWAR TRUST FUND SHALL BE A PERMANENT TRUST FUND OF THE STATE OF NORTH DAKOTA

Section 25. The veterans' postwar trust fund shall be a permanent trust fund of the state of North Dakota and shall consist of moneys transferred or credited to the fund as authorized by legislative enactment. Investment of the fund shall be the responsibility of the state treasurer who shall have full authority to invest the fund only in the same manner as the state investment board is authorized to make investments. All income received from investments is to be utilized for programs which must be of benefit and service to veterans, who are defined by legislative enactment, or their dependents, and such income is hereby appropriated to the administrative committee on veterans' affairs on a continuing basis for expenditure upon those programs selected at the discretion of the administrative committee on veterans' affairs.

The Legislature implemented this section by creating NDCC Chapter 37-14 Veterans' Relief and Rehabilitation. This chapter creates a revolving fund of $700,000 to be "used solely for the purpose of making loans to any veteran . . . and the surviving spouse of a veteran if the spouse has not remarried."[677]

[677] NDCC Section 37-14-03.3 Revolving fund.

Article XI

General Provisions

THE NAME OF THE STATE SHALL BE "NORTH DAKOTA"

Section 1. The name of the state shall be "North Dakota." The state of North Dakota shall consist of all the territory included within the following boundary, to wit: Commencing at a point in the main channel of the Red River of the North, where the forty-ninth degree of north latitude crosses the same; thence south up the main channel of the same and along the boundary line of the state of Minnesota to a point where the seventh standard parallel intersects the same; thence west along said seventh standard parallel produced due west to a point where it intersects the twenty-seventh meridian of longitude west from Washington; thence north on said meridian to a point where it intersects the forty-ninth degree of north latitude; then east along said line to place of beginning.

Section 2. The following described seal is hereby declared to be and hereby constituted the great seal of the state of North Dakota, to wit: A tree in the open field, the trunk of which is surrounded by three bundles of wheat; on the right a plow, anvil and sledge; on the left a bow crossed with three arrows; and an Indian on horseback pursuing a buffalo toward the setting sun; the foliage of the tree arched by a half circle of forty-two stars, surrounded by the motto "Liberty and Union Now and Forever, One and Inseparable"; the words "Great Seal" at the top; the words "State of North Dakota" at the bottom; "October 1st" on the left and "1889" on the right. The seal to be two and one-half inches in diameter.

The Legislature has provided that the secretary of state shall have custody of the "Great Seal,"[678] and made it a crime to use the seal for any political or commercial purpose.[679]

NATURAL WATERCOURSES SHALL FOREVER REMAIN THE PROPERTY OF THE STATE FOR MINING, IRRIGATING AND MANUFACTURING

> **Section 3.** All flowing streams and natural watercourses shall forever remain the property of the state for mining, irrigating and manufacturing purposes.

The Supreme Court was called upon to construe this section in 1896. The Court first pointed out that under common law principles in effect when North Dakota became a state, "the riparian owners in the territory were vested with the specified property rights in the bed of all natural water courses, and in the water itself."[680] Because such rights were protected by the Fourteenth Amendment Due Process Clause, the Court said that this section of the "state constitution would be unconstitutional in so far as it attempted to destroy those vested rights of property."[681] This led the Court to conclude:

> So far as . . . [this section] can have constitutional effect, it should be construed as placing the integrity of our water courses beyond the control of individual owners. Should all the riparian proprietors along the course of a stream so join in the sale of their riparian rights as to work an utter destruction of the stream . . . it might be that the sovereignty of the state could invoke the provision of the constitution against attempted annihilation of the water course.[682]

In addressing the ownership of beds of lakes and streams, the Court has declared:

> When North Dakota became a state it acquired title to lands under all navigable waters within its borders, subject to the limitation of the commerce clause of the federal constitution. . . . Admission to statehood vests no title in the state in the lands underlying non-navigable bodies of water. Title to such lands remained in the federal government or in persons to whom it had transferred title. . . . If before statehood the United States issued an unrestricted grant of land to riparian owners the patentee's title extended to the center of the adjacent non-navigable body of water.[683]

---

678 NDCC Section 54-09-01. Records in custody of the secretary of state.

679 NDCC Section 54-02-01. Great seal—Permitted uses—Penalty for commercial use.

680 Bigelow v. Draper, 69 N.W. 570, 573 (1896).

681 Id.

682 Id.

683 State v. Brace, 36 N.W.2d 330, 332 (1949).

Whether a body of water is navigable or not depends upon facts surrounding its character and use. In finding that Grenora Lake, located in the northwestern corner of the state, was not navigable, the Court wrote:

> There is no evidence that any use ever has been or could be made of the waters of the lake either for pleasure or for profit, for travel, or for trade. No boats were used thereon. The water at all times has been of such a character that it was not habitable for fish. Neither the lake nor its surroundings are suitable for any purposes of pleasure. It is true that aquatic birds sometimes rested on its surface and there is evidence that hunters occasionally shot waterfowl that flew to or from the lake, but this was an infrequent occurrence.[684]

The question of whether Grenora Lake was navigable was of great importance in the dispute over the ownership of the lake bed because the bed consisted of a solid body of sodium sulfate, which, if the lake was navigable, would have belonged to the state.

Because the shorelines of navigable waters sometimes fluctuate, the Court has been called upon to determine the ownership of the land between the high watermark and low watermark. One such case is *State ex rel. Sprynczynatyk v. Mills*.[685] In this case, the riparian landowner claimed ownership of the shoreline to the low watermark while the state asserted the right to the land up to the high watermark.

After an extensive review of legal authorities, Justice William A. Neumann wrote for the Court: "The parties' interests in the shore zone are coexistent and overlap, but in this case no specific right or claim for use of the shore zone is contested. The shore zone presents a complex bundle of correlative, and sometimes conflicting, rights and claims which are better suited for determination as they arise."[686]

Justice Beryl J. Levine, in a concurring opinion, pointed out that: "While I concur in the opinion, and believe we have dutifully counted the angels on the pin, we have left both parties in limbo to speculate over what their 'correlative' rights are and probably to dream the impossible dream about the parameters of those rights."[687]

In placing limitations on the use of waters in the state, the Legislature has provided that: "All waters within the limits of the state . . . belong to the public and are subject to appropriation for beneficial use and the right to the use of these waters for such use must be acquired pursuant to law."[688]

---

684 Ozark-Mahoning Co. v. State, 37 N.W.2d 488, 491 (1949).

685 523 N.W.2d 537 (1994).

686 Id., p. 544.

687 Id., p. 545.

688 NDCC Section 61-01-01.

The Supreme Court has construed this section as creating a public trust. "North Dakota," the Court has written,

> is, in part, a semi-arid State. Therefore, concern for the general welfare could well require that the water resources of the State be put to beneficial use to the fullest extent of which they are capable, and that the waste or unreasonable method of use of water be prevented, and that the conservation of such water be exercised with a view to the reasonable and beneficial use thereof in the interests of the people and the public welfare. We feel that the foregoing factors formed the basis for the legislative enactment of Section 61-01-01, N.D.C.C.[689]

MEMBERS OF THE LEGISLATIVE ASSEMBLY AND JUDICIAL DEPARTMENT. . . . SHALL. . . . TAKE. . . . [AN] OATH

> **Section 4.** Members of the legislative assembly and judicial department, except such inferior officers as may be by law exempted shall, before they enter on the duties of their respective offices, take and subscribe the following oath or affirmation: "I do solemnly swear (or affirm as the case may be) that I will support the Constitution of the United States and the Constitution of North Dakota; and that I will faithfully discharge the duties of the office of ______ according to the best of my ability, so help me God" (if an oath), (under pains and penalties of perjury) if an affirmation, and no other oath, declaration, or test shall be required as a qualification for any office or public trust.

The Primary Election Law of 1907 provided that "the petitions of all . . . candidates for members of the legislative assembly shall contain a pledge to the people that they will support and vote for the candidate of their party, for United States Senator."[690]

Herschel James, a qualified voter, brought an action claiming that this part of the Election Law was unconstitutional as a violation of this section and the Supreme Court agreed.

> The candidate is required by such pledge to obligate himself to discharge certain of his public duties, if elected, in a certain way. He by such pledge divests himself of all discretion and freedom of action in the discharge of a portion of his official duties, if elected. This necessarily operates to hamper and restrict persons in becoming candidates for such office, and is therefore void. . . . We conclude that the requirement of such pledge violates . . . [this section] of our Constitution in that it exacts an additional test in contravention thereof.[691]

---

[689] Baeth v. Hoisveen, 157 N.W.2d 728, 733 (1968).

[690] State v. Blaisdell, 118 N.W. 141, 142 (1908).

[691] Id., pp. 144–145.

The Supreme Court discussed the effect of an oath upon judges in the case of *State v. First State Bank*.[692] The Court wrote that "as a condition precedent to the performance of any official act, each judge is required to take an official oath, whereby he, in the most solemn manner, pledges himself to support the federal and state Constitutions and to faithfully discharge the duties of his office."[693]

Although this section specifically applies to members of the legislative assembly and judicial department, the Legislature has provided that persons elected or appointed to any of the many boards or commissions in the state shall also take an oath prior to taking office. If a person fails to take such an oath, he or she cannot perform the duties of the office to which they were appointed. That was the situation that J. L. Cahill found himself in when he failed to file the oath required of members of the Board of Administration. "This is not a case," the Court declared, "where an officer in qualifying has inadvertently failed to comply literally with the statute, as for instance, by filing a defective oath of office; but this is a case where there was not even an attempt on the part of the officer to qualify within the time prescribed by the statute."[694]

The Supreme Court has interpreted the words "judicial department" in this section to require lawyers to take the oath set forth therein.[695]

MEETINGS OF PUBLIC OR GOVERNMENTAL BODIES. . . . SUPPORTED IN WHOLE OR IN PART BY PUBLIC FUNDS . . . SHALL BE OPEN

Section 5. Unless otherwise provided by law, all meetings of public or governmental bodies, boards, bureaus, commissions, or agencies of the state or of any political subdivision of the state, or organizations or agencies supported in whole or in part by public funds, or expending public funds, shall be open to the public.

The Legislature has implemented this section by providing that "all meetings of a public entity must be open to the public."[696] This code section, however, permits meetings to be closed when no public business is being considered. Governing bodies may also hold executive sessions "to consider or discuss closed or confidential records."[697]

The nonrenewal of teachers' contracts by school boards taking action in private meetings has been before the Supreme Court in several cases. For example, in considering whether to renew the contract of teacher George Peters, the

---

692 202 N.W. 391 (1924).

693 Id., p. 396.

694 State v. Cahill, 193 N.W. 938, 939–940 (1923).

695 Menz v. Coyle, 117 N.W.2d 290, 295 (1962). See also: NDCC Section 27-11-20.

696 NDCC Section 44-04-19. Access to public meetings; and 44-04-19.1 Open records and open meetings—Exemptions for attorney work product, attorney consultation, and negotiation prepration.

697 NDCC Section 44-04-19.2. Confidential or closed meetings.

Bowman Public School District School Board met in an executive session and discussed the issue. Later, during an open meeting, the Board agreed not to renew Peters' contract. The Supreme Court concluded that this procedure was illegal. "When the official action of the school district," Justice Vernon Pederson declared, "is clearly the product of an illegal meeting, documented in the minutes, and not clearly denied in the testimony, such official action is invalid even though such official action is taken at an otherwise legal meeting."[698]

The Supreme Court has not, however, demanded strict compliance with the constitutional and legislative open records requirements in school board decisions regarding renewal of teachers' contracts. For example, the Court refused to condemn secret consultations by Board members held early in contract negotiations between the teachers' organization and the school board, which lasted over a five-month period. The Court was of the opinion that secret consultations were "harmless error."[699] The Court also upheld action by a school board, taken at a public meeting, not to renew a teacher's contract even though the Board had held a prior executive session to discuss teacher evaluations.[700]

RECORDS OF PUBLIC . . . BODIES . . . SHALL BE PUBLIC RECORDS, OPEN AND ACCESSIBLE FOR INSPECTION

> **Section 6.** Unless otherwise provided by law, all records of public or governmental bodies, boards, bureaus, commissions, or agencies of the state or any political subdivision of the state, or organizations or agencies supported in whole or in part by public funds, or expending public funds, shall be public records, open and accessible for inspection during reasonable office hours.

The Legislature implemented this section with the adoption of NDCC Section 44-04-18 Access to Public Records—Electronically Stored Information. This legislation sets forth detailed guidelines for the agencies and organizations subject to the open records requirements. In deciding cases involving open records, the Supreme Court sometimes cites the constitutional requirements and sometimes the statutory requirements and sometimes both.

When S. D. Knutson, former Chief of Police of the City of Grand Forks, became a candidate for County Commissioner of Grand Forks County, a reporter for the *Grand Forks Herald* sought to examine Knutson's personnel file previously maintained by the city. The city, after refusing the reporter's request, commenced legal action to determine whether it was obligated to open Knutson's file to the newspaper. District Judge Kirk Smith held that the

---

[698] Peters v. Bowman Pub. Sch. Dist. No. 1, 231 N.W.2d 817, 820 (1975).

[699] Dickinson Ed. Assn. v. Dickinson Pub. Sch. Dist. No. 1, 252 N.W.2d 205, 213 (1977).

[700] Danroth v. Mandaree Pub. Sch. Dist. No. 36, 320 N.W.2d 780 (1982). See also: Retzlaff v. Grand Forks Pub. Sch. Dist. No. 1, 424 N.W.2d 637 (1988).

municipal personnel files were public records and therefore must be open and available to the press. The Supreme Court agreed. Writing for the Court, Justice William L. Paulson declared: "The City is a political subdivision of the State and, as such, all of its records are public records open for inspection equally to members of the public, which includes the news media. A personnel file maintained by a personnel director of a political subdivision is a public record open to public inspection."[701]

Justices Gerald W. VandeWalle and Paul M. Sand concurred. Writing for both, Justice VandeWalle expressed concern as to the meaning of the word "record" as used in this section of the constitution and in NDCC Section 44-04-18. "By . . . [concurring]," Justice VandeWalle wrote, "I do not imply that every scrap of paper a public official or a pubic employee might retain in the course of his tenure with a public body is a public record."[702]

Justice VandeWalle then suggested that the remedy for those seeking to close personnel files is through the legislative process. In 1987 and 1999, the Legislature responded and enacted legislation defining "Public employee personal, medical and employee assistance records"[703] that are to be confidential.

When the Forum Publishing Company of Fargo, publisher of the newspaper *The Forum*, sought the names and qualifications of applicants for the position of Chief of Police of Fargo, District Judge John Garaas ordered disclosure and the Supreme Court affirmed.[704]

This section of the constitution together with state statutes also require that teachers' personnel files, like those of municipal employees, be open. That was District Judge William F. Hodney's decision, which was affirmed by the Supreme Court.[705]

In responding to teacher Meredith Hovet's argument that an exception should be made for teachers' personnel files, Justice VandeWalle explained: "Thus, for an exception to the open-records law to exist under our constitutional and statutory provisions, it must be specific, i.e., the Legislature must directly address the status of the record in question, for a specific exception, by the plain terms of those provisions, may not be implied."[706]

The Court also denied an exception from the open-records requirements for the records of the Public Service Commission. Citing the *Hovet* case, the Court again pointed out: "There is no specific legislated exception to the open-records

---

[701] City of Grand Forks v. Grand Forks Herald, 307 N.W.2d 572, 578 (1981).

[702] Id., p. 579.

[703] NDCC Section 44-04-18.1. Public employee, personal medical, and employee assistance records—Confidentiality—Personal information maintained by professional boards.

[704] Forum Publishing Co. v. City of Fargo, 391 N.W.2d 169 (1986).

[705] Hovet v. Hebron Pub. Sch. Dist., 419 N.W.2d 189 (1988).

[706] Id., p. 191.

law for public utility contracts that are required by law to be publicly filed which a regulatory agency."[707]

The far-reaching effect of the open-records requirement is illustrated by the case of *Toth v. Disciplinary Bd. of Supreme Court.*[708] Assistant Attorney General JoAnn C. Toth was disciplined by the Disciplinary Board for revealing information contained in a confidential settlement agreement between the State Board of Chiropractic Examiners and Dr. Jeffry T. Vendsel. Dr. Vendsel, who had been charged with having sexual contact with his patients, entered into the confidential agreement with the Chiropractic Board whereby his license was suspended for six months.

At the request of a television station, Attorney Toth revealed the substance of the Vendsel settlement agreement, being of the opinion that the settlement agreement was subject to the open-records requirements.

The Disciplinary Board of the Supreme Court admonished Toth for revealing the confidential information contained in the Vendsel settlement agreement. The Supreme Court reversed. Citing this section and state law, the Court declared: "North Dakota's open records law provides that, unless specifically exempted by law, all records of public governmental bodies, boards, bureaus, commissions or agencies of the state are 'open and accessible for inspection during reasonable hours.' . . . The settlement agreement was an open record accessible for public inspection under North Dakota law."[709]

In 1997, the Supreme Court was confronted with the question of whether the Greater North Dakota Association (GNDA) was an organization "supported in whole or in part by public funds," thereby making it subject to the requirements of this section.

The case involved a $60,000 legislative appropriation to GNDA for the publication of a magazine titled *North Dakota Horizons*, which the *Adams County Record* claimed made GNDA's records open and available for public examination. This required the Court to define the meaning of the word "support" as used in this section.

The Court wrote:

> Upon reviewing decisions of this Court and those of other jurisdictions, we conclude the term support, as used in the open records law, means something other than an exchange of money for identifiable and specific goods and services. When there is a bargained-for exchange of value, *quid pro quo*, the entity is not supported by public funds. As such, those agencies or organizations carrying out business with the state or employed by the state are not subjected to the open records law.[710]

---

[707] NSP v. North Dakota Public Service Com'n., 502 N.W.2d 240, 243 (1993).

[708] 562 N.W.2d 744 (1997).

[709] Id., p. 748.

[710] Adams County Record v. GNDA, 529 N.W.2d 830, 835–836 (1995).

Having reached that conclusion, the Court sent the case back to the District Court to determine whether there was a *quid pro quo* in the arrangements between the state and GNDA. District Judge Benny A. Graff concluded that there was a *quid pro quo* and not support and therefore GNDA's records were not subject to the open-records law. The Supreme Court affirmed Judge Graff's decision.[711]

TO ENSURE CONTINUITY OF . . . GOVERNMENTAL OPERATIONS IN PERIODS OF EMERGENCY . . . [ASSEMBLY] SHALL [ACT]

Section 7. The legislative assembly, in order to ensure continuity of state and local governmental operations in periods of emergency resulting from disasters caused by enemy attack, shall have the power and immediate duty (1) to provide prompt and temporary succession to the powers and duties of public offices, of whatever nature and whether filled by election or appointment, the incumbents of which may become unavailable for carrying on the powers and duties of such offices, and (2) to adopt such other measures as may be necessary and proper for ensuring the continuity of governmental operations including, but not limited to, waiver of constitutional restrictions upon the place of transaction of governmental business, upon the calling of sessions of the legislative assembly, length of sessions, quorum and voting requirements, subject to legislation and appropriation bill requirements, upon eligibility of legislators to hold other offices, residence requirements for legislators, and upon expenditures, loans or donations of public moneys. In the exercise of the powers hereby conferred the legislative assembly shall in all respects conform to the requirements of this constitution except to the extent that in the judgment of the legislative assembly so to do would be impracticable or would admit of undue delay.

This section deals generally with the continuity of state and local governments in periods of emergencies resulting "from disasters caused by enemy attack." The Legislature has, however, enacted broad legislation for dealing with disasters generally. This legislation places the responsibility to respond to such disasters on the governor.[712]

THE GOVERNOR AND OTHER STATE AND JUDICIAL OFFICERS . . . SHALL BE LIABLE TO IMPEACHMENT

Section 8. The house of representatives shall have the sole power of impeachment. The concurrence of a majority of all members elected shall be necessary for an impeachment.

---

[711] Adams County Record v. Greater North Dakota Ass'n., 564 N.W.2d 304 (1997).

[712] NDCC Chapter 37-17.1.

Section 9. All impeachments shall be tried by the senate. When sitting for that purpose the senators shall be upon oath or affirmation to do justice according to the law and evidence. No person shall be convicted without the concurrence of two-thirds of the members elected. When the governor or lieutenant governor is on trial, the presiding judge of the supreme court shall preside.

Section 10. The governor and other state and judicial officers, except county judges, justices of the peace and police magistrates, shall be liable to impeachment for habitual drunkenness, crimes, corrupt conduct, or malfeasance or misdemeanor in office but judgment in such cases shall not extend further than removal from office and disqualification to hold any office of trust or profit under the state. The person accused, whether convicted or acquitted, shall nevertheless be liable to indictment, trial, judgment and punishment according to law.[713]

In discussing the impeachment process, Justice John Burke wrote:

The voting of an impeachment by the House of Representatives follows upon what is little more than a preliminary examination or investigation. The articles of impeachment in themselves constitute the information or charge upon which the party impeached is prosecuted and tried by the Senate. Yet, before the officer impeached is even tried upon this information, he is, . . . suspended from office and deprived of the right to exercise any of the duties thereof.[714]

When the Supreme Court was confronted with the question of whether the Legislature could give the governor the authority to remove state officers, the Court responded that such authority would be in violation of Section 10. "State officers," Justice Guy C. H. Corliss wrote, "can be removed from office only by impeachment. The legislature cannot vest in the governor the power to remove them from office for any cause."[715]

In the case of *State v. Langer*,[716] the Supreme Court held that impeachment was not the only way that a governor could be removed from office. In this case Governor William Langer, who had been convicted in a federal court of defrauding the U.S. Government, was removed from office by the Supreme Court acting on a petition submitted to them by Lieutenant Governor Ole H. Olson.

The Court reasoned that after Langer's conviction he was no longer an elector (i.e., a person qualified to vote), and being an elector was one of the qualifications of a governor.

Writing for the Court, Justice Burke declared: "We therefore conclude from a review of the authorities that, when a defendant is convicted of a felony in this state, his disqualification as an elector attaches immediately, and that this

[713] See: NDCC Chapter 44-09. REMOVAL BY IMPEACHMENT.

[714] State v. Langer, 256 N.W. 377, 389 (1934).

[715] State v. Miller, 57 N.W. 193, 196 (1893).

[716] 256 N.W. 377 (1934).

disqualification is not suspended by his appeal and the furnishing of a supersedeas bond."[717]

OFFICERS NOT LIABLE TO IMPEACHMENT SHALL BE SUBJECT TO REMOVAL FOR MISCONDUCT

> **Section 11.** All officers not liable to impeachment shall be subject to removal for misconduct, malfeasance, crime or misdemeanor in office, or for habitual drunkenness or gross incompetency in such manner as may be provided by law.[718]

This section does not prohibit the Legislature from providing other methods of removal of officials from office. Such a situation came before the Court when the Board of Trustees of the State Hospital for the Insane, acting on behalf of Dwight S. Moore, sought to oust O. Wellington Archibald from the position of superintendent of that hospital.

The Board of Trustees voted to remove Archibald as superintendent and to appoint Moore, but Archibald refused to give up the office. Among the arguments Archibald made was that this section was a limitation upon the Board's power to remove him. The Supreme Court disagreed. "The constitution does not declare," Justice Corliss wrote, "that the officers therein referred to [in this section] cannot be removed in any other way. It merely provides that for certain causes they may be removed in such manner as the legislature may prescribe."[719]

NO OFFICER SHALL EXERCISE THE DUTIES OF HIS OFFICE AFTER HE SHALL HAVE BEEN IMPEACHED

> **Section 12.** No officer shall exercise the duties of his office after he shall have been impeached and before his acquittal.

The Court had an occasion to apply this section in the case of *State v. Myers*.[720] Myers was serving as the manager of the North Dakota Hail Insurance Department under an appointment by Commissioner of Insurance Oscar E. Erickson. When Erickson was impeached by the House of Representatives, Governor Fred Aandahl immediately appointed S. A. Olsness as the new Commissioner of Insurance. Olsness then removed Myers as manager.

When Erickson was acquitted of the charges against him in the impeachment proceedings, he assumed the position of Commissioner of Insurance and reappointed Myers as manager, but without the approval of Governor Aandahl.

---

[717] Id., p. 391.

[718] See: NDCC Chapter 44-10. REMOVAL BY JUDICIAL PROCEEDINGS; and NDCC Chapter 44-11. REMOVAL BY GOVERNOR.

[719] State v. Archibald, 66 N.W. 234, 242 (1896).

[720] 19 N.W.2d 745 (1945).

Action was then commenced in the Supreme Court to remove Myers from office. The question before the Court was whether Erickson retained any authority as commissioner while his impeachment trial was pending in the Legislature and thus the new commissioner, Olsness, was without power to remove Myers.

The Supreme Court, relying upon this section, said Erickson did not have any powers after being impeached until he was later acquitted. "The fact that the elected Commissioner of Insurance [Erickson] held a naked legal title to the office at the time of . . . [Myers'] removal in no way alters the situation. He was stripped of all the powers of the office."[721]

NO PERSON SHALL BE TRIED ON IMPEACHMENT BEFORE HE SHALL HAVE BEEN SERVED A COPY THEREOF

Section 13. On trial of impeachment against the governor, the lieutenant governor shall not act as a member of the court.

Section 14. No person shall be tried on impeachment before he shall have been served with a copy thereof, at least twenty days previous to the day set for trial.

Section 15. No person shall be liable to impeachment twice for the same offense.

The Supreme Court has not decided any cases involving Sections 13, 14, and 15.

THE MILITIA . . . SHALL CONSIST OF ALL ABLE-BODIED MALE PERSONS . . . BETWEEN THE AGES OF EIGHTEEN AND FORTY-FIVE

Section 16. The militia of this state shall consist of all able-bodied male persons residing in the state, between the ages of eighteen and forty-five years, except such as may be exempted by the laws of the United States or of this state. Persons whose religious tenets or conscientious scruples forbid them to bear arms shall not be compelled to do so in times of peace, but shall pay an equivalent for a personal service.

Section 17. The militia shall be enrolled, organized, uniformed, armed and disciplined in such a manner as shall be provided by law, not incompatible with the constitution of the United States.

Section 18. The legislative assembly shall provide by law for the establishment of volunteer organizations of the several arms of the service, which shall be classified as active militia; and no other organized body of armed men shall be permitted to perform military duty in this state except the army of the United States, without the proclamation of the governor of the state.

---

[721] Id., p. 751.

Section 19. All militia officers shall be appointed or elected in such manner as the legislative assembly shall provide.

Section 20. The commissioned officers of the militia shall be commissioned by the governor, and no commissioned officer shall be removed from office except by sentence of court-martial, pursuant to law.

Section 21. The militia forces shall in all cases, except treason, felony, or breach of the peace, be privileged from arrest during their attendance at musters, parades and elections of officers, and in going to and returning from the same.[722]

On January 12, 1909, Brigadier General Thomas H. Poole (retired) was tried and convicted of violating certain sections of the Articles of War.[723]

Poole petitioned the District Court asserting that his conviction was null and void and Judge W. H. Winchester agreed as did the Supreme Court.

The Court pointed out:

The Military Code in force in this state at the time . . . [Poole] was tried and convicted . . . expressly provided that "the militia *while in active service* shall be governed by the military law of the state, and the rules and Articles of War of the United States." . . . but such Code shall be searched in vain for any provision adopting the Articles of War for its government when not in active service, or in other words, in time of peace, and such statute nowhere defines any military offenses punishable by court-martial or otherwise in time of peace.[724]

THE RIGHT OF THE DEBTOR TO ENJOY THE COMFORTS . . . OF LIFE SHALL BE RECOGNIZED BY WHOLESOME LAWS

Section 22. The right of the debtor to enjoy the comforts and necessaries of life shall be recognized by wholesome laws, exempting from forced sale to all heads of families a homestead, the value of which shall be limited and defined by law; and a reasonable amount of personal property; the kind and value shall be fixed by law. This section shall not be construed to prevent liens against the homestead for labor done and materials furnished in the improvement thereof, in such manner as may be prescribed by law.[725]

In describing the homestead, the Supreme Court has written:

It is settled beyond all cavil by previous holdings of this court that the constitutional and statutory provisions of homestead right are wholesome and salutary regulations

---

[722] NDCC Chapters 37-01. MILITARY—GENERAL PROVISIONS; 37-02. ORGANIZATION OF MILITIA; 37-03. ADJUTANT GENERAL; 37-04. COMMISSIONED OFFICERS.

[723] Articles of War. Code framed for the government of a nation's army or navy; for example, Code of Military Justice (*Black's Law Dictionary*) (St. Paul, MN: West Publishing Co., 1990), p. 112.

[724] State v. Peake, 135 N.W. 197, 200 (1912).

[725] See: NDCC Chapter 47-18. HOMESTEAD; and Chapter 28-22. EXEMPTIONS.

> in furtherance of a wise, generous, and humane public policy, encouraging the establishment and maintenance of homes; that statutes providing for homestead exemptions are remedial in character, and should be liberally construed with a view of carrying into effect the obvious purpose of their enactment; and that the object sought by the adoption of this constitutional provision and the enactment of statutes in furtherance thereof, "was to protect and preserve the home, not for the benefit of the head of the family, but for the benefit of the family as a whole. * * * It was the protection of the family which was the purpose in view, and, this being true, it is the duty of the courts, in construing said provisions to give effect to such plain intent."[726]

Furthermore, "when once established it continues to exist after the death of the husband or wife for the benefit of the surviving husband or wife or minor children."[727]

A homestead may be established by the filing with the Register of Deeds "a declaration of homestead."[728] It is not necessary, however, to file such a declaration in order to establish a homestead in any particular piece of property.[729]

Property will qualify as a homestead if the claimant is the head of the family residing on the land even though his wife has title to the property.[730] And property may qualify as a homestead even if part of the premises is leased out to a business. Such was the case of *In re Teiten's Estate*.[731] In this case, Anna Teiten sought a homestead interest in a two-story building in which the family lived at the time of the death of her husband. Part of the ground floor of the building was leased and used as a general hardware store. In agreeing that the building was a homestead, the Court declared: "The law does not say what kind of a home or what kind of buildings shall be built upon the homestead premises."[732]

While it is possible to abandon a homestead, there must be clear and convincing evidence that that was the intention of the owner. For example, Andrew Nelson and his wife took a homestead in Griggs County, North Dakota, in the early 1880s. The Nelsons lived on and farmed the land until ill health forced them to move to a nearby town in 1918. They then leased the land to their son but retained a room in the farmhouse to which they frequently returned.

A judgment was obtained and docketed against Andrew Nelson in 1922, but no levy was made upon the land. In 1926, the Nelsons moved back to the farm

---

[726] Dieter v. Fraine, 128 N.W. 684, 686 (1910).

[727] Meidinger v. Security State Bank, 213 N.W. 850, 852 (1927).

[728] NDCC Section 47-18-18. Declaration of homestead—How executed and acknowledged.

[729] NDCC Section 47-18-17. Who may make declaration of homestead. See also: Larson v. Cole, 33 N.W.2d 325, 330 (1948).

[730] Bremseth v. Olson, 112 N.W. 1056, 1058 (1907).

[731] 249 N.W. 913 (1933). See also: Birks v. Globe International Protective Bureau, 218 N.W. 864 (1928).

[732] Id., p. 916.

and later when a question arose as to whether the judgment was valid as against the land, the District Court held that it was not and the Supreme Court affirmed.

Justice A. G. Burr explained the Court's decision: "This case is not without difficulty, but the trial court found it was the honest intention of Andrew Nelson to keep and consider this farm as his homestead. He took his wife, some of his furniture, and his horse and buggy back to the farm home, to end his days there, as the faithful old horse had done. We do not feel justified in disagreeing with the trial court."[733]

When a married couple has a homestead interest in a particular piece of property, it cannot be encumbered or conveyed to a third person unless "executed and acknowledged by both the husband and wife."[734] Where a mortgage of a homestead is properly executed, however, this section is not violated when the mortgage is foreclosed and the property sold at a forced sale.[735]

This section also provides that "a reasonable amount of personal property; the kind and value shall be fixed by law" shall be exempt. Acting pursuant to this command, the Legislature has listed the property that is absolutely exempt in NDCC Section 28-22-02. That property includes:

> **Absolute exemption.** The property mentioned in this section is absolutely exempt from all process, levy, or sale:
>
> 1. All family pictures.
> 2. A pew or other sitting in any house of worship.
> 3. A lot or lots in any burial ground.
> 4. The family Bible and all schoolbooks used by the family and all other books used as a part of the family library not exceeding in value one hundred dollars.
> 5. All wearing apparel and clothing of the debtor and his family.
> 6 The provisions for the debtor and the debtor's family necessary for one year's supply, either provided or growing, or both, and fuel necessary for one year.
> 7. The homestead as created, defined, and limited by law.
> 8. All crops and grain, both threshed and unthreshed, raised by the debtor on not to exceed one hundred sixty acres [64.75 hectares] of land in one tract occupied by the debtor, either as owner or tenant, as the debtor's home, . . .
> 9. All insurance benefits resulting from insurance covering any or all of the absolute exemptions.

---

[733] Nelson v. Griggs County, 219 N.W. 225, 227 (1928). See also: Larson v. Cole, 33 N.W.2d 325 (1948); Portland Credit Union v. Hauge, 169 N.W.2d 106 (1969); Falconer v. Farmers Union Oil Co., 260 N.W.2d 1 (1977); and Farmers State Bank v. Stambaugh, 366 N.W.2d 804 (1985).

[734] NDCC Section 47-18-05. Homestead—How conveyed. See also: Dixon v. Kaufman, 58 N.W.2d 797, 805 (1953).

[735] Federal Land Bank of St. Paul v. Ziebarth, 520 N.W.2d 51, 53–54 (1994). See also: Farm Credit Bank of St. Paul v. Stedman, 449 N.W.2d 562 (1989), and State v. Bladow, 462 N.W.2d 453 (1990).

10. Any housetrailer or mobile home occupied as a residence by the debtor or the debtor's family, except that it is not exempt from process, levy, or sale for taxes levied on it pursuant to chapter 57–55.

PROPERTY OF ANY WOMAN . . . SHALL BE HER SEPARATE PROPERTY

Section 23. The real and personal property of any woman in this state, acquired before marriage, and all property to which she may, after marriage become in any manner rightfully entitled, shall be her separate property, and shall not be liable for the debts of her husband.

In 1907, the Legislature provided "that husband and wife shall be jointly and severally liable for any debts contracted by either while living together, for necessary household supplies of food, clothing and fuel for themselves and family, and for the education of their minor children."[736]

Pursuant to the above law, Banner Mercantile Co. sought and obtained a judgment against C. J. Hendricks and Anna Hendricks, husband and wife, for household supplies, food and clothing. Anna Hendricks appealed arguing that the judgment was void because the statute violated this section of the constitution. The Supreme Court disagreed. Justice Charles J. Fisk declared: "The statute in question does not seek to make the wife liable for the husband's debts, but it merely modifies and broadens the common-law rule regarding liability for family necessities."[737]

THE LABOR OF CHILDREN UNDER TWELVE YEARS OF AGE SHALL BE PROHIBITED IN MINES, FACTORIES AND WORKSHOPS

Section 24. The labor of children under twelve years of age, shall be prohibited in mines, factories and workshops in this state.

The Legislature has adopted comprehensive legislation governing child labor[738] and has increased the number of occupations which may not employ persons under the age of fourteen.[739]

---

[736] NDCC Chapter 136. SESSION LAWS OF 1907. This Chapter is now NDCC Section 14-07-10.

[737] Banner Mercantile Co. v. Hendricks, 138 N.W. 993, 995 (1912).

[738] NDCC Chapter 34-07. CHILD LABOR.

[739] NDCC Section 34-07-16. Prohibited employments and occupations of minors.

The Supreme Court has held that an underage plaintiff giving his/her age in a pleading is sufficient to allege negligence on the part of a defendant and that such an allegation also sufficiently alleges proximate cause of an injury.[740]

ASSEMBLY SHALL NOT AUTHORIZE ANY GAME OF CHANCE . . . [EXCEPT FOR] BONA FIDE NONPROFIT . . . ORGANIZATIONS, CIVIC AND SERVICE CLUBS

Section 25. The legislative assembly shall not authorize any game of chance, lottery, or gift enterprises, under any pretense, or for any purpose whatever. However, the legislative assembly shall authorize the State of North Dakota to join a multi-state lottery for the benefit of the State of North Dakota, and, the legislative assembly may authorize by law bona fide nonprofit veterans', charitable, educational, religious, or fraternal organizations, civic and service clubs, or such other public-spirited organizations as it may recognize, to conduct games of chance when the entire net proceeds of such games of chance are to be devoted to educational, charitable, patriotic, fraternal, religious, or other public-spirited uses.

The 2003 Legislature is considering authorizing the state to join a multi-state lottery.

In 1915, the Legislature provided that each year the counties send to the state treasurer 10 cents for each school-age child, such funds to be used for the retirement of teachers. Ransom County Treasurer A. E. Hauge refused to comply with the law, claiming that it was unconstitutional. The Teachers' Insurance and Retirement Fund brought an action seeking to force Hauge to comply with the law.

The Supreme Court upheld the law, but Justice James E. Robinson dissented, and wrote:

> As there are few who are so stupid as to make teaching a life business, the chances are that 100 persons must contribute to the fund for every person who wins a prize or pension. Hence the action does in effect provide for a kind of lottery. . . . Were it competent to give such prizes or pensions to the school-teaching class, it would be equally competent to give them to the clergy, farming class or to any other class of persons.[741]

District Judge Lawrence Leclerc was confronted with the question of whether a phone-card dispensing machine was a lottery and thus a violation of state law. The machine, which looks like a slot machine, "dispenses a perforated slip of paper for each dollar inserted. Half of the slip of paper is the two-minute pre-paid phone card, the other half is a game piece giving the buyer a chance to win

---

[740] Schnoor v. Meinecke, 33 N.W.2d 66 (1948).

[741] State v. Hauge, 164 N.W. 289, 292 (1917).

up to $500 in cash."[742] At the time the money is inserted, wheels spin, lights blink, and music plays, and if a certain combination of symbols is aligned, the player wins and he or she can collect the prize from an attendant at the business establishment.

Judge Leclerc concluded that the machine violated the state lottery laws and the Supreme Court agreed.

Writing for the Court, Chief Justice VandeWalle declared: "The Lucky Strike device incorporates visual and audio 'gambling features.' Also, the Lucky Strike device randomly dispenses a chance for cash prizes with each dollar risked, with a payout rate of sixty-five percent. The Lucky Strike device accepts one, five, ten and twenty dollar bills in payment for the two-minute phone cards, but does not give change. These are functional 'gambling features' incorporated into the Lucky Strike device."[743]

THE LEGISLATIVE, EXECUTIVE, AND JUDICIAL BRANCHES ARE COEQUAL BRANCHES OF GOVERNMENT

Section 26. The legislative, executive, and judicial branches are coequal branches of government. Elected members and officials of each branch shall receive as compensation for their services only such amounts as may be specifically set by law. Payment for necessary expenses shall not exceed those allowed for other state employees.

Although this section did not become part of the constitution until 1982, in 1902 the Supreme Court held that the theory of the separation of powers of the three branches of government was part of the law of the state. At that time, the Court considered the validity of the Political Code of 1899, which gave courts the power to exclude territory from city limits. In discussing the relationship between the three branches of government, Justice D. E. Morgan declared that "it is undisputed that the delegation of legislative functions to the district courts is not contemplated by the constitution, and that the three departments of government provided for in the constitution are distinct from each other; the powers of each being therein separately defined. It is therein provided that the executive department shall enforce the laws, the legislative department shall enact, repeal, or amend the laws, and the judicial department shall construe them."[744]

The Supreme Court has been somewhat willing to allow the Legislature to assign some administrative decisions to the courts and to give courts power to review such decisions. For example, the Supreme Court approved the Legislature's giving district judges the power to issue druggists' permits.

---

[742] Midwestern Enterprises, Inc. v. Stenehjem, 625 N.W.2d 234, 235 (2001).

[743] Id., p. 241.

[744] Glaspell v. City of Jamestown, 88 N.W. 1023, 1024 (1902). See also: City of Carrington v. Foster County, 166 N.W.2d 337 (1969) for a similar result.

In approving this delegation of power, the Supreme Court was of the opinion that this task was "quasi judicial" and therefore not a violation of the separations of powers doctrine.[745]

The Court has also held that the Legislature can give courts a limited power to review administrative decisions. For example, the Court upheld a statute giving the District Court the authority to review decisions of a Board of County Commissioners. That review, however, is limited to a determination "whether or not the county's legislative body acted arbitrarily, capriciously, or unreasonably in reaching its decision."[746]

In explaining this standard of review, Justice William A. Neumann has written: "A decision is not arbitrary, capricious, or unreasonable if the exercise of discretion is the product of a rational mental process by which the facts and the law relied upon are considered together for the purpose of achieving a reasoned and reasonable interpretation."[747]

When the Constitution specifically grants certain powers to the Supreme Court, the Legislature's power to legislate in that area is limited. The Supreme Court was confronted with such an issue when, acting pursuant to a state law, the state sought to obtain certain information from a defendant being prosecuted for driving under the influence of alcohol. The defendant, however, argued that he was not obligated to furnish such information, because the state law conflicted with the Rules of Criminal Procedure adopted by the Supreme Court pursuant to Article VI, Section 3 of the constitution.

The Supreme Court agreed and held that the Rules of Criminal Procedure prevailed. "When, as here," Justice Neumann declared, "the legislative branch fails to exercise restraint and intervenes in a matter entrusted by the Constitution exclusively to the judicial branch, we have an obligation under the Constitution to say so."[748]

The Supreme Court, relying on this section, has refused to become involved in a dispute between the President Pro Tempore of the State Senate and the House of Representatives. Senator Rolland W. Redlin, President Pro Tempore of the Senate, being of the opinion that a certain House bill should have been passed in the House by a two-thirds majority, returned the bill to the House thus preventing the Senate from considering it.

Richard Kloubec, the Speaker of the House, then sought an order of the Supreme Court requiring Senator Redlin to accept the bill but the Supreme Court refused to issue such order. "This Court has long recognized," Justice Levine pointed out, "that the creation of the three branches of government by

---

[745] Kermott v. Bagley, 124 N.W. 397 (1910).

[746] Shaw v. Burleigh County, 286 N.W.2d 797 (1979). See also: Ulvedal v. Board of County Com'rs., 434 N.W.2d 707 (1989).

[747] Fandrich v. Wells Cty. Bd of County Com'rs., 618 N.W.2d 166, 170 (2000).

[748] State v. Hanson, 558 N.W.2d 611, 615 (1996).

our constitution operates as an apportionment of the different classes of power whereby there is an implied exclusion of each branch from the exercise of the functions of the others. . . . In recognition of these abiding principles, the judiciary exercises great restraint when requested to intervene in matters entrusted to the other branches of government."[749]

HUNTING, TRAPPING, AND FISHING AND THE TAKING OF GAME AND FISH ARE A VALUED PART OF OUR HERITAGE

> **Section 27.** Hunting, trapping, and fishing and the taking of game and fish are a valued part of our heritage and will be forever preserved for the people and managed by law and regulation for the public good.

During its 1999 session, the North Dakota Legislature overwhelmingly adopted a resolution to submit to the voters at the November 2000 election an amendment to the state's constitution embodying what is now this section. The voters in Minnesota had adopted a similar measure in 1998, and Alaska, Arizona, and Virginia had placed similar resolutions on their 2000 election ballots.

The motivation for the adoption of these measures was concern that national organizations opposed to the killing of wild game and fish would seek to have state legislatures adopt legislation curtailing hunting, trapping, and fishing. In support of the resolution, Dean Hildebrand, Director of the State Game and Fish Department wrote: "A strong majority vote will help ensure that those in opposition to hunting, fishing and trapping will not target our state as they have other states to stop the harvest of wildlife."[750]

There being very little organized opposition to the resolution, it passed with a large margin. Commenting upon the election, one of the strong proponents of the measure, Russ Johnson, declared: "It's a done deal. We are happy. This is something that is so near and dear in the hearts of North Dakotans. We just thought it was a very significant measure and the people of North Dakota agreed."[751]

---

[749] State v. Meiers, 403 N.W.2d 392, 394 (1987).

[750] News Release, State Game and Fish Department.

[751] AP News Release, 11/08/01.

Article XII

Corporations Other Than Municipal

THE ASSEMBLY SHALL PROVIDE BY GENERAL LAWS FOR THE ORGANIZATION OF ALL CORPORATIONS HEREAFTER CREATED

Section 1. The term "corporation", as used in this article, shall not be understood as embracing municipalities or political divisions of the state unless otherwise expressly stated, but it shall be held and construed to include all associations and joint stock companies having any of the powers or privileges of corporations not possessed by individuals or partnerships.

Section 2. No charter of incorporation shall be granted, changed or amended by special law, except in the case of such municipal, charitable, educational, penal or reformatory corporations as may be under the control of the state; but the legislative assembly shall provide by general laws for the organization of all corporations hereafter to be created, and any such law, so passed, shall be subject to future repeal or alteration.

These sections grant the Legislature virtually unlimited power over the organization, maintenance, and dissolution of corporations. In discussing the Legislature's authority over banking, for example, Justice A. M. Christianson, writing for the Court, declared: "It is well settled that the Legislature is vested with constitutional authority to regulate the business of banking, and may even prohibit the business from being carried on at all, except under such conditions as it may prescribe. . . . And the Legislature has power, by general law, to alter or even withdraw franchises granted to banking corporations."[752]

The state's power over corporations organized under the laws of another state was before the Court in *Asbury Hospital v. Cass County*.[753] In this case, the hospital brought an action in the District Court seeking a judgment that a state law prohibiting corporations from owning farmland in the state could not be applied to them. The District Court concluded that the hospital was subject to the law and the Supreme Court affirmed. In concluding that the hospital was subject to the law, the Supreme Court pointed out that "the State may repeal at any time a statute granting permission to do . . . business (within the state), and may withdraw or revoke such license, and may withdraw its implied consent to a foreign corporation which has been allowed on principles of comity to engage in business therein without express permission and may evict such corporation, provided its action does not operate to deprive the corporation of its property without due process."[754]

The law prohibiting corporations from owning farmland in the state was adopted as an initiated measure in 1932 because low prices for farm products caused foreclosures of mortgages on much farmland throughout the state. These foreclosures resulted in much land being owned by nonresident lending institutions. But the statute prohibiting corporations from owning farmland also applies to domestic corporations. For example, the Supreme Court upheld the decision of the secretary of state to deny corporate existence for an organization that proposed to engage in the business of farming.

Justice Obert C. Teigen, in discussing the authority of the Legislature to enact the anti-corporate farming law, pointed out: "The State's objective in enacting the Corporate Farming Law is to prohibit all corporations, except qualified cooperative corporations, from engaging in the business of farming or agriculture. Thus if the General Motors Corporation and the Ford Motor Corporation, . . . are authorized under their foreign charters to engage in the business of farming in addition to the manufacture and sale of motor vehicles, such corporations are, under the Corporate Farming Law, prohibited from engaging in the business of farming or agriculture in North Dakota."[755]

---

[752] State v. First State Bank, 202 N.W. 391, 397 (1924).

[753] 7 N.W.2d 438 (1943).

[754] Id., p. 450.

[755] Coal Harbor Stock Farm, Inc. v. Meier, 191 N.W.2d 583, 590 (1971). See also: State v. J. P. Lamb Land Company, 401 N.W.2d 713 (1987); NDCC Chapter 10-06.1. CORPORATE OR LIMITED LIABILITY COMPANY FARMING; and *North Dakota's Corporate Farming Statute: An Analysis of the Recent Change in the Law*, 58 North Dakota Law Review 283 (1982).

ASSEMBLY SHALL NOT REMIT THE FORFEITURE OF THE CHARTER OF ANY CORPORATION NOW EXISTING, NOR ALTER OR AMEND THE SAME

Section 3. All existing charters or grants of special or exclusive privileges, under which a bona fide organization shall not have taken place and business been commenced in good faith at the time this constitution takes effect, shall thereafter have no validity.

Section 4. The legislative assembly shall not remit the forfeiture of the charter of any corporation now existing, nor alter or amend the same, nor pass any other general or special law for the benefit of such corporation, except upon the condition that such corporation shall thereafter hold its charter subject to the provisions of this constitution.

The Supreme Court has not decided any cases involving the above two sections.

EXERCISE OF THE RIGHT OF EMINENT DOMAIN SHALL NEVER BE ABRIDGED

Section 5. The exercise of the right of eminent domain shall never be abridged, or so construed as to prevent the legislative assembly from taking the property and franchises of incorporated companies and subjecting them to public use; the same as the property of individuals; and the exercise of the police power of this state shall never be abridged, or so construed as to permit corporations to conduct their business in such a manner as to infringe the equal rights of individuals or the general well-being of the state.

Although the intent of this section is to prevent limitations on the state's police power, what constitutes such a limitation is not clearly defined. The Supreme Court pointed this out when it wrote: "'The development of the law relating to the proper exercise of the police power of the state clearly demonstrates that it is very broad and comprehensive, and is exercised to promote the general welfare of the state, as well as its health and comfort. And the limit of this power cannot and never will be accurately defined, and the courts have never been willing, if able, to circumscribe it with any definiteness.'"[756]

The Court did not find a limitation of the state's police power, however, when the Legislature provided that utilities forced to relocate their facilities to accommodate highway development must be reimbursed for the cost of such relocation. "The police power inherent under the common law," Justice Obert C. Teigen declared, "is not destroyed by the reimbursement statute. The statute

[756] State v. Cromwell, 9 N.W.2d 914, 919 (1943).

specifically gives the commissioner statutory power to order the removal, relocation or change of the utility facility. The state in no way has bartered or bargained away its right to use the police power and has not divested itself of the power to remove utility facilities without payment, as the law may be repealed by any subsequent legislature. The statute while in force is not invalid as a surrender or an abridgement of the state's police power."[757]

IN ALL ELECTIONS FOR . . . MANAGERS OF A CORPORATION, EACH MEMBER . . . MAY CAST THE WHOLE NUMBER OF HIS VOTES FOR ONE CANDIDATE

Section 6. In all elections for directors or managers of a corporation, each member or shareholder may cast the whole number of his votes for one candidate, or distribute them upon two or more candidates, as he may prefer, provided, any cooperative corporation may adopt bylaws limiting the voting power of its stockholders.

The intent of this section was examined in *State v. Thompson.*[758] The issue in that case was whether or not state law permitted cumulative voting for city commissioners. In answering that question in the negative, the Court pointed out that in adopting Section 6, the delegates at the constitutional convention understood the concept of cumulative voting. "In the light of history of this state," Justice E. B. Goss pointed out, "we may conclude . . . that the Legislature did not, if they had an eye to the past, intend to declare cumulative voting permissible"[759] for city commissioners.

Justice C. J. Fisk concurred. He said: "It is a significant fact that the only place in the Constitution recognizing the right of cumulative voting is in . . . [this section] relating to elections of directors and managers of private corporations, and I think it clearly apparent that it was the intention of the framers of our Constitution to restrict such right to such elections, and to none others."[760]

FOREIGN CORPORATION . . . [MUST HAVE] AN AUTHORIZED AGENT . . . UPON WHOM PROCESS MAY BE SERVED

Section 7. No foreign corporation shall do business in this state without having one or more places of business and an authorized agent or agents in the same, upon whom process may be served.

---

757 Northwestern Bell Telephone Company v. Wentz, 103 N.W.2d 245, 257 (1960). See also: S. E. Cass Water Res. v. Burlington Northern Railroad Company. 527 N.W.2d 884, 893 (1995).

758 131 N.W. 231 (1911).

759 Id., p. 239.

760 Id., p. 240.

Plaintiff Hart-Parr Company, a foreign corporation, brought suit against defendant Robb-Lawrence Co., a public warehouseman in Cass County, North Dakota, to recover property which plaintiff had delivered to the defendant's warehouse. Defendant Robb-Lawrence Co. responded that the plaintiff could not maintain the action because it had not qualified to do business in the state as a foreign corporation. Although District Judge Charles A. Pollock agreed with the defendant, the Supreme Court reversed, concluding that doing an isolated transaction is not doing business in the state. "The fact that foreign corporations," Justice Edward Engerud declared, "proposing to do business here are required to establish a place of business within the state makes it clear that the term 'doing business' does not mean a single isolated transaction. It is not reasonable to suppose that the Constitution or the statute intended that a foreign corporation, without intending a continuance of its business in the state, could not collect a debt or make any contract or demand that its property rights should be respected unless it had previously acquired a situs or domicile within our borders."[761]

The Supreme Court has also held "that the burden is not on a foreign corporation to either prove compliance with the . . . [law] or that it was not doing business in the state contrary to the . . . [law]; that the presumption is in favor of their right to do business; that he who asserts that there is illegality in the transaction, fair on its face, must plead and prove it."[762]

In granting foreign corporations authority to do business in the state, " 'such assent may be granted upon such terms and conditions as those States may think proper to impose. They may exclude the foreign corporation entirely; they may restrict its business to particular localities, or they may exact such security for the performance of its contracts with their citizens as in their judgment will best promote the public interest.' "[763]

NO CORPORATION SHALL ISSUE STOCK OR BONDS EXCEPT FOR MONEY, LABOR DONE, OR MONEY OR PROPERTY ACTUALLY RECEIVED

Section 8. No corporation shall engage in any business other than that expressly authorized in its charter.

Section 9. No corporation shall issue stock or bonds except for money, labor done, or money or property actually received; and all fictitious increase of stock or indebtedness shall be void. The stock and indebtedness of corporations shall not be increased except in pursuance of general law, nor without the consent of the persons holding the larger amount in value of the stock first obtained.

---

[761] State v. Robb-Lawrence Co., 106 N.W. 406, 408 (1906).

[762] Brioschi-Minuti Co. v. Elson-Williams Const. Co., 172 N.W. 239, 240–241 (1919).

[763] Asbury Hospital v. Cass County, 7 N.W.2d 438, 450 (1943). See also: J. R. Watkins Company v. Vangen, 116 N.W.2d 641, 647 (1962).

The part that a promissory note plays in the purchase of stock has been considered by the Supreme Court. For example, in an action on a note issued in payment of the purchase of stock, the Court declared: "Had he [the purchaser of the stock] given a check for his stock, and the check been dishonored, he would not be absolved. No more is he relieved from liability by the fact that he gave a note which shall not be considered as payment; that is, shall not be received as actual payment."[764]

Because this section prohibits the issuance of stock or bonds except for "money or property actually received," the Court has said: "It is well settled in this jurisdiction that a pledge of unissued stock of a corporation as collateral security for an existing indebtedness is prohibited by . . . constitutional and statutory provisions."[765] "The purpose of . . . [this] constitutional provision," the Court has written, "is to protect stockholders and creditors, so that the stock of a corporation may not be issued without the corporation actually receiving full value therefor."[766]

In anticipation of the passage of a law permitting the sale of liquor in the state, Leon Bryan spent considerable time and effort to secure potential customers for a corporation he intended to create to sell and distribute liquor. After the passage of the act, Bryan, together with several other individuals, organized Northwest Beverages, Inc., as a liquor wholesaler. For his organizational efforts, Bryan was to receive $16,000 in stock, which the corporation issued, but did not deliver to Bryan, and which it later cancelled.

Bryan brought an action seeking to recover the value of his services to the corporation. One of the questions the Court considered was whether Bryan's efforts qualified as "money or property actually received" by Northwest Beverages. In giving an affirmative answer, the Court declared: "We are of the opinion that the services performed by . . . [Bryan], and the property and good-will taken by the . . . [corporation] in exchange for the stock to be issued, were a sufficient consideration to support the contract in question."[767]

NO LAW SHALL BE PASSED . . . TO CONSTRUCT . . . A STREET RAILWAY . . . WITHOUT . . . THE CONSENT OF LOCAL AUTHORITIES

Section 10. No law shall be passed by the legislative assembly granting the right to construct and operate a street railway, telegraph, telephone or electric light plant within any city, town or incorporated village, without requiring the consent of the

[764] German Mercantile Co. v. Wanner, 142 N.W. 463, 465 (1913). See also: Baird v. Kilene, 205 N.W. 681 (1925).

[765] Dakota Trust Co. v. Lucky Strike Coal Co., 215 N.W. 89, 92 (1927).

[766] McAndrews v. Iowa Gold Mining Co., 210 N.W. 514, 520 (1926).

[767] Bryan v. Northwest Beverages, 285 N.W. 689, 694–695 (1939).

local authorities having the control of the street or highway proposed to be occupied for such purposes.

Justice James Morris, writing for the Supreme Court, discussed the intent of this section in the case of *City of Grafton v. Otter Tail Power Company*.[768] Justice Morris pointed out:

Section ... [10] of the Constitution is not a grant of power to municipalities but a restriction upon the legislature designed to prevent it from authorizing indiscriminate use of the streets of a municipality by certain enumerated public utilities without control by the local authorities. To that extent it is a limitation upon the sovereign power of the state.[769]

Furthermore, the Court has declared:

The power reserved by ... [this section] of the Constitution to a village or city to either grant or refuse permission to an electric light company to occupy the streets of such village or city with the structures of such lighting company is not limited to a simple granting or denial of permission to use the city streets for such purposes; a village or city may permit such use of its streets on certain conditions only, and, if the electric light company accepts the permission or franchise so granted, all valid conditions or restrictions attached thereto become binding upon it.[770]

EVERY RAILROAD ... SHALL HAVE AND MAINTAIN A PUBLIC OFFICE ... IN THE STATE FOR THE TRANSACTION OF ITS BUSINESS

Section 11. Every railroad corporation organized and doing business in this state, under the laws or authority thereof, shall have and maintain a public office or place in the state for the transaction of its business, where transfers of its stock shall be made and in which shall be kept for public inspection, books in which shall be recorded the amount of capital stock subscribed, and by whom, the names of the owners of its stock and the amount owned by them respectively, the amount of stock paid in and by whom, and the transfers of said stock; the amount of its assets and liabilities and the names and place of residence of its officers. The directors of every railroad corporation shall annually make a report, under oath, to the auditor of public accounts, or some officer or officers to be designated by law, of all their acts and doings, which report shall include such matters relating to railroads as may be prescribed by law, and the legislative assembly shall pass laws enforcing by suitable penalties the provisions

[768] 86 N.W.2d 197 (1957).

[769] Id., p. 205.

[770] Chrysler Light & Power Co. v. City of Belfield, 224 N.W. 871, 874 (1929).

> of this section; provided, the provisions of this section shall not be so construed as to apply to foreign corporations.

In commenting on this, and Sections 12, 13, and 14, Chief Justice VandeWalle pointed out:

> There is no doubt that North Dakota has historically considered railroads separate and apart from ordinary corporations. . . . The reason for separate treatment of railroads is their special status in the development of our State. Railroads were instrumental if not integral to populating North Dakota. Because of this significance to settlement of the State, some railroads were given land grants by Congress for extending their rail lines through North Dakota, as well as other western states, and for the benefits resulting from that extension. Many of the benefits and many of the problems our State faces today, at least demographically, are due to the foresight or lack thereof of the railroads.[20771]

ASSEMBLY SHALL . . . ENACT LAWS REGULATING . . . THE RATES OF CHARGES FOR THE TRANSPORTATION OF PASSENGERS, . . . AND FREIGHT

> **Section 12.** No railroad corporation shall consolidate its stock, property or franchises with any other railroad corporation owning a parallel or competing line; and in no case shall any consolidation take place except upon public notice given at least sixty days to all stockholders, in such manner as may be provided by law. Any attempt to evade the provisions of this section, by any railroad corporation, by lease or otherwise, shall work a forfeiture of its charter.

> **Section 13.** Railways heretofore constructed or that may hereafter be constructed in this state are hereby declared public highways, and all railroad, sleeping car, telegraph, telephone and transportation companies of passengers, intelligence and freight, are declared to be common carriers and subject to legislative control; and the legislative assembly shall have power to enact laws regulating and controlling the rates of charges for the transportation of passengers, intelligence and freight, as such common carriers from one point to another in this state; provided, that appeal may be had to the courts of this state from the rates so fixed; but the rates fixed by the legislative assembly or board of railroad commissioners shall remain in force pending the decision of the courts.

> **Section 14.** Any association or corporation organized for the purpose shall have the right to construct and operate a railroad between any points within this state, and to connect at the state line with the railroads of other states. Every railroad company

---

[771] S. E. Cass Water Res. v. Burlington Northern Railroad Company, 527, N.W.2d 894, 896–897 (1995).

> shall have the right with its road to intersect, connect with or cross any other, and shall receive and transport each other's passengers, tonnage and cars, loaded or empty, without delay or discrimination.

In commenting on the Legislature's authority under Section 13, the Supreme Court has pointed out: "The rule is, of course, too well settled to admit of dispute that the Legislature has the power to fix and regulate rates to be charged by common carriers upon intrastate traffic, provided such rates are not confiscatory, but are reasonably remunerative. . . . [This] Section . . . of our Constitution expressly confers such power upon the Legislature."[772]

SECURITY TO THE FULL AMOUNT THEREOF SHALL BE DEPOSITED . . . FOR THE REDEMPTION OF SUCH NOTES OR BILLS

> **Section 15.** If a general banking law be enacted, it shall provide the registry and countersigning by an officer of the state, of all notes or bills designed for circulation, and that ample security to the full amount thereof shall be deposited with the state treasurer for the redemption of such notes or bills.

By a Concurrent Resolution, the 1999 Legislature proposed that the office of state treasurer be abolished, and that Section 15 be repealed. The voters, however, rejected the Concurrent Resolution at the June 2001 primary election.

CONTROLLING OF THE PRICE OF ANY PRODUCT OF THE SOIL OR ANY ARTICLE OF MANUFACTURE OF COMMERCE . . . IS PROHIBITED

> **Section 16.** Any combination between individuals, corporations, associations, or either having for its object or effect the controlling of the price of any product of the soil or any article of manufacture of commerce, or the cost of exchange or transportation, is prohibited and hereby declared unlawful and against public policy; and any and all franchises heretofore granted or extended, or that may hereafter be granted or extended in this state, whenever the owner or owners thereof violate this article shall be deemed annulled and become void.

When Attorney General William Langer sought to cancel the corporate charters of Gamble-Robinson Fruit Co. and Stacy Bismarck Company for combining to control the prices of fruits and berries, the defendants argued that the

---

[772] State v. Northern Pac. Ry. Co., 120 N.W. 869, 870 (1909).

attorney general must proceed by way of a criminal action. The Supreme Court disagreed. Writing for the Court, Justice Luther E. Birdzell declared:

> The provisions of the Constitution and of the statute . . . in so far as they affect the manner in which corporations may conduct their business, form the terms of the implied contract upon which the corporate franchise is granted, and therefore enter into the franchise itself. When the corporation breaks this contract in such a way as to work injury to the public, the state has a right to institute an inquiry into the extent of the abuse of the powers granted to it, and, in proper cases, to annul the franchise for the abuse.[773]

Section 17. The exchange of "black lists" between corporations shall be prohibited.

The Supreme Court has not considered any cases involving this section.

[773] State v. Gamble-Robinson Fruit Co., 176 N.W. 103, 108 (1919).

Article XIII

Compact with the United States

JURISDICTION . . . OF THIS STATE EXTENDS OVER THOSE RESERVATIONS . . . WHICH . . . JURISDICTION IS NOT VESTED IN THE UNITED STATES

Section 1. Perfect toleration of religious sentiment must be secured, and no inhabitant of this state may ever be molested in person or property on account of that person's mode of religious worship.

Section 2. Jurisdiction is ceded to the United States over the military reservations of Fort Abraham Lincoln, Fort Buford, Fort Pembina, and Fort Totten, heretofore declared by the president of the United States; provided, legal process, civil and criminal, of this state extends over those reservations in all cases in which exclusive jurisdiction is not vested in the United States, or of crimes not committed within the limits of those reservations. The legislative assembly may provide, upon the terms and conditions it adopts, for the acceptance of any jurisdiction as may be delegated to the state by an act of Congress.

In an attempt to clarify when the state may exercise jurisdiction over an Indian, the Legislature enacted legislation by which reservation Indians may vote to accept state jurisdiction.[774] The U.S. Supreme Court, however, has held

[774] NDCC Chapter 27–19. INDIAN CIVIL JURISDICTION.

that some of these provisions violate federal law.[775] The exercise of jurisdiction over Indians is therefore being decided on a case-by-case basis.[776]

NORTH DAKOTA HEREBY ACCEPTS THE SEVERAL GRANTS OF LAND GRANTED BY THE UNITED STATES TO THE STATE OF NORTH DAKOTA

Section 3. The state of North Dakota hereby accepts the several grants of land granted by the United States to the state of North Dakota by an Act of Congress entitled "An act to provide for the division of Dakota into two states, and to enable the people of North Dakota, South Dakota, Montana and Washington to form constitutions and state governments, and to be admitted into the union on equal footing with the original states, and to make donations of public lands to such states," under the conditions and limitations therein mentioned; reserving the right, however, to apply to Congress for modification of said conditions and limitations in case of necessity.

By this section, the state acknowledges receipt of land granted to it by the U.S. Government. The management and disposition of this land is governed by Article IX of the state constitution.

PROVISIONS OF THE ENABLING ACT . . . ARE CONTINUED IN EFFECT AS THOUGH FULLY RECITED AND CONTINUE TO BE IRREVOCABLE

Section 4. All other provisions of the Enabling Act of Congress approved on February 22, 1889, 25 United States Statutes at Large 676, chapter 180, and section 1 of the article of the Constitution of North Dakota, as section 1 existed immediately before the adoption of this section, are continued in effect as though fully recited and continue to be irrevocable without the consent of the United States and the people of this state.

The Supreme Court has not decided any cases involving this section.

---

775 Three Affiliated Tribes v. Wold Engineering, 476 U.S. 877 (1986).

776 In Interest of M.L.M., 529 N.W.2d 184 (1995); Application of Otter Tail Power Co., 451 N.W.2d 95 (1990); Byzewski v. Byzewski, 429 N.W.2d 394 (1988); McKenzie County Social Services Bd. v. V. G., 392 N.W.2d 399 (1986); McKenzie County Social Service Bd. et al. v. C. G., 633 N.W.2d 157 (2001).

Transition Schedule

THE . . . ASSEMBLY SHALL PROVIDE FOR THE EDITING, AND FOR THE PUBLICATION IN AN INDEPENDENT VOLUME, OF THIS CONSTITUTION[777]

Section 26. The legislative assembly shall provide for the editing, and for the publication in an independent volume, of this constitution as soon as it shall take effect, and whenever it shall be altered or amended and shall cause to be published in the same volume the Declaration of Independence, and the Constitution of the United States and the Enabling Act.

Done at Bismarck, Dakota, in open convention, this 17th day of August A. D. 1889.

JOHN G. HAMILTON, Chief Clerk — B. B. FANCHER, President

[777] Sections 1 through 25 were repealed. See Notes, Constitution of North Dakota, p. 309.

■ BIBLIOGRAPHY

American Jurisprudence, 2nd ed., "Constitutional Law." Danvers, MA: West Group, 1998, Vol. 16B, Section 671, pp. 160–161.

American Jurisprudence, 2nd ed., "Jury." Danvers, MA: West Group, 1998, Vol. 47, Section 15, p. 723.

Black, Henry Campbell. *Black's Law Dictionary*. St. Paul, MN: West Publishing Co., 1990.

Bouvier, John. *Bouvier's Law Dictionary*. Kansas City, MO: Vernon Law Book Company, 1914, Vol. 1.

Compendium of History and Biography of North Dakota. Chicago: Geo. A. Ogle & Co., 1900.

Compton's Interactive Encyclopedia, "North Dakota." Softkey Multimedia, 1999.

Corpus Juris Secundum. *Constitutional Law*. St. Paul, MN: West Publishing Co., 1984, Vol. 16A.

Crockett, Richard B. *Constitutional Autonomy and the North Dakota State Board of Education*. 54 North Dakota Law Review 530 (1977–1978).

The Encyclopedia Americana, Int. ed., "Fifth Amendment." Danbury, CT: Grolier, 1996, Vol. 11, p. 187.

Eule, Julian N. *Judicial Review of Direct Democracy*. 99 Yale Law Journal 1503 (1990).

Grolier Multimedia Encyclopedia, 1999, "Indians, American, (II)." Grolier Interactive.

Guy, Daniel, and Jack McDonald. *Government in the Sunshine*. 53 North Dakota Law Review 51 (1976).

Journal of the Constitutional Convention Held at Bismarck, Thursday, July 4 to August 17, 1889, pp. 357–360.

Lamar, Howard Roberts. *Dakota Territory, 1861–1889*. Fargo: Institute for Regional Studies, 1997.

Leahy, James E. *"The Constitution Is What the Judges Say It Is."* 65 North Dakota Law Review 491, 499 Note 50 (1989).

Leifur, Conrad W. *Our State North Dakota*. New York: American Book Company, 1953.

Meschke, Herbert L., and Lawrence D. Spears. *Digging for Roots: The North Dakota Constitution and the Thayer Correspondence*. 65 North Dakota Law Review 343 (1989).

North Dakota's Corporate Farming Statute: An Analysis of the Recent Change in the Law. 58 North Dakota Law Review 283 (1982).

Robinson, Elwyn B. *History of North Dakota*. Lincoln: University of Nebraska Press, 1986.

Smith, Thomas O. *State Lands! What Are We Doing*. 51 North Dakota Law Review 477 (1975).

Sovereign Immunity: An Outdated Doctrine Faces Demise in a Changing Judicial Arena. 69 North Dakota Law Review 401 (1993).

Sovereign Immunity—Judicial Abrogation of North Dakota's Sovereign Immunity Results in Its Possible Legislative Reassertion and Legislation to Provide Injured Parties a Remedy for the Torts Committed by the State or Its Agents. 71 North Dakota Law Review 761 (1995).

Tabor, Sandra L. *Apportionment in North Dakota: The Saga of Continuing Controversy*. 57 North Dakota Law Review 447 (1981).

Vogel, Robert. *Justice Robinson and the Supreme Court of North Dakota*. 58 North Dakota Law Review 83 (1982).
Vogel, Robert. *Sources of the North Dakota Constitution*. 65 North Dakota Law Review 331 (1989).
Wills, Brent Lloyd. *North Dakota Geography and Early History*. Grand Forks: University of North Dakota Press, 1967.

■ TABLE OF CASES

D

E

F

G

H

M

N

O

P

R

S

T

U

V

W

■ INDEX

About the Author

JAMES E. LEAHY is Professor Emeritus of Constitutional Law, California Western School of Law, San Diego. He is the author of *Supreme Court Justices Who Voted with the Government* (1999), *Freedom Fighters of the United States Supreme Court* (1996), and *Liberty, Justice, and Equality* (1992).

www.ingramcontent.com/pod-product-compliance
Ingram Content Group UK Ltd.
Pitfield, Milton Keynes, MK11 3LW, UK
UKHW020924170926
475595UK00031B/55

9 780199 778737